THE MISCELLANIES COMPANION

THE MISCELLANIES
COMPANION

Edited by ROBERT L. BOSS *and* SARAH B. BOSS

Foreword by DOUGLAS A. SWEENEY

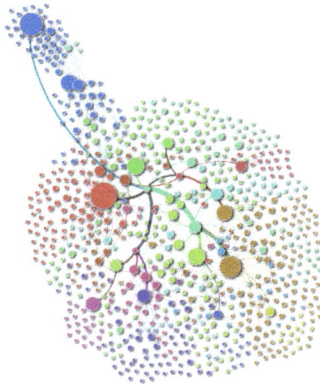

JESociety
Press

WWW.JESOCIETY.ORG

Hardcover Edition December 18, 2018
ISBN 978-0-578-43206-9
© 2018 Robert L. Boss

A publication of JESociety Press
Visit https://www.jesociety.org

For permission requests and inquiries,
Email: info@jesociety.org
Web: www.jesociety.org

PRAISE FOR THIS VOLUME

The Miscellanies Companion wonderfully sheds light on Edwards's private theological workshop: his cavernous "Miscellanies" notebooks. The twenty-one essays here are packed with Edwards's stimulating theological reflections on numerous topics, both well-known (the Trinity, Hell, the Millennium) and not-so-well-known (like China, the Sabbath, and comets!). The addition of Robert Boss's visual maps of Edwards's thought dramatically increases the appeal of this volume. An outstanding contribution to Edwards scholarship that I shall be returning to for years to come!

ROBERT CALDWELL

Associate Professor of Church History
Southwestern Baptist Theological Seminary, Fort Worth, Texas

During the length of his ministry, and through the breadth of their focus, the "Miscellanies" represent the raw Edwards. First thoughts, perhaps reimagined, a number of times, offer insights into his developing mind. In this sweeping book, we not only read summaries of themes in the "Miscellanies" but are provided with a cartographic interpretation of interconnections between the entries. The visual plates are stunning in both their impact and in their academic possibilities. If you want to learn about causality, China, or comets, there is something here for you.

RHYS BEZZANT

Director of the Jonathan Edwards Center, Lecturer in Christian Thought
Ridley College, Melbourne, Australia

To date, there is a mixed reception amongst Edwards scholars concerning the role of the "Miscellanies" in his theology. *The Miscellanies Companion* exposes the student of Edwards to a sampling of Edwards's creative mind as the first attempt to analyze part of the "Miscellanies" in light of Edwards's other works. Composed of a set of new and seasoned Edwards scholars, the reader is guided through some of Edwards's most fruitful ideas. Even more, the editors of the *Companion* help the reader grasp the mind of Edwards using an illustration piece–akin to a neural network. And, it is in this way, that the *Companion* acquaints us with the latest cutting-edge Edwards scholarship issued by JESociety Press.

JOSHUA FARRIS
Assistant Professor of Theology
Houston Baptist University, Houston, Texas

This captivating collection of essays stems from Rob Boss's multimodal interpretation of the writing of Jonathan Edwards. Using digital methods of visualization, Boss succeeds in translating words and thoughts into images, uncovering many aspects of Edwards's thoughts that would otherwise remain hidden. This innovative approach initiates a whole new area of research in Jonathan Edwards Studies and adds to the recent contributions of Digital Humanities to the study of American letters as such.

MICHAŁ CHOIŃSKI
Assistant Professor in the Institute of English Studies
Jagiellonian University, Krakow, Poland

Soli Deo gloria

ACKNOWLEDGEMENTS

A project such as this does not come about without many words of encouragement and support. Much gratitude is due to the authors and their excellent contributions, without which this volume would not exist. Of inestimable value were the helpful conversations and prompts of S. Mark Hamilton. Many thanks are due Douglas Sweeney for cheering on JESociety these past few years. Kenneth Minkema's early affirmation of this project was a major encouragement. I am also grateful to Chris Chun and the new Jonathan Edwards Center at Gateway Seminary for our future collaboration on "The Miscellanies Project." Finally, I cannot give a high enough tribute to my wife Stephanie who has been an unfailing encouragement and my greatest support.

The cover art is a visualization (sans labels) of the theological system inherent in Jonathan Edwards' notebook "Images of Divine Things."

Robert L. Boss
Fort Worth, Texas

Contents

Acknowledgments   i

Contributors   vii

Foreword
  — *Douglas A. Sweeney*   ix

Introduction
  — *Robert L. Boss*   xi

What does Hell have to do with the Trinity?
  — *Christopher Woznicki*   1

Edwards' Doctrine of The Immanent Trinity
  — *Adam G. Cavalier*   19

A New Trinity: The Trinity *ad extra* in Edwards
  — *Obbie Tyler Todd*   41

Edwards on Reason, Revelation, and Mystery
  — *Jonathan S. Marko*   65

Edwards on Reasonable Christianity and
  Necessary Revelation
  — *Jonathan S. Marko*   79

Edwards' Comet: "Miscellanies," Meteors,
and the End of the World
— *Sarah B. Boss*   89

A World that Excites Devotion
— *Robert L. Boss*   105

Edwards on God's Immediate and
Arbitrary Operations
— *S. Mark Hamilton*   119

Preparationism in Edwards' Theology of
Evangelism and Missions
— *Adam G. Cavalier*   149

Edwards on China
— *Victor Zhu*   169

Edwards on Covenant Theology
— *David Mark Rathel*   185

Edwards' Vision of the Millennium
— *Victor Zhu*   199

A Millennial Vision of One Glorious
and Amiable Society
— *Bonghyun Yoo*   209

Edwards in Defense of a Literal Millennium
— *Bonghyun Yoo*   221

Edwards on Happiness
— *Matthew Everhard*   233

Edwards' Vision of Happiness as the Divine
and Human Goals of God's Creation
— *David Luke*   245

Edwards and the Timeless Time of God's Decrees
  — *Toby K. Easley*   257

Providence and Prayer for Advancing
  the Kingdom on Earth
  — *Bonghyun Yoo*   277

Edwards on Gospel Holiness as God's
  Perfect Salvation
  — *Roy Mellor*   289

Edwards on the Importance of the Sabbath
  — *David J. Arnold*   301

Edwards on Glory as the End of Creation
  — *Brandon James Crawford*   311

Index   323

CONTRIBUTORS

DAVID J. ARNOLD
Bridge City Ministries
Detroit/Ann Arbor, MI

ROBERT L. BOSS
JESociety
Fort Worth, TX

SARAH B. BOSS
Károli Gáspár University
Budapest, Hungary

ADAM G. CAVALIER
Southwestern Baptist
Theological Seminary
Fort Worth, TX

BRANDON JAMES CRAWFORD
Grace Baptist Church
Marshall, MI

TOBY K. EASLEY
Fort Worth, TX

MATTHEW V. EVERHARD
Faith Evangelical
Presbyterian Church
Brooksville, FL

S. MARK HAMILTON
Free University of Amsterdam
Amsterdam, The Netherlands

DAVID LUKE
Irish Baptist College
Moira, Northern Ireland

JONATHAN S. MARKO
Cornerstone University
Grand Rapids, MI

ROY MELLOR
Durham, UK

DAVID MARK RATHEL
St. Andrews University
St. Andrews, Scotland

OBBIE TYLER TODD
New Orleans Baptist
Theological Seminary
New Orleans, LA

CHRISTOPHER WOZNICKI
Fuller Theological Seminary
Pasadena, CA

BONGHYUN YOO
McMaster Divinity College
Hamilton, Ontario

VICTOR ZHU
University of Edinburgh
Edinburgh, Scotland

FOREWORD

Rob Boss is a busy man—and a creative one to boot. His Jonathan Edwards Society (a.k.a. JESociety) is quickly picking up steam as it promotes the study of Edwards "through innovation, collaboration and publication," as he summarizes its mission on the organization's website.

The cutting edge of its work today is "The Miscellanies Project." Inspired by a diagram in Wilson Kimnach's "General Introduction" to the sermons in *The Works of Jonathan Edwards* (Yale University Press, 1957-), which depicts conceptual links between the "Miscellanies," "Blank Bible," sermons, and other manuscripts in Edwards' vast corpus, Boss is wielding new technology to craft beautiful pictures of the ways in which the topics in Edwards' writings hang together. These "visualizations" help researchers see the number of times Edwards wrote on various topics, the emphases he placed on these topics during his lifetime, and the relationships between them in his "Miscellanies" notebooks and theology as a whole.

The book you hold in your hands represents the first fruits of scholarly labor on these pictures. Each contributor to *The Miscellanies Companion* was given two "visualizations" on his or her topic–some of which appear below, and all of which are available at JESociety.org— one that "maps" Edwards' comments on that topic in the "Miscellanies," another that "maps" the range of his comments on that topic in Yale's letterpress edition of *The Works of Jonathan Edwards*. Each scholar was asked to reflect on the frequency and emphases of Edwards' varied commentary on his or her topic and develop new interpretations of Edwards as a result.

Readers can judge for themselves whether this project bears good fruit. What I want to highlight here is that computers are revolutionizing the study of Jonathan Edwards. We can access and analyze the work of this prolific man like never before in history, and entrepreneurs like Boss can publish our findings much more cheaply and efficiently than traditional publishing houses (though without their editorial and marketing expertise). At least for those who have access to computers and the Web, the study of Edwards is being democratized, accelerated, and globalized.

Boss is not the only one to do this kind of work. Michał Choiński of Jagiellonian University in Kraków is performing stylometric work on Edwards' extant sermon corpus: publishing statistical computations and analyses of the semantic range, structure, and significance of Edwards' work.

But in the United States, Boss's work is gaining the most attention, and his Society is attracting the most investment from other scholars. Older academics like me mainly admire this from afar, snatching insights on occasion that make a difference in our work. But younger scholars are catching on, learning to do this work themselves, and improving on the studies of their pre-digital forebears. Big data is here to stay—even in Jonathan Edwards studies. Here's hoping that those who use it can make the interpretation of Edwards more accurate, visually impressive, and compelling.

Douglas A. Sweeney
Trinity Evangelical Divinity School

INTRODUCTION

Robert L. Boss

THIS PRESENT VOLUME is a print companion to "The Miscellanies Project." The essays within were contributed by an international body of scholars hailing from East Asia, Europe, the UK, and North America. The contributions canvas a wide range of topics contained in Edwards' "Miscellanies," including Trinitarianism, millennialism, reason and revelation, evangelism, happiness, salvation, and more. With much gratitude I thank these scholars for their participation and excellent contributions to this project.

What is "The Miscellanies Project"?

To begin to answer this question, one must note that *The Works of Jonathan Edwards,* print and online, have been lauded as a singular monument to America's Theologian, "the single most sustained, scholarly, editorial undertaking in the United States alongside the Founding Fathers papers projects."[1] The works of Edwards brim with a creative genius unparalleled among evangelical theologians. The quality of his thought calls for an approach that attempts to answer his creativity.

    An explanation of a *visual* Edwards might be helped by a brief history of typography. Edwards' works were initially printed with press technology not far removed from Gutenberg's of the fifteenth century, which used individual letters cast from lead. Developments in the nineteenth century witnessed the advent of automated typesetting machines. The latter twentieth century gave rise to personal computers and the Internet which began to displace paper with screens and hypertext. Following this digital revolution, digital fonts were born. Type was no longer produced through physical means. Instead, mathematical descriptions defined each character's outline. Today is a day of typographic experimentation—digital typefaces are sophisticated software and old physical limitations no longer apply. Fonts can now contain advanced algorithms which automatically change size and shape depending on their context and even respond to the rhythm and tempo in which they are typed.[2]

The advances which precipitated the revolution in typography are now occurring, in a similar way, in our ability to read and understand large bodies of text. The digital age enabled the creation of fonts with unlimited scalability and flexibility. The unlimited computational attributes of a small individual letter or point of punctuation also extends to a large corpus ... including the writings of Edwards. A *visual* Edwards project grants a new view of America's theologian. *Visual Edwards* is, as it were, an advanced computational material which can be stretched, bent, and zoomed to direct the scholar to areas of interest. As a cartographic tool, it grants the reader a new visual access to Edwards in his own words.

Why Map Edwards?

There are a number of benefits. First, maps can reduce the cognitive load of the researcher—a greater amount of information can be communicated in a detailed map more quickly than having to scan through thousands of lines of Edwards' text. Yet, at the same time, the maps direct the user to *read* Edwards. Maps reveal the presence of unseen seismic structures in Edwards' writings and direct the user where to "drill for oil." This is especially helpful for new students of Edwards who desire direct contact with his writings.

Second, maps of Edwards' writings are beautiful confluences of theology, technology, and art. The colors and connections guide the eye, and in a blink the reader can assess the content. This can be described as "Edwards at a glance." Maps reveal new context and detail which combine to deepen understanding—visualizations which are both aesthetic and accurate.

Visualizing Edwards is not entirely new. Wilson Kimnach's conceptual diagram in volume 10 of *The Works of Jonathan Edwards* illustrates the intertextuality of Edwards' notebooks and sermons, reflecting the formidable intellectual and spiritual effort Edwards famously exerted in his study for up to 13 hours a day.[3] The complex and aesthetically profound nature of Edwards' writings beg for a visual exegesis that is exhaustive, vibrant, and tactile. The interrelated character of Edwards' thought births a desire to visualize the beautiful complexity within his writings.

The project goal is cartographic in nature—a visualized interior of his *Works*. A *visual* Edwards provides a distant or meta-reading of Edwards which displays shapes, contours, and conjunctions within his writings, providing the reader with immediate reference to his text with exact page locations in volumes 1–26 of the Yale edition of his *Works*.

The Team Process

"The Miscellanies Project" is a team-oriented project: Contributors first selected topics and "Miscellanies" of interest, along with submitted key vocabulary words occurring within the selected entries. This information was used to create a contributors topic map which served to prevent overlap in the essays.

The selected "Miscellanies" and keywords were then used to construct visual maps of the chosen topics which spanned the twenty-six volume print edition of *The Works of Jonathan Edwards*. These maps were comprised of labeled nodes and lines. The nodes were labeled with keywords and volume/page locations in *WJE* 1–26. Lines radiating out from the vocabulary nodes connected to corresponding nodes with the exact volume/page location of the term for the reader to look up in the print or online edition of *The Works of Jonathan Edwards*. Clusters of location nodes indicated the shared presence of multiple keywords. The maps were provided to the contributors to assist them in their research, as well as provided the basis for a future digital exhibition.[4]

Project Goals

The purpose of "The Miscellanies Project" is to visually unlock Edwards' notebooks, map intricate connections in his thought, and produce an interface(s) that is navigable by touchscreen, mouse, and keyboard. The main goals are:

1. Produce deep, comparative, visual analyses based on "Miscellanies," nos. a–1360 and canvas a wide range of theological topics which reveal the weave of Edwards' thought throughout *WJE* 1–26.[5]

2. Publish collections of contributed essays.

3. Establish a *Visual Edwards Library*—a digital archive of maps suitable for annotation and presentation.

4. Develop JEViewer—desktop software for viewing, annotating, animating, and presenting the *Visual Edwards Library*. JEViewer will empower users to visually navigate and annotate the *Visual Edwards* via a zoomable map interface, as well as export snapshots of maps and notes for use in word processing documents, websites, social media, video and animation software, and more.

5. Host a special exhibition of "The Miscellanies Project" and resources at the Jonathan Edwards Center at Gateway Seminary.

The Miscellanies Companion is a first step towards the Himalayan task of visualizing Jonathan Edwards—an ongoing project seemingly without end. To echo Edwards' sentiment in *Types,* "there is room for persons to be learning more and more ... to the end of the world without discovering all."[6]

Notes

[1]http://edwards.yale.edu/about-us

[2]Casey Reas and Ben Fry, *Processing: A Programming Handbook for Visual Designers and Artists,* (Cambridge, MA: MIT Press, 2014), 149.

[3]*WJE* 10:90.

[4]Condensed subsets of these maps appear throughout this volume.

[5]Maps will be based, in part, on Edwards' Table to his "Miscellanies."

[6]*WJE* 11:152.

WHAT DOES HELL HAVE TO DO WITH THE TRINITY?

Christopher Woznicki

No reasonable creature can be happy, we find, without society and communion, not only because he finds something in others that is not in himself, but because he delights to communicate himself to another. This cannot be because of our imperfection, but because we are made in the image of God; for the more perfect any creature is, the more strong this inclination.

— Jonathan Edwards, *Miscellany no. 96*

AMONG CONTEMPORARY THEOLOGIANS Jonathan Edwards is best known as a Trinitarian theologian. Although the Northampton pastor never published any of his explicit Trinitarian works, his writing on the topic can be found in several places including "Observations concerning the Trinity and the Covenant of Redemption," the "Discourse on the Trinity," *The End of Creation,* and several "Miscellanies." Among non-theologians, however, Edwards' fame is not primarily due to his creative yet orthodox Trinitarian formulations; rather, it is due to his (supposed) hellfire and brimstone style preaching.[1] This is due mainly to the fact that Edwards' most famous work is his 1741 sermon "Sinners in the Hands of an Angry God." This sermon, which is still standard reading material in American high school literature classes, depicts a horrific, ghoulish, and terrorizing portrayal of the future that awaits the reprobate.[2] But what do the "Trinitarian" Edwards and the (supposed) "Hellfire and Brimstone" Edwards have to do with one another? Or better yet, what does Edwards' doctrine of the Trinity have to do with his doctrine of hell? Are there any clear links between these two aspects of Jonathan Edwards' thought? In order to answer these questions, we shall turn our attention to two of his "Miscellanies": nos. 96 and 279.

In what follows I provide an introduction to "Miscellanies" 96 and 279. In the first section we turn our attention to Miscellany 96 "Trinity." We will look briefly at some of the historical disputes Edwards entered into when reflecting upon the Trinity. We will then carefully examine his arguments for the Trinity in Miscellany 96. In the second section, we will turn our attention to Miscellany 279 "Eternity of Hell Torments." We will begin by covering some background concerning Enlightenment disputes about the doctrine of hell that Edwards sought to address. I will then provide a reconstruction of his argument for the eternity of hell in Miscellany 279.[3] In the final section I will tie together what I have said about both "Miscellanies" in order to answer the question, "What does hell have to do with the Trinity?"

Miscellany no. 96: Trinity

The seventeenth and eighteenth centuries were periods in which "rational" and "scriptural" criticisms of the doctrine of the Trinity were on the rise. Edwards himself notes this tendency when he exclaims that "there has been much cry of late against saying one word, particularly about the Trinity, but what the Scripture has said."[4] The challenges to orthodox Trinitarianism which Edwards decries primarily were centered in England. These challenges were put forth by a number of famous thinkers including Isaac Newton, John Milton, and John Locke. Although these thinkers differed in significant ways, they all were united in their doubts concerning the doctrine's reasonable-

ness and its basis in Scripture. Perhaps the most notable challenge to the reasonableness and scriptural nature of the doctrine that Edwards would have been familiar with came from the Anglican Bishop, Samuel Clarke. In his 1712 publication, *The Scripture-Doctrine of the Trinity,* Clarke argues that the doctrine is not plainly revealed in the Bible, and thus it cannot be an essential component of the Christian faith. Edwards was aware of Clarke's work, evidence of which is his *Catalogues of Books.*[5] In his catalogue Edwards lists Clarke's book, responses to Clarke's book by James Knight and Daniel Waterland, and a defense of Clarke's book by John Jackson.[6]

Anti-Trinitarian controversies, however, were not limited to England, they also made their way across the Atlantic to New England. Peter Thuesen notes that in 1736 the New Hampshire association "had accused Edwards' Arminian nemesis Robert Breck of denying the authenticity of 1 John 5:7."[7] Additionally, a prominent Boston minister Jonathan Mayhew became the object of investigation when he complained that orthodox pastors "contend and foam, and curse their brethren, for the sake of the Athanasian Trinity, 'till 'tis evident they do not love and fear the one living and true God as they ought to do."[8] Edwards was aware of Mayhew's position and comments upon it in a letter to Edward Wigglesworth.[9]

Because this central Christian doctrine was under attack by a number of notable theologians, philosophers, and ministers, Edwards took it upon himself to defend the doctrine. Edwards had a fourfold strategy for defending this teaching. First, to those who accept the authority of Scripture he argues that Trinitarian doctrine can, in fact, be found in the Old and New Testaments. Second, to those who are more enamored with Greco-Roman philosophy and world religions he argues that even non-Christian works provide hints or shadows of the Trinity. For example, Edwards cites a section of Chevalier Ramsay's paraphrase of *Tao Te Ching,* which, according to Edwards, is proof that a Trinitarian concept exists in Chinese thought.[10] Edwards also claims that Trinitarian claims can be found in the work of Plato, Parmenides, and Indian philosophy.[11] Third, he argues for the Trinity from the claim that one can find Trinitarian types in creation, e.g., the sun and the human person. Finally, Edwards provides rational arguments for the Trinity.

Concerning rational arguments, Edwards claims that

> There may be deductions of reason from what has been said of the most mysterious matters, besides what has been said, and safe and certain deductions too as well as about the most obvious and easy matters. I think that it is within the reach of naked reason to perceive certainly that there are three distinct in God, each of which is the same [God], three that must be distinct.[12]

These rational arguments take on three primary forms: arguments from 1) idealism, 2) consent,[13] and 3) goodness.[14] Examples of each will be given, but we will focus on the argument from goodness. The first argument amounts to something like the following:

1. God infinitely and perfectly delights in himself.

2. God's delights in the perfect idea of himself.[15]

3. A perfect idea of a thing is the very thing itself. (*The Idealism Premise*) Therefore,

4. The perfect idea of God just is God himself.

Having established that God and God's own idea of himself (the Son) are divine, Edwards believes it is a small move to show that the bond of love between the Father and the Son constitutes the third person of the Trinity.

Edwards' second rational argument for the Trinity is an argument from "consent." This second argument goes as follows:

1. God is excellent.

2. Excellency involves the notions of harmony and consent.

3. Harmony and consent require relations.

4. Relations require plurality.

5. If God is excellent, there must be harmony and consent in God. Therefore, following 1 and 5,

6. There is harmony and consent in God. Therefore, following 6, 3, and 4,

7. There is plurality in God.

Edwards' third rational argument for the Trinity is the argument from goodness. This argument is found in Miscellany 96, our object of study.

In this argument, Edwards seeks to prove that "there must be more than a unity in infinite and eternal essence, otherwise the goodness of God can have no perfect exercise."[16] In order to make this claim he makes the following argument:

1. To be perfectly good is for A to incline to and delight in making another, B, happy in the same proportion as A.

2. God is perfectly good. Therefore,

3. God is inclined to and delights in making another, B, happy in the same proportion as God himself is happy.

This argument, however, does not deliver Trinitarianism just yet. In fact, as this argument stands, a Unitarian could affirm it by suggesting that "B" is some created entity, e.g., creation in general or an Arian Christ. More is needed to get a true Trinitarian argument. Edwards provides the missing piece in the second paragraph of Miscellany 96. This argument can be reconstructed as follows:

1. Goodness is delight in communicating happiness.

2. If goodness is perfect, the delight in communicating happiness must be perfect.

3. A delight in communicating happiness is perfect if and only if the inclination to communicate happiness to another is equal to the communicating agent's own inclination to be happy.

4. To be an object of one's perfect delight in communicating happiness, an object, X, must be the right kind of object.

5. To be capable of being the object of God's perfect delight in communicating happiness, X must be the kind of object that is (a) loved by God as much as God loves himself and (b) capable of receiving the fullness of God's communication.

6. A creature cannot (a) be loved by God as much as God loves himself and (b) cannot receive the fullness of God's communication. Therefore, from 4,5,6,

7. A creature is not the right kind of object to receive God's perfect delight in communicating happiness.

8. If God is good, then God must exercise perfect goodness.

9. If God will exercise perfect goodness there must be an object which meets criteria (a) and (b).

10. God is good. Therefore, from 8–10,

11. God exercises perfect goodness. It follows from 9–11 that

12. There is an object, X, that meets criteria (a) and (b). It follows from 7 and 12 that

13. There is an object, X, toward which God perfectly delights in communicating his happiness, and X is not a creature. It follows from this that

14. There must be more than a unity in the infinite and eternal essence; God must have fellowship with a person equal to himself.

In addition to the rational argument from goodness, Edwards makes a secondary argument in Miscellany 96.[17] However, rather than starting from theology proper, Edwards begins with theological anthropology. Edwards explains that we know that "reasonable" creatures—here he has in mind human beings—cannot be happy apart from communion and fellowship with other reasonable creatures. This, Edwards says, is because reasonable creatures, i.e., human beings, delight in communicating themselves to reasonable creatures other than themselves. We know that reasonable creatures are, in fact, happy sometimes. Therefore, it must be the case that human beings have communion and fellowship with other human beings. Following this logic, Edwards makes a "lesser to greater" type argument and claims that if this line of thinking is true of human beings, who are made in the image of God, how much more must this be true of God who is perfectly and eternally happy? Edwards thus reasons that "Jehovah's happiness consists in communion, as well as the creature's."[18]

What we have seen so far is that in the face of threats to the reasonableness of the doctrine of the Trinity, Edwards was unafraid to defend the doctrine by arguing that it was eminently reasonable. Thus, Amy Plantinga Pauw is right when she claims that "Edwards thought it appropriate to counter attacks on the reasonableness of the doctrine of the Trinity with reasonable arguments."[19] Despite his confidence in using reason to *defend* the Trinity we should remember that Edwards did not believe that such rational arguments fully *explained* the doctrine. Edwards himself claims that "[I am] far from pretending to explain the Trinity so as to render it no longer a mystery. I think it to be the highest and deepest of all divine mysteries still, not withstanding anything I have said or conceived about it. I do not pretend to explain the Trinity."[20] Edwards' approach, which holds reason and mystery together, reflects how much of the Christian tradition has approached the doctrine of Trinity. His approach also serves as an example to Christians today, especially those who are philosophically or analytically inclined, for how they might approach this grand doctrine.

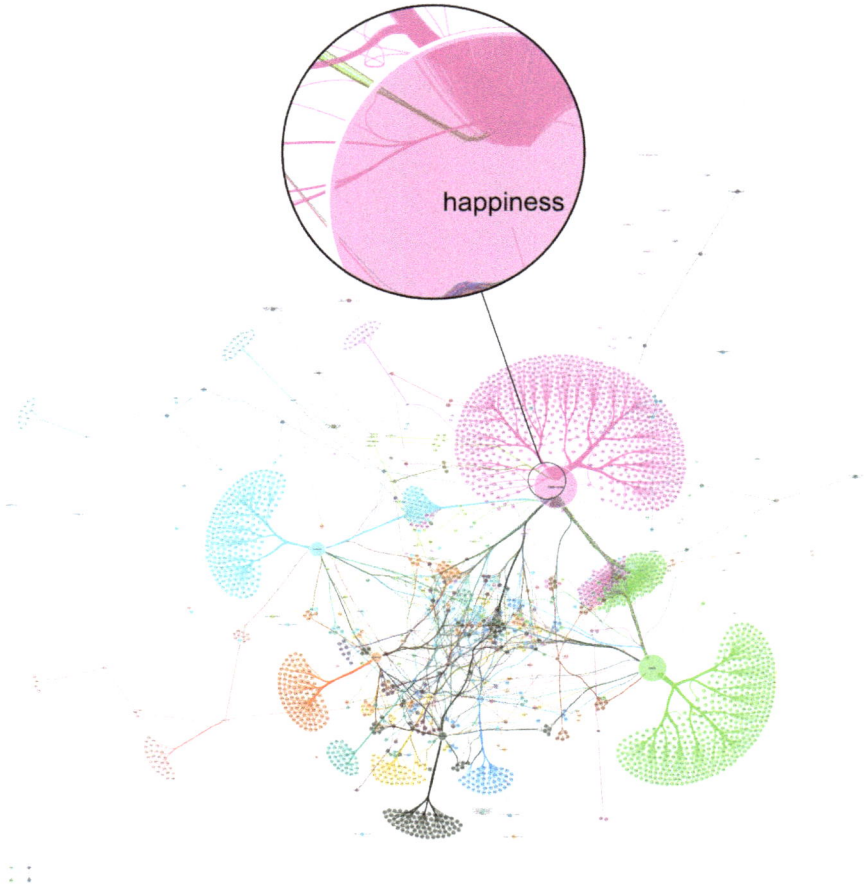

COMMUNION *and* HAPPINESS—*a map of communicability, communicable, communicant, communicants, communicate, communicated, communicates, communicating, communication, communications, communicative, communicativeness, communing, communion, communions, communities, community, happier, happiest, happifying, happily, happiness, happinesses, happy with interconnections and page locations in WJE 1–26.*

Miscellany no. 279: Eternity of Hell Torments

Like the doctrine of the Trinity, which was an object of criticism in Edwards' day, the doctrine of hell also bore the brunt of a number of critics. This is partly due to shifting attitudes concerning reason's relationship to revelation and the nature of punishment.[21]

Traditionally the doctrine of hell has consisted of four parts:

(H1) The Anti-Universalism Thesis: Some persons are consigned to hell.

(H2) The Existence Thesis: Hell is a place where people exist; if a person exists in hell, her existence never ceases.

(H3) The No Escape Thesis: There is no possibility of leaving hell once one is consigned there.

(H4) The Retribution Thesis: The justification for and purpose of hell is retributive in nature, hell being constituted so as to mete out punishment to those who deserve it.[22]

These four theses are all challenged in various ways by Edwards' theological and pastoral peers; however, since Miscellany 279 deals specifically with the eternity of punishment in hell, we will limit our focus to challenges brought against (H2).

Philip Almond notes that early in the eighteenth century supporting the doctrine of eternal punishment in hell was "socially, politically, and theologically correct."[23] However, by the middle of the century, it was being publicly challenged and rejected by a number of significant figures. One way this doctrine was challenged was by challenging the meaning of the term "everlasting" in Matthew 25:46. Henry More for example suggests that "everlasting" has "the signification of long continuance, though not of everlastingness."[24] Although More believed in the eternality of hell's torments, arguments like his concerning the meaning of the terms in use were used by others to challenge the traditional doctrine. Isaac Barrow, a Cambridge mathematician, took a different approach to challenging this doctrine; he argued that the notion of eternal punishment reflected "a severity of justice far above all example of repeated cruelty in the worst of men."[25] Given the principle that when the literal sense is disagreeable to beliefs concerning the nature of God one ought to prefer a "spiritual sense," Barrow argues that the "everlasting fire" of Matthew 25:41 should be interpreted metaphorically, meaning everlasting destruction. Others like Thomas Samuel Clarke, Matthew Tindal, and Samuel Bourn reject the notion of eternal punishment because such actions are not befitting of a morally good God. In addition to these notable critics Thomas Hobbes offers moral opposition to the Existence Thesis. Hobbes claims that he cannot believe that God "who is the Father of Mercies... should punish men's transgressions without any end of time, and with all the extremity of torture that men can imagine."[26] Thus Hobbes denies the traditional doctrine of hell. Given these numerous critiques of the belief that the punishments of hell never cease, it appears that Edwards swam against the intellectual tide of his day.

How does Edwards go about defending the Existence Thesis? In general, he employed two approaches: Scriptural defenses and rational defenses. One finds examples of his scriptural defenses in several of his sermons. For example, in a sermon titled "They That Are Gone to Hell," Edwards uses Revelation 9:6 and 22:11 to make a case that all change after death is "expressly denied" and that "there will never be any end or death by annihilation."[27] In another sermon, "The Eternity of Hell Torments," Edwards turns to Matthew 25:46 in order to oppose those who believe "the punishment of the wicked shall consist in sensible misery, yet it shall not be absolutely eternal, but only of a very long continuance."[28] This belief, that the punishment of the wicked will consist in sensible misery but only for a "very long continuance," might be read in one of two ways. First, it may be read as sort of "Escape Thesis"; that is, there are some persons in hell who experience some time in hell as a punishment, but, once they exhaust their punishment, it is possible for them to be "released" from hell. This, however, is not likely the view Edwards opposes in this sermon. Another way the statement may be read is in support of an "anti-Existence Thesis." On this reading, a person is consigned to hell for some period, and after experiencing punishment for some amount of time, the person is then annihilated. This second reading has some support given that Edwards believed in two judgements: "a particular one at death after which the disembodied soul proceeds to either heaven or hell, and a general one at the end of history in which all human beings who have ever lived (plus the devil and his wicked angels) will be judged publicly by Jesus Christ."[29]

One can find examples of Edwards' second type of defense, rational defenses, in a number of his "Miscellanies" including Miscellany 279.[30] Edwards bases the argument for the eternity of hell upon several concepts including happiness, love, and thanksgiving. One can reconstruct his argument as follows:

1. If the elect in heaven are to be happy and thankful, they must have a "lively sense" of God's love, justice, and holiness.[31]

2. If the elect have a "lively sense" of God's love, justice, and holiness, it is necessary that there be a state of affairs which induces a "lively sense" of God's love, justice, and holiness.

3. Seeing God punish the wicked necessarily induces a "lively sense" of God's love, justice, and holiness.

4. The elect in heaven are in fact happy and thankful. It follows that

5. There is some state of affairs which induces a "lively sense" of God's love, justice, and justice, namely the punishment of the wicked.

According to Edwards the reason that seeing God punish the wicked induces a lively sense of God's love is that when the elect see the wicked punished they get a "lively sense of opposite misery" that would have been their destiny had not God elected to rescue them from his wrath. Additionally, seeing God punish the wicked induces a sense of thankfulness to God because "he chose them out from the rest to make them thus happy" and because they realize that "God did not make them such vessels of wrath."[32] Thus in the condemnation of the wicked, the elect are made happy. Furthermore, upon seeing God punish the wicked, the elect catch a glimpse of God's power, his "great and dreadful majesty and authority," and his "awful justice and holiness."[33] Seeing these attributes on display incites love towards God and leads the elect to glorify him.

Although Edwards' logic thus far provides a reason for why God would punish the wicked, it does not yet show why the punishment of the wicked in hell must be eternal. In order to argue for the eternity of the punishment of the wicked in hell Edwards must add something to his argument. I suggest that the following, which is implicit in Miscellany 279, should be added in order make explicit the conclusion that "the misery of the damned will be eternal."[34]

6. If the elect are eternally happy, then they are happy at $time_1$, $time_2$, $time_3$, and so on *ad infinitum*.

7. If the elect are happy at $time_1$, $time_2$, $time_3 \ldots time_\infty$, then there is some state of affairs that necessarily induces a lively sense of God's love and justice, namely the punishment of the wicked at $time_1$, $time_2$, $time_3 \ldots time_\infty$.

8. The saints are eternally happy. It follows from 6, 7, and 8 that

9. There is some state of affairs that necessarily induces a lively sense of God's love, and justice, namely the punishment of the wicked at $time_1$, $time_2$, $time_3 \ldots time_\infty$.

By reasoning in this manner Edwards concludes that the punishment of the wicked must be eternal, thus addressing the critique offered by the leading thinkers of his day.

Before explaining what hell has to do with the Trinity, we should make one comment regarding Edwards' approach to defending the traditional doctrine of hell. Much like his defense of the Trinity,

Edwards unashamedly used scripture to defend his views about hell. Also, like his defense of the Trinity, he supplemented his scriptural arguments with rational arguments. This dual-defense (Scripture and reason) approach is by no means unique to Edwards; nevertheless, it is an approach that marks much of his writing.[35] Those who are inclined to defend the traditional doctrine of hell, including the Existence Thesis, ought to pay careful attention to his method, for it may prove helpful in light of contemporary critiques of the doctrine.[36]

What Does Hell Have to Do with the Trinity?

So far, we have briefly examined Edwards' defense of the reasonableness of the doctrines of the Trinity and hell as they appear in "Miscellanies" 96 and 279, but we might still wonder, "How do these apparently unrelated doctrines hang together?" I suggest that the answer lies in God's overarching Trinitarian purposes.

According to Edwards, God's ultimate end in all things is the communication of his glory. Given that this is God's ultimate end, God's self-communication transpires from all eternity among the three persons of the Trinity and overflows to creatures who participate in God's glorification. Because the communication of his glory is central to who God is, Edwards claims that God is a "communicative being."[37] By calling God a communicative being, Edwards means that God essentially inclines to communicate himself.[38] And when God does communicate himself, he communicates his own glory.

How does this divine self-communication (or self-glorification) occur? It occurs *ad intra* and *ad extra*—that is, within the inner life of the Trinity and the external workings of the Trinity. Regarding God's *ad intra* self-communication, Edwards says that God glorifies himself in two ways. First, by appearing to himself in his own idea of himself (corresponding to the person of the Son). Second, by enjoying and delighting in himself (corresponding to the person of the Holy Spirit). Regarding God's *ad extra* self-communication, Edwards again says that God glorifies himself in two ways. First, by appearing to the saints in their understanding. This corresponds to knowledge through the Son. Second, by communicating himself to their heart. In doing so, the saints rejoice, delight, and find joy in God's communication to them. This corresponds to the work of the Holy Spirit.[39] Thus Edwards explains that "God is glorified not only by his glory being seen, but by its being rejoiced in, when those that see delight in it."[40] The key phrase here is that God is glorified when his glory is *rejoiced in*. This only occurs as God's knowledge of himself (in the Son) and God's delight and joy in himself (the Holy Spirit) is received by the mind and heart of the saints. With these preliminary points regarding God's Trinitarian self-glorifying purposes we can now see how the doctrine of the Trinity in "Miscellanies" nos. 96 and 279 relate.

I suggest that Trinity and hell relate in Edwards' thought in the following way: God is essentially the type of being who communicates his goodness. He does this *ad intra* and *ad extra*. This communication of goodness, addressed in Miscellany no. 96, which is essential if God is a Trinitarian God, leads to God's *ad intra* glorification. Because God is essentially the kind of being who communicates his goodness, God also communicates his goodness *ad extra* to the saints. According to Miscellany no. 279, when the saints see the eternal punishment of the wicked in hell, not only do they understand, they also rejoice in God's goodness, i.e., his love, mercy, justice, majesty, etc. Rejoicing in God's goodness, the saints glorify God, and in turn they return God's *ad extra* communication of his glory. The end result of this process is God's glorification, or as Edward puts it elsewhere, "In the creature's knowing, esteeming, loving, rejoicing in, and praising God, the glory of God is both exhibited and acknowledged; his fullness is received and returned."[41]

Conclusion

At first glance Edwards' doctrine of the Trinity and doctrine of hell may appear to be unrelated. However, after a careful examination of "Miscellanies" nos. 96 and 279, we find that both doctrines find unity in the Edwards' idea that God is essentially a God of goodness and glory.

Notes

[1] Here I say "supposed" because Norman Fiering has shown that Edwards almost never addressed hell in his major writings and that only two percent of his sermons focused on hell. See Norman Fiering, *Jonathan Edwards' Moral Thought and Its British Context* (Chapel Hill: University of North Carolina Press, 1981), 204.

[2] Jonathan Edwards. "Sinners in the Hands of an Angry God." *Norton Anthology of American Literature,* ed. Nina Baym and Robert Levine (New York: W.W. Norton & Co., 2012), 430–41.

[3] In theological vocabulary "eternal" typically refers to something which has no beginning or end. Clearly this is not what Edwards means when he speaks of the "eternity" of hell's torments. By speaking of the "eternity" of hell's torments Edwards is speaking of the "unendingness" of hell's torments.

[4] Jonathan Edwards, *The Works of Jonathan Edwards,* Vol 13, ed., Thomas Schafer (New Haven: Yale University Press, 1994), 256. (Hereafter, the *Works of Jonathan Edwards* shall simply appear as WJE followed by the volume number and page number, e.g. "Miscellanies," no. 94, in *WJE* 13:256.

[5] Peter Thuesen, "Editor's Introduction," *WJE* 26:74.

[6] See *WJE* 26, "Catalogue" nos. 537, 104, 674, and 518 respectively.

[7] Thuesen, "Editor's Introduction," *WJE* 26:61. "For there are three that testify:" (1 John 5:7, ESV).

[8] Quoted in Thuesen, "Editor's Introduction," *WJE* 26:74.

[9] Thuesen, "Editor's Introduction," *WJE* 26:74.

[10] "Miscellanies," no. 1181, in *WJE* 23:98.

[11] See for example "Miscellanies," no. 1351, in *WJE* 23:468 and "Miscellanies," no. 1355, in *WJE* 23:562–63.

[12] "Miscellanies," no. 94, in *WJE* 13:256-7.

[13] For Edwards, "consent" is a technical term meaning "agreement, or union of being to being." *WJE* 8:561. It can also be thought of an agreement between relations or parts.

[14] For commentary on the first two arguments see Oliver Crisp, *Jonathan Edwards on God and Creation* (Oxford University Press: New York, 2012), 118–21 and 96–100 respectively.

[15] "Miscellanies," no. 94, in *WJE* 13:259.

[16] "Miscellanies," no. 96, in *WJE* 13:263.

[17] There is an alternative way to understand Edwards' comments in the second half of this Miscellany whereby one reads these comments not as an "argument" or "proof" of the Trinity, but rather as commentary on a principle of theological anthropology

that follows from his Trinitarian argument in the first half of the Miscellany. However, I take it that it is a secondary argument.

[18] "Miscellanies," no. 946, in *WJE* 13:264.

[19] Amy Plantinga Pauw, "Trinity" in *The Jonathan Edwards Encyclopedia,* ed. Harry S. Stout, Kenneth P. Minkema, and Adrian Neele (Grand Rapids: Eerdmans, 2017), 572.

[20] *WJE* 21:134

[21] Philip Almond, *Heaven and Hell in Enlightenment England* (New York: Cambridge University Press, 1994), 149 and 155–61.

[22] These four theses are adapted from Jonathan Kvanvig's articulation of the four components of the traditional doctrine of hell in, *The Problem of Hell* (New York: Oxford University Press, 1993), 19.

[23] Almond, *Heaven and Hell,* 145.

[24] Henry More, *Annotations upon the Two Foregoing Treatises, Lux Orientalis, or, An Enquiry into the Opinion of the Prae-existence of Souls; and the Discourse of Truth. . .* (London: J. Collins and S. Lounds, 1682), 74.

[25] Cited in Almond, *Heaven and Hell,* 148.

[26] Thomas Hobbes, *Leviathan,* vol. 1, ed. G.A.J Rogers and Karl Schuhmann (New York: Continuum, 2005), 497.

[27] Jonathan Edwards, "They That Are Gone to Hell," in *The Torments of Hell: Jonathan Edwards on Eternal Damnation,* ed. William C. Nichols (Ames, IA: International Outreach, 2006), 206.

[28] Jonathan Edwards, "The Eternity of Hell Torments," in *The Torments of Hell: Jonathan Edwards on Eternal Damnation,* ed. William C. Nichols (Ames, IA: International Outreach, 2006), 111–12. The language of "long continuance" is reminiscent of Henry More's Language in *Annotations.* However, Edwards' catalogue of books does not list this book as being in Edwards' possession.

[29] Michael J. McClymond and Gerald R. McDermott, *The Theology of Jonathan Edwards* (New York: Oxford, 2011), 66. See "Miscellanies," no. 777, in *WJE* 18:431 and *WJEO* 50.

[30] For other "rational" defenses see: "Miscellanies," no. 117, in *WJE* 13:283, "Miscellanies," no. 238, in *WJE* 13:353–4, "Miscellanies," no. 260, in *WJE* 13:360, "Miscellanies," no. 308, in *WJE* 13:392.

[31] Although Edwards does not explicitly state what he means by "lively sense," I take it that a "lively sense" refers to an immediate perception of some reality.

[32] "Miscellanies," no. 279, in *WJE* 13:379.

[33] "Miscellanies," no. 279, in *WJE* 13:379.

[34] "Miscellanies," no. 279, in *WJE* 13:379.

[35] For another example of this approach see how Edwards organizes *The End of Creation,* especially *WJE* 8:419.

[36]For an example of how looking to Edwards might serve as a resource for defending the traditional doctrine of hell see Christopher Woznicki, "Redeeming Edwards' Doctrine of Hell: An 'Edwardsean' Account" in *Themelios* 42.2 (2017).

[37]"Miscellanies," no. 332, in *WJE* 13:410.

[38]"Miscellanies," no. 107b, in *WJE* 13: 277–78.

[39]"Miscellanies," no. 448, in *WJE* 13:495.

[40]"Miscellanies," no. 448, in *WJE* 13:495.

[41]*WJE* 8:531.

EDWARDS' DOCTRINE OF THE IMMANENT TRINITY

Adam G. Cavalier

I think that it is within the reach of naked reason to perceive certainly that there are three distinct in God, each of which is the same [God], three that must be distinct; and that there are not nor can be any more distinct, really and truly distinct, but three, either distinct persons or properties or anything else; and that of these three, one is (more properly than anything else) begotten of the other, and that the third proceeds alike from both, and that the first neither is begotten nor proceeds.

— Jonathan Edwards, *Miscellany no. 94*

THE DOCTRINE OF THE TRINITY for Jonathan Edwards has long been a point of interest for scholars who study his writings. The path of historical and theological inquiry has been full of intrigue and controversy on the one hand and devotion and improvement on the other. For example, in the mid-nineteenth century, there was great speculation as to whether or not Edwards was fully orthodox in his theology. This divergent path was due in large part to conjecture and speculations sparked from a theologian who was denied access to part of the Edwardsian corpus. He generated critical inquiry when he suggested that Edwards might hold Arian or even Sabellian views on the Trinity. However, now that all manuscripts have been released to the public, Edwards has been praised as a theologian who simultaneously held to the orthodox position and yet expressed that doctrine in innovative ways.[1] With the publication of these manuscripts a deluge of scholarship has followed. Today, Edwards is widely praised for his contribution to the doctrine, especially within Reformed tradition. He furthered a stream of constructive theological discourse, particularly the psychological analogy of the Trinity.

Edwardsian scholars are in full agreement that the doctrine of the Trinity is both fundamental and predominant in Edwards' writings.[2] This claim does not mean that Edwards simple affirmed the traditional position and then went on to focus his primary attention on other doctrinal issues. Edwards' Trinitarianism was at the forefront of all of his theological discourse. Moreover, the doctrine brought all of his other theological teachings and philosophical reasoning into proper focus. Kyle Strobel writes of the priority of Edwards' doctrine, "Jonathan Edwards' theology is fundamentally trinitarian. Edwards' account of the Trinity is the anchor, or in his words, the *fountain* of all that is. Edwards' theology traces the contours of the Trinity so that the ordering, emphasis and teleology of his thought finds its home in his trinitarian analysis."[3] Similarly, Oliver Crisp writes, "[Edwards is] a divine for whom the three persons of the Godhead are a touchstone for all other doctrines."[4] Edwards reasoned that because God created everything and is sovereign over all things, doctrinal connections can be made between the two. Therefore, seeing that the foundation for all of Edwards' theology is the Trinity, a critical engagement with the doctrine is of paramount importance for any detailed work in Edwardsian studies.

This chapter will outline the broad contours of Jonathan Edwards doctrine of the immanent Trinity as it is found within the "Miscellanies." While enigmatic and brief at times, this body of literature can help the reader understand a robust and coherent doctrine that innovatively advances the doctrine of the immanent Trinity within the Reformed tradition. Pauw draws the connection, "The 'Miscellanies' notebooks . . . reflect his lifelong interest in the doctrine [of the Trinity]." This sustained engagement with the doctrine provides a wide scope of information. This extensive data allows the scholar to evaluate potential changes, developments, and progress in Edwards' doctrine of the Trinity. Considering this broad collection of data that now exists, the scholar is able to make a much better analysis than was available just a few decades ago.[5]

This chapter will begin with an analysis of the intellectual milieu in which Edwards formulated his doctrine. This approach will shed light on the broader historical context which will in turn inform the reader as to the purpose and background of his theological formulations. Moreover, the "Miscellanies" not only constitute a window into the theological and philosophical ruminations of the scholar, they also provide insight into the historical progression of his thought. Finally, this chapter will discuss the the contemporary theological debates over Edward's use of Trinitarian models. These debates center on Edwards' analogical language and reasoning. Scholars are asking and answering the following question: Is Edwards to be placed squarely within an Augustinian framework, which primarily centers on a psychological analogy, or should one see Edwards as adding a new model to this tradition to suit a theological argument at a given point? In short, all scholars agree that Edwards works from within the Augustinian tradition, yet a new thesis claims something slightly different. It proposes that Edwards used this tradition in dialogue with another model. This proposal asserts Edwards adopted a non-Western model alongside the Augustinian model which employs a social analogy to understand the immanent Trinity. He used this analogy when he wanted to highlight a different ontology aspect of God's triunity. In other words, did Edwards employ one model—that is, the Augustinian model which uses a psychological analogy—or did Edwards employ two models?

Enlightenment Rationalist Intellectual Milieu

Rationality and Practicality of the Doctrine

Edwards' theological formulations on the doctrine occurred within a polemical context. Fierce attacks against the traditional orthodox position came primarily from Deists, Socinians, Unitarians, and other Enlightenment Rationalists. While many intellectuals within the movement were not altogether anti-religious, orthodox positions came under heavy scrutiny. Placing Edwards' theology of immanent Trinity within its intellectual milieu will give greater insight as to the relevance of his conclusions.

William Pitts, a contemporary scholar in American religion, aptly summarizes one of the core tenants of the Enlightenment in America, "The doctrine of the Trinity is contrary to reason and therefore must be abandoned."[6] The movement fostered a spirit of distrust in the doctrine of the Trinity. It was seen as irrational and useless, an archaic relic of the past that needed to be discarded. Natural religion was to supersede special revelation. Aristotelian scholasticism along with its presumptive authority of the past was to be thrown off as a burdensome weight. Deductive reasoning was a methodological aberrance that falsely reasoned from *a priori* assumptions. Reason, unaided by any divine assistance, was lauded as the reliable guide that could progress religion and society towards true flourishing. Thus, the doctrine of the Trinity was seen as untenable. It was a doctrine that was birthed out of arcane philosophical speculation and impractical in contemporary morality.

At one point in his writings, a young Edwards also questioned the usefulness of the doctrine. This hesitancy to accept the practical implications of the Trinity would have come in part due to his engagement with reading Enlightenment scholars. He wrote, "I used to think sometimes with myself, if such doctrines as those of the Trinity and decrees are true, yet what need was there of revealing of them in the gospel? what good do they do towards the advancing [of] holiness?"[7] At least initially, Edwards shared the concerns of the Enlightenment ethos. However, Edwards was led to a different conclusion from that of the rationalist skeptics:

> But now I don't wonder at all at their being revealed, for such doctrines as these are glorious inlets into the knowledge and view of the spiritual world, and the contemplation of supreme things; the knowledge of which I have experienced how much it contributes to the betterment of the heart. If such doctrines as these had not been revealed, the church would never have been let half so far into the view of the spiritual world, as God intends it shall be before the world is at an end. I know by experience, how useful these doctrines be to lead to this knowledge. God doubtless knew what was needful to be revealed.[8]

Edwards reasons that although a person may not initially receive a doctrine such as the Trinity as logically coherent or practical, it should not necessarily be rejected. He would eventually come to sense the religious and practical benefits of the doctrine. Writing that he experienced its effect on his heart, the doctrine provided emotional comfort and spiritual improvement. Edwards writes that he has come to know this truth by way of experience. The revelation of the Trinity is able to effect the person with empirical evidence, engaging the person with firsthand involvement. In short, a Christian is able to experience the doctrine's practical use in everyday piety. Moreover, the doctrine affected more than just his own personal life. It is for the benefit of the church at large. The church is able to gain insight into the spiritual world that affects its daily faith life.

Edwards saw a strong connection between the doctrine of the Trinity and ethics, refuting the claim that the doctrine was useless and irrelevant in everyday life.[9] Edwards writes in one of his entries, "Duties are founded on doctrines; and the revelation we now have of the Trinity . . . [makes] a vast alteration with respect to the reason and obligations to many amiable and exalted duties, so that they are as it were new."[10] A Christian's duties are enlivened and empowered through a proper understanding of the Trinity. When this Trinitarian ethic is understood and applied, there is an added social effect.[11] As the persons of the Godhead are unified in intimate affection and will, Christians are to live in harmony with one another. They live selflessly and help others. God is the fountain and source of all love. God's intra-Trinitarian love is beautiful and glorious. This divine love is communicated to his creatures. Their love to one another reflects this divine love. Writing on Edward's connection of Trinitarianism and ethics, Craig Biehl says, "Since all things in the universe are an emanation of the internal glory of the Trinity 'diffused' and 'overflowing,' all beauty and love are an emanation of God's intra-Trinitarian love and excellence. All moral beauty is a communication of God's moral beauty."[12] For Edwards, a creature's moral duties to their neighbor reflect God's love and delight within himself. However, when this ethic is not understood and applied, discord and division arises. Selfishness, pride, and envy all result in societal unrest. This moral friction reflects the antithesis of the triune relations. In sum, a society of persons is to mirror the persons of the Godhead. All are to be living in one accord, perfectly happy and unified with the other. Societal ethics are to reflect Trinitarian ontology.

Not only did Edwards believe the doctrine to be logical and rational, but he also believed the doctrine to be immensely practical, affecting everyday life and piety. Far from being an impenetrable and irrelevant relic of the past, the doctrine of the Trinity is practical and intelligible.

Retaining the Mystery

Edwards claimed that certain elements of the doctrine could be understood by human reasoning. Scriptural revelation allows humans to comprehend essential facts about God. By divine grace, creatures can know particular fact about God, yet they cannot fully comprehend every aspect of God's nature and his inner workings. Thus, Edwards retained an element of unexplainable divine mystery when seeking to understand the Trinity. This approach sought to communicate God's utter transcendence beyond human understanding. Edwards writes,

> I am far from pretending to explaining the Trinity so as to render it no longer a mystery. I think it to be the highest and deepest of all divine mysteries still, notwithstanding anything that I have said or conceived about it. I don't pretend to explain the Trinity, but in time, with reason, may [be] led to say something further of it than has been wont to be said, though there are still left many things pertaining to it incomprehensible.[13]

Not seeking to capitulate core doctrinal points to Enlightenment rationalism, Edwards retained the preeminence and excellency of God. In one sense, the doctrine of the Trinity is knowable. Yet in another sense, it is beyond comprehension. God created all things and stands above all things. None of his creatures could ever grasp the depths of God. Edwards recounts a story in one of his "Miscellanies" that illustrates this point well:

> I once told a boy of about thirteen years of age that a piece of any matter of two inches square was eight times so big as one of but one inch square, or that it might be cut into eight pieces, all of them as big as that of but an inch square. He seemed at first to think me not in earnest ... and cried out of the impossibility and absurdity of it ... And when I afterwards showed him the truth of it by cutting out two cubes, one an inch and another two inches square, and let him examine the measures ... he seemed to [be] astonished as though there were some witchcraft in the case and hardly to believe it after all, for he did not yet at all see the reason of it.[14]

The proposed experiment was dismissed as incompatible with natural logic and reason. How could the block be that much bigger when—to the natural eye's perception—it was not so? Initially, the difference was imperceptible to reason. The claim was thought to be preposterous. Yet upon close examination, the truth was found to be just as reported. The same is so with regards to certain matters of orthodox Christian theology. In this case, Edwards made the case specifically in parallel to the doctrine of the Trinity. The orthodox claim seemed to be incompatible with both mathematics and reason. The same was true of the wooden boxes to the young lad. In both cases, they reasoned that because they could not understand the claim, it was absurd. Edwards concluded that the doctrine of the Trinity is infinitely greater than any geometric puzzle that could stupefy young boys.

Edwards' point in conducting the experiment was to show how unassisted reason is not always correct. Thus, it should not be used as an infallible guide to truth. He links the boy's perception to that of the critics of the doctrine of the Trinity: "I believe it was a much more difficult mystery to him than the Trinity ordinarily is to men. And there seemed to him more evidently to be a contradiction in it than ever there did in any mystery of religion to a Socinian or deist."[15] These detractors are guilty of rejecting something simply because they cannot understand it. Thus, Edwards is claiming that the fault lies not with the doctrine itself, but with the person. They do not have the intellectual capacity to understand it. This shortcoming should not lead one to the reject the traditional teaching on the subject. Rather, it should cause them to wonder at a transcendent God who is above human attempts at comprehension. Instead of rejecting the doctrine on grounds of incompatibility with natural reasoning, the critics should reckon that the doctrine is compatible with supernatural revelation. In one of Edwards' very last entries on the Trinity in the "Miscellanies," he writes, "The Trinity [is] not absurd and [a] contradiction."[16] Thus, Edwards claimed that the orthodox position was logical and acceptable, contrary to modern claims of the Deists, Socinians, Unitarians, and other non-Trinitarians.

Finally, Edwards sought to build upon the orthodox position. He believed that reason could assist the theologian in constructing theological formulations. These formulations would be rooted in Scriptural truth, but would be logical deductions from that special revelation. He writes in his earliest Miscellany on the Trinity, "I am not afraid to say twenty things about the Trinity which the Scripture never said. There may be deductions of reason from what has been said of the most mysterious matters, besides what has been said."[17] Thus, Edwards sought to construct new paradigms for understanding the Trinity. He was not content to simply rehearse old doctrinal formulations, although he accepted the traditional standards. Edwards sought to use new philosophical categories to create new ways of understanding ontological and experiential truths about the Trinity.

Edwards did not fully reject all aspects of the Enlightenment. Surely, he rejected the claims from some within the movement that sought to attack traditional Christian doctrines. Yet he sought to use the new methods of reason and logic found in the intellectual milieu of the movement, and sought to apply it to Christian orthodoxy. In an ironic turn, Edwards used the movement's intellectual currents to validate the traditional position. Edwards writes that indeed there can be "results from the putting [together] of reason and Scripture, though it has not been said in Scripture in express words."[18]

Divine Excellency

Related to his position on moral thought and the divine nature, Edwards wrote extensively on the concept of excellency. [19] Indeed, E. Brooks Holifield argues that the idea permeated all of Edwards' thinking. He writes, "Notions of excellency . . . affected the way Edwards thought about almost everything."[20] This term implies love, harmony, consent, agreement, congruence, symmetry, proportion, and beauty. The starting point is rooted in aesthetics.[21] Whenever something meets the senses that conforms to these quality, the beholder is struck with a sense of the thing's excellency. This beauty is experienced regularly in the natural world. Music, art, mathematics, etc., all have expressions of this concept. Then, the term must be understood in terms of relation. One thing is rightly aligned and ordered to an-

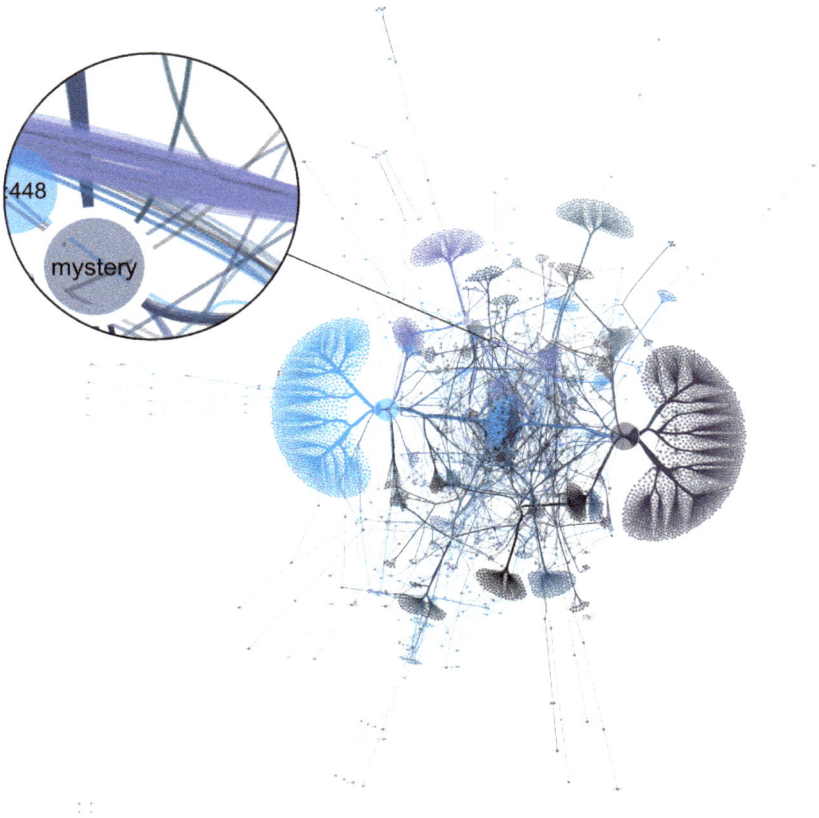

MYSTERY, REASON, SCRIPTURE, *and* TRINITY—*a map of antiscriptural, mysteries, mysterious, mysteriously, mysteriousness, mystery, reason, reasonable, reasonableness, reasonably, reasoned, reasoner, reasoners, reasoning, reasonings, reasons, scriptural, scripture, scriptures, trinity, unreasonable, unreasonableness, unreasonably, unscriptural, unscripturalness with interconnections and page locations in WJE 1–26.*

other. In order for things to be congruent or agreeable, there must be something to compare it.

This term is most exemplified in love. This is the highest of all excellencies. Edwards writes, "Love is certainly the perfection as well as happiness of a spirit."[22] When two people love each other, they display excellency in their approval of one another. There is harmony, consent, and agreement between the two. They delight in one another. Further, a greater communication of excellency is in a creature's love to the Creator. When a human loves God, they experience enjoyment in him. This unifying love to God has excellency in its relations. The highest and perfect expression of this concept is God's love to himself. Agreement and delight go back and forth in perfect harmony. This intra-Trinitarian love is the fountain from which all love is communicated. It is also a paradigm and archetype for all other loves because that is where love finds its perfect form.

Since God is love and there must be another to make love possible, Edwards concludes in an entry on the Trinity,

> That 'tis necessary that that object which God infinitely loves must be infinitely and perfectly consenting and agreeable to him; but that which infinitely and perfectly agrees is the very same essence . . . One alone cannot be excellent, inasmuch as, in such case, there can be no consent. Therefore, if God is excellent, there must be a plurality in God; otherwise, there can be no consent in him.[23]

God must delight in that which is most excellent. So, he fully loves himself. If he did not love what is most excellent, he would be an idolater. Thus, there must be a plurality within God. Edwards writes that the Son is "infinitely happy in the enjoyment of the Father's love."[24] This claim gives greater context to the opening line of Edwards' *Discourse on the Trinity*, which says, "God is infinitely happy in the enjoyment of himself, in perfectly beholding and infinitely loving, and rejoicing in, his own essence and perfections."[25]

God is perfectly excellent because he delights in what is completely harmonious, agreeable, lovely, and beautiful—that is, himself.

Edwards' Response to Intellectual Hostility

Edwards' doctrine of the Trinity was formed in a hostile intellectual environment. The rise of natural religion appealed to the ability of unassisted human reason. Special revelation must conform to whatever common sense and reason could confirm. Intellectual currents within the Enlightenment rejected traditional doctrines such as the Trinity. They were artifacts of a bygone age that needed to be discarded. In response, Edwards held to the orthodox position, rejecting the claims that the doctrine was illogical and impractical. Edwards held that although the Trinity could not be fully comprehended, it could be believed on reasonable grounds. Simply because human reason could not immediately arrive at the doctrine using the intellectual means of the day does not necessarily lead to the conclusion that it is false and should be discarded. Moreover, Edwards was not simply content to have a defensive posture regarding the doctrine. He sought to relate it to all areas of his theology. Yet Edwards' most unique contribution to the doctrine is to be found in his analogical language when talking about the Trinity.

Analogies of the Trinity

Edwards held that while God could not be fully comprehended, theologians can make proper use of human logic and reasoning in order to probe deeper into divine revelation. Thus, Edwards sought to better understand the Trinity by making use of analogies of the Trinity. Although Edwards was cautious of employing such models to describe the Trinity, he found a solid Reformed tradition from which to make theological inquiry.

The locus of contemporary scholarly debate within Edwards' doctrine of the immanent Trinity concerns his use of analogies. In this section, the current debate over the different models will be presented and explained. Then, a conclusion will be drawn from these two perspectives which will see the historical outworking and theological content of the "Miscellanies" as a key to solving this contemporary debate.

Augustinian Model

Augustine's *De Trinitatae* presents a systematic analysis of triune relations. He reasons that a unity of essence exists like a human soul exists. The human soul is one just as the divine essence is one. In both cases, a plurality exists within the one. The divine essence (*essentia*) has three substances (*personae*).[26] Similarly, a human soul has a triad of intellectual systems.[27] There is a threefold combination of a mind, heart, and volition all acting within one person. These faculties are all independent, yet they are also integrated into a singular whole. Augustine writes, "Behold, there is a Trinity, namely, wisdom, the knowledge of itself, and the love of itself. For so do we find a trinity in man, that is, the mind, and the knowledge by which it knows itself, and the love by which it loves itself."[28] He succinctly summarizes that these three can be seen in a single person's understanding, memory, and will.[29] Thus, a person's mind, heart, and volition all work together, yet they are separate within a person. They are not confused within one another; they maintain distinctiveness; yet, they all coalesce into an integrated system inside the human soul. Thus, Augustine lays out a model for the Trinity that has been often called the psychological model (or analogy).

Thus, Augustine introduced a profound and original contribution to the church's doctrine of the Trinity. In his psychological model of the Trinity, the Christian is able to have a window into the inner life of God by self-introspection guided by Scriptural revelation. He reasoned that one created in the image of God could understand the very nature of God by this reflective approach.

Within the present scholarly debate in Edwardsian studies, there is one point that remains uncontested: Edwards employed this psychological model when talking about the Trinity. Furthermore, Edwards built upon the tradition expressed in this Western analogy. Whereas in previous expressions of this model, the Trinity was seen as various faculties within a person, Edwards recast the analogy as an image, self-image, and the love that connects the two. The former way of articulating the analogy rested upon a framework which sought to ground the human psyche as the primary illustration. Edwards slightly altered this schema by grounding the image in philosophical idealism.

Edwards reasoned that metaphysical reality is grounded in ideas. He writes, "An absolutely perfect idea of a thing is the very thing ... Whatsoever is perfectly and absolutely like a thing, is that thing."[30] Humans perceive imperfectly and can view nothing immediately. However, God can perceive perfectly. Edwards continues the logic, "God's idea is absolutely perfect."[31] Then Edwards says that ideas are the images of things. Pointing to biblical passages that identify the Son as the image of God, Edwards concludes his point: The Father is the perfect idea and the Son is the expressed image of that idea.[32] Further, the love between the idea and the image are so strong that the bond that unites them eternally generates into reality. Edwards identifies this bond as the third person of the Trinity, "The Holy Spirit is the the act of God between the Father and the Son infinitely loving and delighting in each other."[33] Again, Edwards cites multiple Scripture passages in support of his claim.[34] Thus, there are three: the Father, the Son, and the Holy Spirit. Edwards posits a model of the Trinity building on the same tradition as Augustine. The Trinity can be likened to a psychological analogy of self-introspection: the self, its knowledge, and its love. This logic forms the philosophical framework for all of Edwards' subsequent philosophical deductions on the doctrine of the Trinity.

Edwards would go on to recount this proposal numerous times in his "Miscellanies." He writes consistently, expansively, and repeatedly on this analogy. Edwards would often compare images in the natural world to to describe the Godhead. For example, he would often reference the sun as a picture of the Trinity:

> We have a lively image of this Trinity in the sun. The Father is as the substance of the sun; the Son is as the brightness and glory of the disk of the sun, . . . the Holy Ghost is as the heat and powerful influence which enlightens, warms, enlivens and comforts the world. The Spirit, as it is God's infinite love and happiness, is as the internal heat of the sun; but as it is that by which God communicates himself, is as the emitted beams of God's glory.[35]

Yet the most frequented analogy to which he returns is that of the human psyche. Edwards clearly saw an image of the Trinity within the human intellect. He would return to this image as the foundation of all his Trinitarian discourse. Later in that Miscellany, he writes, "There is yet more of an image of the Trinity in the soul of man: there is the mind, and its understanding or idea, and the will or affection or love—the heart, comprising inclination, affection, etc.—answering to God, the idea of God, and the love of God." This concept is communicated numerous times in the "Miscellanies" in various forms. After elaborating on its many dimensions, Edwards will typically summarize the analogy, putting it into a concise formula. He writes, "The Son is God's idea of himself, and the Spirit is God's love to and delight in himself."[36] Putting a distinct emphasis on the Holy Spirit in this paradigm, Edwards contends that the Holy Spirit is the bond of love that connects the Father and the Son. He says succinctly, "God's love to himself, that is, to his Son, I suppose to be the Holy Spirit."[37] This insight is unquestionably his most unique contribution to this model.[38] Augustine used the human psyche to say that the unity of God is like a single person in his intellect, emotions, and will. Edwards cast the paradigm in a different light. He claimed that the unity of God is like a single person's psyche. It consists of a self, a self-image, and the connection which binds the self together with the self image.

Again, within this model of the Trinity, Edwards regularly connects concrete images in Scripture with the third person of the Trinity. A clear example can be found in his Miscellany 98. He writes, "The Holy Spirit is nothing but the infinite love and delight of God, by his symbol, a dove; which is the symbol of love, and which is a bird ... remarkable and wonderful for its love to its mate."[39] The dove is a bird that shows remarkable love to its mate. This love represents the love by which the Father and Son are unified together. As is typical with Edwards' examples, a flurry of Scriptural references are provided for support.[40] Edwards also likens the Holy Spirit to oil. Just as oil beautifies the face, the Holy Spirit is meant to beautify God.[41] Moreover, oil is used to provide fuel for a lamp which illuminates. The oil also gives a fragrant smell to those within its proximity. Through this sensory experience one can partake in the nature of the elements. This communication is paradigmatic for the Holy Spirit, and thus he is referred to as such. He also says that the Spirit is the breath of God.[42] He then asks rhetorically, "What are so properly said to be the breathings of the soul, as its affections?" The love of God is an affection. This can properly be understood to be the bond of love which connects the Father and the Son. Therefore, not only does the image of God's breath characterize the Holy Spirit as a non-material being (a spirit), it characterizes him in his relations to the other two persons of the Godhead. Edwards would go on to liken the Holy Spirit to numerous images from the natural world. He says that the Holy Spirit is like a river, a spring, water, a shower, precious ointment, oil, wind, and fire.[43] Edwards would go on to say that these images should be kept in their proper place. They do not fully encapsulate all that God is in his being. Yet, Edwards often employed these images to help understand the persons and their relations.[44]

Social Model

A recent thesis by Amy Plantinga Pauw has taken Edwardsian scholarship in an altogether new direction.[45] She has concluded that Edwards employed the Augustinian model alongside another model—the social analogy.[46] She argues that Edwards accepted both models of the analogy and intentionally vacillated between the two. Briefly stated, the social model is an analogy that comes from outside the Western tradition. The model presents the members of the Trinity starting as individual members coming together for an agreement (or pact) to unite. This analogy is known by its espousal by the twelfth century theologian Richard of St. Victor. Edwards would employ the Augustinian model when he wanted to emphasize the unity of God, and he would employ the social model when he wanted to highlight the relational diversity of the Trinity. Using this strategy allowed for great diversity and creativity when speaking about the Trinity. Although she has reservations about the stiltedness of the way in which Edwards fluctuated between the two models, Pauw lauds Edwards' brilliance and creativity as a systematic theologian.[47] To this point, Pauw's title for her chapter six calls Edwards' doctrine "A Cobbled Trinitarianism." She says that if taken separately the models do not adequately work. "The psychological model is not sufficient for telling the particular story of God's engagement with the world. It tends towards impersonal, hydraulic metaphors of pouring out and overflowing."[48] She goes on to say that the work of the Son and Spirit are diminished and obscured in this model. She makes the same claim for the social analogy, saying it, too, is insufficient for encapsulating the dynamism of the Trinity. If taken alone, the social image "could denigrate into crude anthropomorphism."[49]

Taken together, the images work in harmony with one another. Edwards oscillates between the two models to fit his theological purposes. They complement each other well and strengthen where the other image has weaknesses. Pauw frames this dual usage in music terminology. She says that the psychological model is like the bottom of sheet music: "Edwards's two models of the Trinity have distinctive roles to play. The psychological analogy serves as the *basso continuo*, anchoring the melodic flights of the salvation narrative."[50] Conversely, the social model is the top line of the sheet music: "The social analogy of the Trinity has a crucial role to play. It takes the melody line, showing how the overflowing gifts of God are communicated to human sinners in the drama of the Son's extraordinary life for others."[51]

These two models are to be taken together. Instead of creating conflict, the two work together balancing and complementing each other.

Expanding Caldwell and Studebaker's Claim

These two models come to their fullest expressions in "Miscellanies" 94 and 1062. These two lengthy entries can be seen at the most important "Miscellanies" for Edwards' Trinitarianism. Furthermore, they can be seen as both representing the two models, respectively. First, Miscellany 94 forms the backbone for all subsequent entries on the Trinity. It clearly articulates a position that falls within the Augustinian tradition. Second, Miscellany 1062 appears to articulate a social model of the Trinity.[52] Much of the social language surrounding this debate finds its root in this entry. It talks about the economic relations between the three persons of the Godhead. Thus, interpreting these two "Miscellanies" correctly will play a critical role in how one should navigate the contemporary debate over Edwards' usage of Trinitarian analogies.

One salient point that seems to be missed in this debate is the location of these particular entries and chronology within the broad corpus of the "Miscellanies." In all of the debates, the scholars properly engage the theological content and analogical language of the subject. Ultimately, this author generally agrees with Caldwell and Studebaker's thesis, yet it will consider another aspect that is neglected. The frequency of Edward's social language is limited. Furthermore, the location in which this substantial entry (1062) is near the end of all his collection. Within the "Miscellanies," there are only two significant instances in more than sixty-five explicit entries on the Trinity that use this type of language. Thus, the idea that Edwards oscillated between the two is an argument that overreaches. Pauw's claim is further stretched when placed within the larger body of evidence in the "Miscellanies." Miscellany 1062 is followed by about ten other entries on the Trinity.[53] Moreover, each one of these later entries do not use that same social language. Edwards' later "Miscellanies" do not dwell on this subject of divine relations. When he was a young theologian, Edwards wrote Miscellany 94, which accounts for this prevalent Augustinian model. It is an idea that is revisited many times and sustained throughout all of his "Miscellanies." However, his Miscellany 1062, which is the entry where he uses this social language, is one of Edwards' last "Miscellanies" on the Trinity. Moreover, the "Miscellanies" that occur after this entry do not return to this use of language. The entries following 1062 tend to be extended quotations from various theologians on other topics related to the Trinity or they are arguments that show the incipient vestiges of the Trinity in Old Testament. Even if the point is conceded that Edwards' indeed used a social analogy for the Trinity, the argument that he returned to this model frequently is forced.

Conclusion

For Edwards, the doctrine of the Trinity is not abstract and irrelevant. Furthermore, it is not intended to be relegated to the speculations of ancient theologians or philosophers. The doctrine exists for delight and edification. It is one that can be relevant in everyday life. Edwards' analogy of the Trinity builds upon a tradition that emphasizes both unity and plurality within the Godhead. While he was certainly aware of the limitations of analogical language, Edwards used vivid imagery from nature to describe the Trinity. This model was intended to appropriate the doctrine into practical use. Edwards used the natural world to illustrate the fact that the Trinity is not some abstract philosophical deduction, which Enlightenment thinkers so despised. The Triune God condescends to the human intellect while fully transcending it as well. Edwards saw the doctrine of the Trinity as both mysterious and logical. Modern debates have sharpened the way in which scholars interpret Edwards' doctrine. While navigating these debates, Edwards' unique contribution should be kept in perspective. Edwards built upon the traditions of previous generations of theologians in order to construct an analogy of a God that maintained both unity and diversity, holding both harmoniously together.

Notes

[1]This historical controversy can be traced back to Horace Bushnell in the mid-nineteenth century. The background and content of this found in a recent monograph on Edwards' Trinitarianism. See Robert W. Caldwell III and Stephen M. Studebaker, *The Trinitarian Theology of Jonathan Edwards: Text, Context, and Application* (Burlington, VT: Ashgate, 2012), 6–15.

[2]Amy Plantinga Pauw, "Trinity," in *The Jonathan Edwards Encyclopedia,* eds. Harry S. Stout, Kenneth P. Minkema, and Adriaan C. Neele (Grand Rapids, MI: Eerdmans, 2017).

[3]Kyle Strobel, *Jonathan Edwards's Theology: A Reinterpretation* (New York: Bloomsbury T&T Clark, 2013), 4.

[4]Oliver Crisp, *Jonathan Edwards Among the Theologians* (Grand Rapids, MI: Eerdmans, 2015), 36.

[5]Amy Plantinga Pauw said in a 2005 publication, "It is only in the last twenty-five years that the doctrine of the Trinity has received much attention in studies in Jonathan Edwards' theology." See Amy Plantinga Pauw, "The Trinity," in *The Princeton Companion to Jonathan Edwards,* ed. Sang Hyun Lee (Princeton: Princeton University Press, 2005), 44.

[6]Bill L. Pitts, "Enlightenment Protestantism," in *Dictionary of Christianity in America,* ed. D.G. Reid (Downers Grove, IL: Intervarsity Press, 1990).

[7]"Miscellanies," no. 181, in *WJE* 13:328.

[8]"Miscellanies," no. 181, in *WJE* 13:328.

[9]An entire dissertation was written on this topic. For further consideration see William J. Danaher, Jr., "The Trinitarian Ethics of Jonathan Edwards." Ph.D. diss., Yale University, 2002.

[10]"Miscellanies," no. 343, in *WJE* 13:416.

[11]David C Brand, "Ethics," in *The Jonathan Edwards Encyclopedia,* eds. Harry S. Stout, Kenneth P. Minkema, and Adriaan C. Neele (Grand Rapids, MI: Eerdmans, 2017).

[12]Craig Biehl, "Complacence," in *The Jonathan Edwards Encyclopedia,* eds. Harry S. Stout, Kenneth P. Minkema, and Adriaan C. Neele (Grand Rapids, MI: Eerdmans, 2017).

[13]*WJE* 21:134.

[14]"Miscellanies," no. 652, in *WJE* 18:192.

[15]"Miscellanies," no. 652, in *WJE* 18:192–93.

[16]"Miscellanies," no. 1234, in *WJE* 23:167.

[17]"Miscellanies," no. 94, in *WJE* 13:257.

[18]"Miscellanies," no. 94, in *WJE* 13:257.

[19]Edwards first outlined this concept in the first of his entries on "The Mind." However, Edwards originally began this entry in the "Miscellanies." He could have separated it from the "Miscellanies" in order to distinguish it as a particularly important concept. He writes, "There has nothing been without more a definition than excellency, although it be what we are more concerned with than anything else whatsoever." See *WJE* 6:332.

[20]E. Brooks Holifield, *Theology in America: Christian Thought from the Age of the Puritans to the Civil War* (New Haven: Yale University Press, 2003), 105.

[21]John Ray Van Wyk, "Excellency," in *The Jonathan Edwards Encyclopedia,* eds. Harry S. Stout, Kenneth P. Minkema, and Adriaan C. Neele (Grand Rapids, MI: Eerdmans, 2017).

[22]"Miscellanies," no. 117, in *WJE* 13:283.

[23]"Miscellanies," no. 117, in *WJE* 13:284.

[24]"Miscellanies," no. 516, in *WJE* 18:62.

[25]*WJE* 21:113.

[26]Augustine's predecessors in the East, the Cappadocian Fathers, would have articulated this same position, using the equivalent Greek terminology: one essence (*ousia*) and three substances (*hypostases*).

[27]For a helpful discussion on Augustine's psychological model for the Trinity, see Lewis Ayres, *Augustine and the Trinity* (New York: Cambridge University Press, 2010), 134–38.

[28]Saint Augustine, *The Trinity,* translated by Stephen McKenna (Washington, D.C.: The Catholic University of America Press, 1963), 464.

[29]Saint Augustine, *The Trinity,* translated by Stephen McKenna (Washington, D.C.: The Catholic University of America Press, 1963), 465.

[30]"Miscellanies," no. 94, in *WJE* 13:258.

[31]"Miscellanies," no. 94, in *WJE* 13:258.

[32]In his first and most important Miscellany on the Trinity, Edwards cites the following passages in support of his conclusion: 2 Cor. 4:4, Col. 1:15, and Heb. 1:3.

[33]"Miscellanies," no. 94, in *WJE* 13:260.

[34]Edwards sees this binding love identified as the Holy Spirit in Isa 42:1, Matt 3:17, and John 3:35.

[35]"Miscellanies," no. 370, in *WJE* 13:441.

[36]"Miscellanies," no. 405, in *WJE* 13:468.

[37]"Miscellanies," no. 151, in *WJE* 13:302.

[38]The point made here is the subject of the following monograph: Robert W. Caldwell III. *Communion in the Spirit: The Holy Spirit as the Bond of Union in the Theology of Jonathan Edwards, Studies in Evangelical History and Thought* (Milton Keynes, UK: Paternoster), 2006.

[39]"Miscellanies," no. 98, in *WJE* 13:265.

[40]Edwards references (in the order of their appearance) Song 1:15, 4:1, 2:14, 5:2, 6:9, and Psa. 74:19. He later cites Matt 3:17 and John 17:26.

[41]Although this image of oil is recounted numerous times, the reference here is to Miscellany 226 and 227. Edwards cites Psa 104:15, 133:2, and Song 4:10 for support. See "Miscellanies," no. 226, in *WJE* 13:347.

[42]"Miscellanies," no. 157, in *WJE* 13:307.

[43]"Miscellanies," no. 1065, in *WJE* 20:445.

[44]In Miscellany 1065, Edwards says that the images he used for the Holy Spirit could not be easily likened to the Son or the Father because of their method of communication. The Holy Spirit is the person who is most clearly represented in their manner and likeness. The analogy would not work properly otherwise.

[45]Amy Plantinga Pauw is the Henry P. Mobley Jr. Professor of Doctrinal Theology at Louisville Presbyterian Seminary.

[46]This thesis is the central argument in her book. See Amy Plantinga Pauw, The Supreme Harmony of All: The Trinitarian Theology of Jonathan Edwards (Grand Rapids: Eerdmans, 2002).

[47]She also calls him a "theological risk-taker." See *Amy Plantinga Pauw, The Supreme Harmony of All: The Trinitarian Theology of Jonathan Edwards* (Grand Rapids: Eerdmans, 2002), 190.

[48]Amy Plantinga Pauw, *The Supreme Harmony of All: The Trinitarian Theology of Jonathan Edwards* (Grand Rapids: Eerdmans, 2002), 185.

[49]Amy Plantinga Pauw, *The Supreme Harmony of All: The Trinitarian Theology of Jonathan Edwards* (Grand Rapids: Eerdmans, 2002), 186.

[50]Amy Plantinga Pauw, *The Supreme Harmony of All: The Trinitarian Theology of Jonathan Edwards* (Grand Rapids: Eerdmans, 2002), 185.

[51]Amy Plantinga Pauw, *The Supreme Harmony of All: The Trinitarian Theology of Jonathan Edwards* (Grand Rapids: Eerdmans, 2002), 186.

[52]Miscellany 571 uses the image of a "household" of God in heaven. It is also used as support for the social model. However, the principle entry is 1062, due to its in-depth analysis and usage of social language.

[53]They are followed in both literary and chronological sequence. In other words, the entries roughly follow a sequential order in number and in Edwards's life. The lower numbers are entries early in his life, whereas the higher numbers are later in his life.

A New Trinity: The Trinity *ad extra* in Edwards

Obbie Tyler Todd

> *From what has been said it appears that, besides that eco-nomical subordination of the persons of the Trinity that arises from the manner and order of their subsisting, there is a new kind of subordination and mutual obligation between two of the persons, arising from this new establishment the covenant of redemption: the Son undertaking and engaging to put himself into a new kind of subjection to the Father, far below that of his oeconomical station, even the subjection of a proper servant to the Father and one under his law . . .*
>
> — Jonathan Edwards, *Miscellany no. 1062*

IN 1793, THE SCOTTISH EDITOR of Jonathan Edwards' "Miscellanies," John Erskine, explained in his preface that one of the primary reasons for publishing Edwards' private manuscripts was the anti-Trinitarian bias that had proliferated among Protestants toward the end of the eighteenth century. Jonathan Edwards, Jr. urged Erskine to publish portions of the "Miscellanies" for its rich repository of Trinitarianism and Christology: "Dr. Edwards was advised to publish them, as they may prove an antidote to the deistical notions spreading in some parts of America."[1] Contrary to Oliver Wendell Holmes's sensational claim in the late 1800s that Edwards was a crypto-Unitarian, for those who had access to them, Edwards' "Miscellanies" exhibited an unmistakable Trinitarian character.[2]

In reality, the seeds of Unitarianism had begun germinating in the soil of New England rationalism during Edwards' own lifetime. Edwards' harshest critic, Charles Chauncy, who himself became a universalist, served as a liberal forerunner to the Unitarianism that would later flourish in the Boston area. In 1755, popular anti-Trinitarian works by Jonathan Mayhew and Thomas Emlyn compelled Edwards to write to Harvard's Edward Wigglesworth, imploring him to openly rebuke the Unitarian heresy. Though agreeing with Edwards about their heterodoxy, Wigglesworth did not believe a public dispute about the Trinity was worth the time and controversy.[3] Wigglesworth's feckless reply is further evidence of eighteenth-century Congregationalism's devolution into nineteenth-century Unitarianism. In such a theological milieu, Edwards' "Miscellanies" were summoned in order to countervail the reemergence of one of the church's most ancient heresies.

Trinity *ad extra*: Newness with Continuity

During the course of his life, Jonathan Edwards' Trinitarianism in his "Miscellanies" underwent a transition that reflected the increasing hostility to the doctrine of the Trinity in eighteenth-century New England. Compared with his initial emphasis upon idealism and consent, Edwards' later thoughts on the Trinity are noticeably more apologetical, focusing on the reasonableness of the doctrine and citing heathen philosophers in addition to scholastic theologians such as John Owen.

Still, perhaps the most obvious progression in Edwards' Trinitarianism in the "Miscellanies" is his shift in focus from the immanent Trinity to the economic Trinity. Edwards' treatment of the Trinity *ad extra* is, in some ways, the third prong to his Trinitarian apologetics: classical (natural theology), historical (pagan philosophy), and presuppositional (God's work of redemption as revealed in Scripture). In

THE TRINITY *ad extra*

Miscellany no. 982, Edwards explains that the Gospel "unfolds the grand mystery of all God's counsels and works, and opens to view the treasures and divine wisdom and knowledge in God's proceedings, which before were, from the beginning of the world, hidden treasures. It discovers the grand scheme of God's proceedings and operations."[4] In other words, the order of the Trinity as seen in the work of redemption is designed to tell us something about the inner life of God from eternity. There is correspondence and continuity between the Trinity *ad extra* and the Trinity *ad intra*. According to Sang Hyun Lee, "Since God ad intra is fully actual, God's further self-actualization *ad extra* can only be a *repetition* of what is already actual *ad intra*."[5] Edwards believed that there was a "new kind of" Trinitarian dynamic in the Gospel that was still consistent in some way with the order and structure of the Trinity before the foundation of the world.[6] This new economy of divine Persons is not "merely arbitrary," but has its basis in God's eternal being.[7] Between the Trinity *ad intra* and *ad extra,* there is newness-with-continuity.

As shown by my colleague Adam Cavalier earlier in this work, Edwards' entries on the Trinity *ad intra* are presented chiefly in an Augustinian model. Miscellany no. 94 is Edwards' first in-depth presentation of his immanent Trinitarianism. In this lengthy Miscellany, Edwards describes the Son as "God's idea of his own essence" and the Holy Spirit as the Father's "infinite happiness" in his spiritual idea.[8] Edwards was bold enough to assert that he was "not afraid to say twenty things about the Trinity which the Scripture never said" and that he believed "it is within the reach of naked reason to perceive certainly that there are three distinct in God."[9] Therefore, for Edwards, the notion that the Son is "God's perfect idea of God" and that the Holy Spirit is "the perfect act of God" was not only biblical; it was perfectly reasonable.[10] Within the Reformed tradition, one of the single most defining features of Edwards' Trinitarianism was not, strictly speaking, its psychology, but rather its effability. Edwards was unafraid to posit that God's idea of himself "must be a substantial idea, having all the perfections of the substance perfectly; so that by

43

God's reflecting on himself the Deity is begotten, there is a substantial image of God begotten."[11]

By Miscellany no. 143, Edwards was willing to call the Father "the fountain of the Godhead."[12] According to Edwards' doctrine of the immanent Trinity, there is equality and consubstantiality among the Persons of the Godhead, yet with clear ranking among them. This divine order persists in the economic Trinity and is clearly visible in the work of redemption. Therefore, Jonathan Edwards' Trinitarianism *ad extra* did not shed its psychological quality. According to Ross Hastings, "Edwards' favored model when it comes to the working of the Trinity to effect human redemption is without doubt, the psychological Trinity."[13] For Edwards, the tri-unity of God *ad extra* was something "new in kind," but still "agreeable to the order" of the Trinity *ad intra*.[14] In other words, Edwards did not envision the three hypostases of the Godhead *ad intra* as simply Person 1, Person 2, and Person 3. Instead the economy of God in the work of redemption unveils an economy of sorts within the immanent Trinity. Contrary to Rahner's Rule, Edwards did not suppose the economic Trinity to be identical to the immanent Trinity; however, they were analogous in a very real way.[15]

Edwards' Four Orders of Trinitarianism

In some sense, for Edwards, the distinction between an immanent Trinity and an economic Trinity was an overly simplistic one. After all, the Trinity *ad intra* contained an "economy" of its own that preceded any intra-Trinitarian covenant or decree. In Edwards' most incisive Miscellany on the Trinity *ad extra,* no. 1062, the Northampton theologian conceived of the inner and outer life of God in terms of four orders:

1. Co-Equality of Divine Persons in terms of Deity and Glory. (*ad intra*)

2. Order of Subsistence in the Godhead (*ad intra*)

3. Order of Acting in Creation (*ad extra*)

4. Covenant of Redemption (*ad extra*)

As will be shown, the Gospel introduces additional relations within the Godhead. However, neither of the Trinitarian orders *ad extra* compromise the integrity and immutability of the orders *ad intra*. Despite his consistent usage of the word "new" to describe the orders *ad extra*, Edwards' reflections on the Trinity were always undergirded by the abiding belief in the equality between the three divine Persons. Contrary to Amy Plantinga Pauw's thesis of "three interconnected levels of trinitarian relationship," in Miscellany no. 1062 Edwards outlines four levels, grounding his Trinitarian ontology in the common "Deity and glory" of the Godhead.[16] In this sense, Edwards was thoroughly Augustinian in his commitment to the unity of God. In Edwards' psychological model of the Trinity, the Son's Deity is a derived essence, but it is also a shared essence. As he makes clear in Miscellany no. 94, there is a "triplicity" in the divine essence, "each of which are the Deity substantially."[17]

This shared "glory of the Deity" is critical for understanding Jonathan Edwards' doctrine of the Trinity *ad extra*. Before establishing any kind of covenant with man or with himself, God first decided to communicate this intra-Trinitarian glory to an audience. Furthermore, due to the consubstantiality of the Spirit with the Son and the Father, in Miscellany no. 1062 Edwards confidently asserts that "his concern in the covenant is as great as theirs, and equally honorable as theirs."[18] Edwardsean Trinitarianism begins with this axiom of divine being. "Tis very manifest," Edwards insists, "that the persons of the Trinity are not inferior one to another in glory and excellency of nature. The Son, for instance, is not inferior to the Father in glory; for he is the brightness of his glory, the very image of the Father and the express and perfect image of his person."[19] In this Nicene framework, the Father possesses no more deity, power, or glory than the Son or the Spirit. After establishing the Father as "Head of the Trinity" at the very beginning of Miscellany no. 1062,

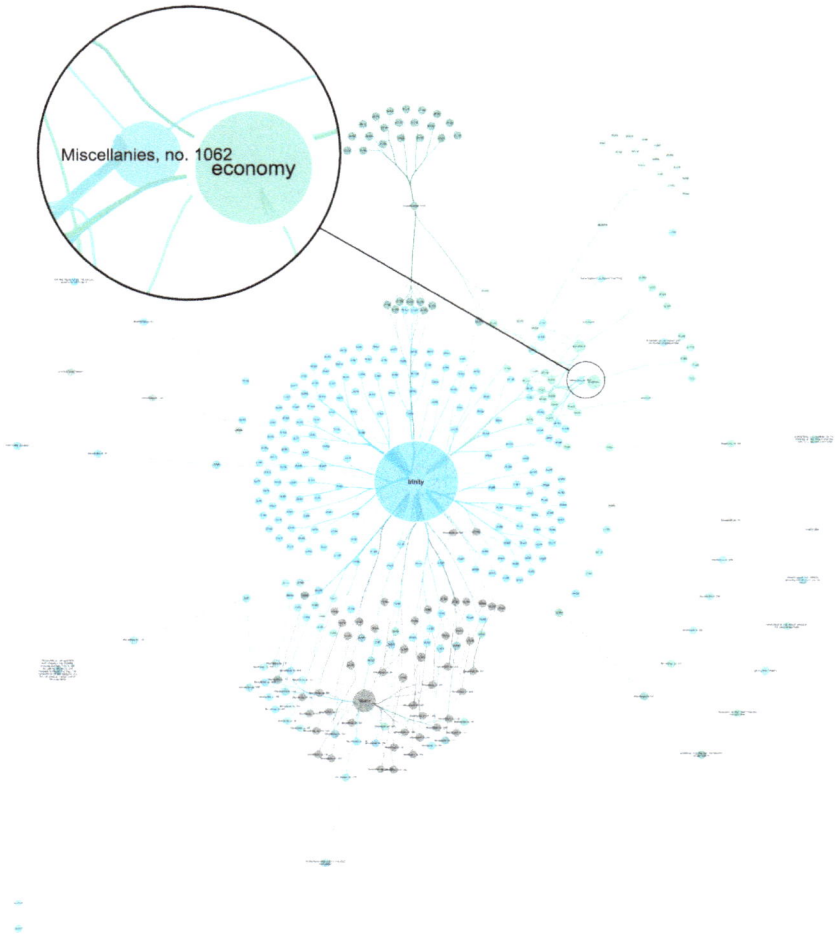

TRINITY, ECONOMY, and AD EXTRA—a map of ad extra, economical, economically, economy, oeconomical, oeconomically, trinity with interconnections and page locations in WJE 1–26.

Edwards then immediately reminds himself of the "glory of the Deity" shared by all three of the heavenly society.[20]

Nevertheless, in Edwards' paternalistic mind, an equality of Persons did not preclude a natural hierarchy within the Godhead *ad intra*. This second order of Trinitarianism was something Edwards called a "priority of subsistence"—a stratum of authority and subordination grounded in the divine nature. Edwards was careful to distance this divine order from any form of henotheism or Neo-Arianism:

> And though there be a priority of subsistence, and so a kind of dependence of the Son, in his subsistence on the Father—because with respect to his subsistence he is wholly from the Father and begotten by him—yet this is more properly called priority than superiority, as we ordinarily use such terms. There is dependence without inferiority of Deity, because in the Son the Deity, the whole Deity and glory of the Father, is as it were repeated or duplicated.[21]

Edwards' psychological model of the Trinity recognized both a strict hierarchy and an equality of divine Persons. Paradoxically, such a view of the Trinity *ad intra* allowed Edwards to ascribe a "dependence" of the Son upon the Father without inferiority. This is the abiding tension of Edwardsean Trinitarianism and the inner divine reality to which his doctrine of the Trinity *ad extra* corresponds: the subsistence-dependence identity of God. As Seng-Kong Tan observes, this particular paradigm differed slightly from the traditional Calvinistic understanding of equality:

> This notion of a necessary, communication of essence *ad intra* entails a modification of Calvin's idea of *autotheos*. As all three divine persons are 'numerically the same' divine essence, they share equally in this one *essentia* and *esse*. But the modes by which this essence is imparted and received and so 'should be here or there' allows the Son

and Spirit to be considered as derived. In short, the Son is both derived and *autotheos* because he receives and so owns the one divine essence from the Father. Such a primordial self-communication in God implies no gradation of being in God but a dynamic, ordering of persons *ad intra*.[22]

While John Calvin did not reject the idea of eternal generation, he found "no solidity" in the Augustinian psychological model.[23] Therefore, by "derived," Edwards means something more than a mere derivation of personhood.[24] Edwards goes a step further than Calvin when he posits that, in addition to his sonship, the Son's essence is also derived.

Edwards avoids the charge of Arianism with the concept of repetition: the Son is a "duplication" of the deity of the Father. As the Father's perfect idea of his own essence, the Son lays claim to the deity of the Father in the same degree that the Father does. There is, as Edwards explains, a "duplicity" in the divine essence.[25] Within God's indivisible being, there are irreducible distinctions. The Son is not *in* the Father's spiritual image; he *is* the Father's image. According to Edwards, "the idea of a thing is, in the most proper sense of all, its image; and God's idea, the most perfect image."[26] He both is "dependent" upon the Father and also is God in and of himself. In Miscellany no. 142 Edwards asks, "Can we believe that this Son of God is of a nature infinitely inferior to the Father? Would he then be so properly called the Son of God?"[27] This subsistence-dependence identity is then mirrored in the life and work of the Son incarnate when Jesus Christ submitted to the Father "not from any proper natural subjection," but rather voluntarily.[28]

The third order of Edwardsean Trinitarianism is the first order of the Trinity *ad extra*. This arrangement is something Edwards calls "the order of the acting." It was not established by necessary compulsion, but rather forged "by mutual free agreement" among the three divine persons of the Godhead "for carrying on the great design of glorifying the Deity and communicating its fullness."[29] Before any decree was issued to create human beings or covenant ratified to save them, God first determined to glorify and communicate himself from "the mere pleasure of the members of this society."[30] However, this was not a flippant, random decision by a needy, capricious God. Edwards understood this doxological disposition as part of the very fullness of God within.[31] Therefore, the order of the triune God *ad extra* reveals the nature of God himself.[32] God's operations in the world are grounded in his operations within himself. Between the second and third orders, there is newness with continuity. Edwards explains,

> But there is a natural decency or fitness in that order and economy that is established. 'Tis fit that the order of the acting of the persons of the Trinity should be agreeable to the order of their subsisting: that as the Father is first in the order of subsisting, so he should be first in the order of acting; that as the other two persons are from the Father in their subsistence, and as to their subsistence naturally originated from him and dependent on him, so that, in all that they act, they should originate from him, act from him and in a dependence on him; that as the Father, with respect to the subsistences, is the fountain of the Deity, wholly and entirely so, so he should be the fountain in all the acts of the Deity. This is fit and decent in itself.[33]

The continuity between God's order of subsisting and his order of acting is fitting. In other words, when Jesus Christ expresses his utter dependence and communion with the Father while on earth, he is disclosing a similar, corresponding intra-Trinitarian relationship that has existed eternally in infinite joy from before the foundation of the world. The incarnation doesn't rescind the Trinity *ad intra*; it reveals it. As Michael McClymond and Gerald McDermott note, this is something Edwards observed in his first "Miscellanies":

> Early in the "Miscellanies," Edwards wrote that just as God is glorified within himself by appearing to himself

in his Son and delighting in that appearance, so too he glorifies himself 'towards the creatures' by appearing to their understandings and communicating to them his own delight. Thus the reality of God's Trinitarian life *ad intra* is known through and replicated in his Trinitarian work *ad extra*.[34]

In this sense, Miscellany no. 1062 is an explication of Edwards' earliest thoughts on the Trinity *ad extra* in the "Miscellanies." The third order of Edwardsean Trinitarianism is indeed more doxological than soteriological, and thus serves as a decretal reminder that salvation for Edwards is not only from the Lord; it is *for* the Lord. Edwards' supralapsarian theology is built upon the edifice of God's own glory revealed and communicated to his elect in the crucified and risen Christ. Without divine glory and a desire to express that glory, there could be no good news of salvation in Edwards' mind. Likewise, without the Father's perfect idea of himself in the Son, and without the mutual love between the Father and Son in the Holy Spirit, there could be no communication of the knowledge and love of God to the saints in the Gospel.[35] For Edwards, covenant theology and conversion have their basis in intra-Trinitarian glory: fountain, idea, and love. This is what Robert Caldwell calls Edwards' "trinitarian blueprint":

> This blueprint consists of an intimate connection between three major areas in his theology: (1) the trinitarian fullness *ad intra,* or his immanent trinitarianism, (b) the trinitarian effulgence *ad extra,* or his economic trinitarian theology of the end for which God created the world, and (c) the trinitarian reception in the redeemed human being created in the image of God. Throughout his "Miscellanies" notebooks we find Edwards consistently refining the connections between the trinitarian fullness, effulgence, and its reception in the redeemed.[36]

The fourth and final order of Edwardsean Trinitarianism is the completion of this trinitarian blueprint in the elect. It clothes doxology with soteriology. For Edwards, the covenant of redemption wasn't God's decree to glorify himself; it was the appointed means. As God's inclination is to communicate his glory, the *pactum salutis* is the "particular, excellent method to gratify that natural inclination."[37] The Gospel scheme was not God's remedial second decree following an initial decree to create. Rather, in their infinite wisdom, the Father and Son transacted a single overarching "agreement" for "the redemption of a certain number of fallen inhabitants of this globe of earth" for the specific purpose of bringing glory to the Father through the Son. This intra-Trinitarian compact was not "required" but was "entirely diverse" from any order *ad intra* or *ad extra*. Despite omitting an initial order of Trinitarianism, Pauw explains the newness-with-continuity principle well when she insists,

> In the covenant of redemption, the equality and hierarchical ordering of the previous two levels are again reflected. The Father's headship and the Son's abject humiliation must be viewed as the result of a prior agreement among the three persons. In the covenant transactions, the Father does not arrogate power for himself; instead, consonant with his authority in the immanent and economical Trinity, he is appointed by the Son and Spirit to act as head in the plan of redemption as well. Nor are the Son and Holy Spirit compelled by the Father into subordinate roles.[38]

The free, voluntary nature of the covenant of redemption is important not simply for Christ's redemptive work as the second Adam; it is also critical for its disclosure of the unique *homoousian* nature of God. Equal with the Father in deity and glory, the Son agrees to take on the incarnate work of redemption not out of compulsion but out of love for the Father. Edwards insists that "the whole tenor of the Gospel" makes evident the free "self-abasing" of the Son for the sake of the Father.[39] His dual submission as Son of God and as Son of Man is twofold in its revelation of Trinitarian order *ad intra*: (1) the Son is one with the Father (2) and He is also subordinate to the Father. (John 10:30, 14:28) The Trinity *ad extra* duly yet freely mirrors the inner life of the Trinity. It is a "new agreement, and not merely from the order already fixed in a preceding establishment founded in the nature of things, together with the new determination of redeeming mankind."[40]

After Christ accomplishes the work given to him by the Father, the covenant of redemption does not remain for the rest of eternity *ceteris paribus*. Edwards interprets Paul's eschatological discourse in 1 Corinthians 15 as a return of sorts to the third order of Trinitarianism: "That the forementioned economy of the persons of the Trinity is diverse from all that [is] established in the covenant of redemption, and prior to it, is further confirmed from this: that this economy remains after the work of redemption is finished."[41] The "order of acting" is an everlasting Trinitarian reality. Edwards believed that, after the fulfillment of the covenant of redemption, this first order *ad extra* will "become more visible and conspicuous; and the establishment of things by the covenant of redemption shall then as it were give place to this economy as prior."[42] The increasing visibility of God's first order *ad extra* is due to the everlasting participation of the church in Trinitarian glory as it beholds the work of the Son. According to McClymond and McDermott, "Since for Edwards God's idea is the Son, and his perfect act that loves the idea is the Holy Spirit, Christian love lifts up the believer into the triune life."[43] Via glorified humanity worshipping the Father through the Son by the Holy Spirit, Edwardsean eschatology is a grand showcase of the covenant of redemption "giving place" to the "order of acting" and hence to the Trinity *ad intra*. For Edwards, the covenant of redemption is a soteriological window into the immanent God, a cascade of *ad intra* reality overflowing into the saints' true worship of God through the Trinity *ad extra*. By witnessing and receiving what God has done *ad extra,* the elect come to know (at least in part) who God is *ad intra*. In contrast with, for instance, B.B. Warfield, Edwards believed that the notion of a disjunction between the orders *ad intra* and *ad extra* is harmful for Christian worship, as it attempts to sever the work of God from the identity of God.[44]

In the end, Christ's wedding to the church is an eternal wedding. The "order of acting" remains, but a new incarnational reality is added to it. While not all terms of the covenant of redemption extend into perpetuity (i.e., the supremacy of the Son), its Gospel effects are never-ending. Therefore the "order of acting" can never lose its new soteriological hue. In turn, Edwards was willing to concede that the death, burial, and resurrection of Jesus inaugurates a "new kind of" Trinity consistent with the Trinity *ad intra*.[45] After the Son hands back all authority and power to the Father, he is appointed to a "new dignity of station" and conferred a new power of "disposal and dispensation" of the Holy Spirit.[46] While the covenant of redemption is transacted exclusively between the Father and the Son, its eschatological telos is fixed primarily in the Son's relationship to the Spirit.

"New in Kind": The Eschatological Trinity

Does the incarnation introduce a change in an immutable God? Jonathan Edwards would certainly have answered in the affirmative. However, for Edwards, the newness of the Trinity *ad extra* is one of order and not of *ousia*. God cannot change in his being, but his relations with himself are dynamic in light of his redemptive plan in Christ. As the fourth order of Edwardsean Trinitarianism comes into view, an alliterative "4-D" scheme of orders takes shape:

1. Deity
2. Dependence
3. Doxology
4. Disposal

Perhaps the single most defining feature of Edwardsean eschatology is not his postmillennialism but rather the way he framed the Son's unique relationship to the Holy Spirit.[47] For this reason, the Son's "disposal" of the Spirit, and the authority given him by the Father to do so, are critical concepts in explicating Edwards' eschatological Trinity.

The covenant of redemption is about much more than salvation; it is a heavenly marriage between Christ and his "spiritual spouse," namely in the covenant of grace.[48] In Miscellany no. 98, Edwards explains that the concept of marriage is germane to the very identity and role of the Holy Spirit: "It further appears that the Holy Spirit is nothing but the infinite love and delight of God, by his symbol, a dove; which is the symbol of love, and which is a bird beyond all other irrational animals in the world is remarkable and wonderful for its love to its mate."[49] This theme of union in the covenant of redemption is consistent with Robert Caldwell's thesis that in "the mystical union believers have with Christ, and the union of fellowship that believers have with each other, the Holy Spirit works *ad extra* in a manner that is patterned after his inner-trinitarian work."[50] The consummation of Trinitarian soteriology is the wedding of God and man in Christ by the very same bond that unites the Father and Son: the Holy Spirit.

According to Edwards, this could only have been accomplished by the Son of God subjecting himself to the Father on a level hitherto unrealized in the immanent Trinity. Before the Son could possess the right of "disposal" of the Holy Spirit—the love of God and the purchased sum of all spiritual blessings—it was necessary that the Son first subject himself to the Father in a way unparalleled in the Son-Spirit relationship: under law. Edwards insists,

> There is a new kind of subordination and mutual obliga-
> tion between two of the persons, arising from this new
> establishment the covenant of redemption: the Son un-
> dertaking and engaging to put himself into a new kind of
> subjection to the Father, far below that of his oeconomical
> station, even the subjection of a proper servant to the Fa-
> ther and one under his law – in the manner that creatures,

that are infinitely below God and absolutely dependent for their being on the mere will of God, are subject to his perceptive will and absolute legislative authority—engaging to become a creature, and so to put himself in the proper circumstances of a servant.[51]

Since only the Son became a man, his subordination is different in kind and degree, serving as the basis for all further subjections in the Trinity. In turn, the Father "acquires a new right of headship and authority over the Son" with a "new obligation" to see that his Son receives all heavenly rewards.[52] Generally speaking, this is the first change in the Trinity *ad extra*: the Son of God subjects himself to the Father as a servant and in return is advanced into the "economical seat" of the Father whereby he is made Lord and Judge of the earth "in the Father's stead."[53]

By debasing himself for the glory of the Father in the covenant of redemption, the Son of God is then elevated to a twofold office "new in kind."[54] The Son becomes (a) viceregent to the Father and (b) husband and head to the church. First, as viceregent, Jesus Christ is established upon the Father's throne and appointed "Disposer" of the world on the Father's behalf.[55] However, this is only a temporary station, abrogated once his authority is given back to the Father. This present scheme wherein the Son rules, "having the Father's authority committed unto him," is ephemeral in the scope of eternity and will cease at the end of the age.[56] On the other hand, with respect to Christ's office as God-man and husband to the church, "he will never resign his dominion."[57] In this eternal marriage, the Trinity *ad extra* emanates the full glory of the Godhead, centered primarily in the Son-Spirit relationship.

The Son's newly established authority over the Spirit in the eschaton is the apogee of Edwards' "new" Trinity, giving credence to Caldwell's assertion that Edwards' Christology exhibits an "Alexandrian flavor" with a "strong pneumatological presence."[58] Due to this "new kind of subjection" of the Spirit to the Son, Edwards was largely incapable of discussing the work of the Son without the work of the Spirit. For Edwards, since the Father grants the Son a "twofold dominion over the world," there is likewise a "twofold subjecting of the Holy Spirit to the Son."[59] However, this subordination is "only circumstantially new" and not like that of the Son's subjection under the law. As viceregent, "the Son will have the disposal of the Spirit in the name of the Father, or as ruling with his authority" until the end of the aeon.

Conversely, as the obedient second Adam, "Christ God-man will continue to all eternity to be the vital head and husband of the church, and the vital good that this vital head will eternally communicate to his church will be the Holy Spirit."[60] The love that Christ bestows upon his church forevermore is the Holy Spirit, himself the infinite goodness and holiness and love of God that Jesus now delivers to the saints by virtue of his deity and his humanity. This is the crescendo of Trinitarian glory in Miscellany no. 1067: in his incarnate Son, God lavishes the delight of himself upon the church as (1) the inheritance Christ purchased for himself as the obedient second Adam and (2) as the inheritance the Father bestowed upon the Son at his ascension. This dual inheritance then becomes the inheritance of the elect, eternally united to the Son and prepared to receive every spiritual blessing the Son himself receives.[61] In this way, the Holy Spirit is not subject to the Son by law or by special covenant, but by the benevolence of the Father. He is a "gift of the Father."[62]

The Elliptical Trinity

With his closing remarks about the dignity of the Holy Spirit, Edwards concludes Miscellany no. 1062 much like he began it: defending the co-equality of the Father, Son, and Holy Spirit. In his fourteenth and fifteenth points, Edwards essentially restates Augustine's doctrine of *opera trinitas ad extra indivisa sunt.*[63] The perichoretic persons of the Godhead are not simply united in their external operations; they are, so to speak, equal in their seats at the table in the divine boardroom. Despite the fact that the covenant of redemption did not include the

Holy Spirit directly, it was nonetheless a "joint agreement of all," even if the Spirit was not a covenanting party per se. The Holy Spirit is more than a passive bystander to God's designs; he is "the great good covenanted for, and the end of the covenant."[64] In other words, the covenant of redemption finds its most tangible telos in the Holy Spirit. "We may well suppose," Edwards insists, "that the affair was as it were concerted among all the persons, and determined by the perfect consent of all, and that there was a consultation among the three persons about it."[65]

Despite Edwards' admitted emphasis upon the Spirit in light of what he perceived to be gross misunderstandings regarding the third divine person during the Great Awakening, his doctrine of the Trinity *ad extra* cannot be said to ignore or eclipse one divine person for another. The covenant of redemption is forged in the Father-Son relationship in order that the Son-Spirit relationship might become the origin of the church's worship to the Father. In this way, the Son stands at the center of the Gospel scheme, and his constant coordination with the Father and the Spirit creates a symmetry of sorts in the Godhead *ad extra*. The Son's "most solemn investiture" by the Father in "his delegated kingdom" includes a twofold authority over the Spirit similar to the Father's twofold authority over the Son.[66] His relationship with the Spirit is in some ways a microcosmic mirror of his relationship with the Father. Instead of eclipsing the Son for the Spirit, as some have charged, Edwards' Trinitarianism view of the Gospel is rather an "ellipsing" of the Son with both the Father and the Spirit.[67] Whether covenanting with the Father before the ages, ruling in the Father's stead in this age, or being wedded to the church under the Father in the next, the Son is positioned in such a way that his respective relationships to the Father and to the Spirit *ad extra,* while dynamic and changing, are always cumulatively the same. Any seeming imbalance in the life of the Trinity sheds light on another relationship within the Trinity *ad extra* and upon the overall proportion of the Godhead. If the Father and Son are central in Edwards' covenantal framework, it is with the Spirit as its telos. Conversely, if the Son and Spirit are prominent in Edwards' conversionist thinking, it is with the Father as its ultimate end. It is through the work of the Son that each foci, the Father and the Spirit, find their relation to one another in Edwards' elliptical Trinity *ad extra*. Therefore, with good reason, Edwards calls Jesus Christ "the middle person" of the Trinity in Misc. no. 772.[68] In his doctrine of the Trinity *ad extra,* Christ is mediator both soteriologically and, literally speaking, theologically.

For Edwards, the Trinitarian Gospel is a window through which the church beholds, albeit darkly, the inner life of God. Consequently, Edwards believed that the doctrine of the Trinity *ad extra* was fundamental not only to a proper understanding of God; it was also critical for Christian spirituality. Thinking back to a time when he questioned the practicality of the doctrine of the Trinity, Edwards then stated in Misc. 181,

> Now I don't wonder at all at their being revealed, for such doctrines as these are glorious inlets into the knowledge and view of the spiritual world, and the contemplation of supreme things; the knowledge of which I have experienced how much it contributes to the betterment of the heart. If such doctrines as these had not been revealed, the church would never have been let half so far into the view of the spiritual world, as God intends it shall be before the world is at an end.[69]

Underneath Edwards' "Miscellanies" on the Trinity *ad extra* is the chief assumption that the works of the Trinity in salvation are indeed "glorious inlets" into the inner life of God and therefore profitable for the soul of the Christian. Through the Gospel of grace, the church of Jesus Christ is privileged to peer into God himself. For the "God-intoxicated" Jonathan Edwards, this is the essence of worship and Christian sanctification.[70]

Appendix: Edwards and Eternal Functional Subordination

With the rise in evangelical feminism, the doctrine of the Trinity has become an arena in which to think through the theology of the sexual revolution. Advocating for the fluidity of gender roles and against a complementarian view of human sexuality, egalitarians have invoked the tri-unity of God as the basis for their ideas. These theologians, such as Gilbert Bilezikian and Rebecca Groothuis, appeal to the Son's ontological equality with the Father in order to deny that the Son is eternally and necessarily subject to the Father in the immanent Trinity.[71] In response, complementarian theologians such as Bruce Ware and Wayne Grudem have advocated for a Trinitarian configuration called "Eternal Functional Subordination" (EFS), which "holds that the Son is eternally and necessarily subordinate to the Father, not in terms of his deity, but in his role in relationship to the Father."[72] This is the idea that the Son's subordination to the Father *ad intra* is not an ontological subordination, but rather a functional subordination based in relation and not in being. It is also virtually the same idea behind Jonathan Edwards' second order of Trinitarianism: "dependence without inferiority of Deity."[73]

Much like the proponents of Eternal Functional Subordination, Edwards understood a natural hierarchy within the immanent Trinity that preceded the incarnation. However, to say that EFS is a mere recapitulation of Edwards' "priority of subsistence" paradigm would be inaccurate. In his psychological understanding of the Trinity, Edwards was willing to derive the essence of the Son from the Father in a way that some modern complementarians are not. Nevertheless, for Edwards, the eternal generation of the Son necessitated an eternal subordination of the Son "more properly called priority than superiority," an important distinction held by Grudem and Ware.[74] This distinction of authority does not seem to exist in the minds of evangelical feminists, both in the Trinity and in the realm of biblical manhood and womanhood. While egalitarians see a mutual exclusion between the concepts of authority and equality in the Trinity *ad extra,* Edwards avoided the Scylla of Arianism and the Charybdis of Sabellianism by emphasizing that the Father's perfect idea of himself is a "repetition" of the divine essence, forming a "duplicity." In this way, Edwards preserves unity of essence and distinction of persons. While aligning with EFS in his view of a hierarchical God *ad intra,* Edwards' Trinitarianism is not so much an historical weapon against evangelical feminists as it should be a clarion call for the church as a whole to rediscover the importance of the doctrine of the eternal generation of the Son, something Ware himself has questioned.[75]

In the preface to their edited volume *One God in Three Persons: Unity of Essence, Distinction of Persons, Implications for Life* (2015), Bruce Ware and John Starke insist, "the human obedience of Christ has a basis in the eternal Son of God, and to affirm otherwise would threaten the integrity of the human and divine nature of the Son or lead to a modalistic error of a 'Christ whose proper being remains hidden behind an improper being.'"[76] Jonathan Edwards would have completely affirmed this statement. His doctrine of the Trinity *ad extra* affirmed the continuity between Christ's obedience to the Father on earth and His subordination to the Father before the foundation of the world. For Edwards, any other Gospel is a Gospel of confusion, proffering knowledge of Christ that does not translate in some way into knowledge of the triune God. Edwards' "newness-with-continuity" principle is defended by advocates of EFS and denied by evangelical feminists. In this way, what is debated is not simply the immanent Trinity but rather the trustworthiness of the Trinity's work *ad extra* to reveal the inner life of God. Going forward, may Jonathan Edwards' doctrine of the Trinity *ad extra* prove to be a resourceful tool to the modern church in its defense of the Trinitarian Gospel.

Notes

[1]"Miscellanies" in *The Works of Jonathan Edwards,* ed. Edward Hickman (Carlisle: Banner of Truth, 2009), 2:459.

[2] Oliver Wendell Holmes, "The Pulpit and the Pew," *Pages from an Old Volume of Life* (Boughton: Houghton Mifflin, 1883), 402–33.

[3] Joseph A. Conforti, *Samuel Hopkins and the New Divinity Movement: Calvinism and Reform in New England between the Great Awakenings* (Eugene: Wipe and Stock Publishers, 1981), 62.

[4] "Miscellanies," no. 982, in *WJE* 20:302.

[5] Sang Hyun Lee, *The Philosophical Theology of Jonathan Edwards* (Princeton, NJ: Princeton University Press, 2000), 203.

[6] "Miscellanies," no. 1062, in *WJE* 20:437.

[7] "Miscellanies," no. 1062, in *WJE* 20:431.

[8] "Miscellanies," no. 94, in *WJE* 13:258–59.

[9] "Miscellanies," no. 94, in *WJE* 13:257.

[10] "Miscellanies," no. 94, in *WJE* 13:260.

[11] "Miscellanies," no. 94, in *WJE* 13:258.

[12] "Miscellanies," no. 143, in *WJE* 13:298.

[13] Ross Hastings, "Jonathan Edwards and the Trinity: Its Place and Its Rich but Controversial Facets," *JETS* 59 No. 3 (2016): 585–600.

[14] "Miscellanies," no. 1062, in *WJE* 20:431.

[15] "Rahner's Rule" denotes a famous dictum by former German Jesuit priest and theologian Karl Rahner. He posited, "The economic Trinity is the immanent Trinity and vice versa."

[16] Amy Plantinga Pauw, *"The Supreme Harmony of All": The Trinitarian Theology of Jonathan Edwards* (Grand Rapids: Eerdmans, 2002), 132. Pauw's first relationship is what she calls the "quasi-genetic order of subsistence."

[17] "Miscellanies," no. 94, in *WJE* 13:262.

[18] "Miscellanies," no. 1062, in *WJE* 20:442.

[19] "Miscellanies," no. 1062, in *WJE* 20:430.

[20] "Miscellanies," no. 1062, in *WJE* 20:430.

[21] "Miscellanies," no. 1062, in *WJE* 20:430.

[22] Seng-Kong Tan, "Trinitarian Action in the Incarnation," in *Jonathan Edwards as Contemporary: Essays in Honor of Sang Hyun Lee,* ed. Don Schweitzer (New York, NY: Peter Lang, 2010), 127.

[23] John Calvin, *Institutes of the Christian Religion,* 1.15.

[24] For a brief discussion on Calvin's acceptance of the eternal generation of the Son, see Robert Letham in "Eternal Generation in the Church Fathers," *One God in Three Persons: Unity of Essence, Distinction of Persons, Implications for Life,* ed. Bruce A. Ware and John Starke (Wheaton, IL: Crossway, 2015), 118.

[25] "Miscellanies," no. 94, in *WJE* 13:262.

[26] "Miscellanies," no. 151, in *WJE* 13:302.

[27] "Miscellanies," no. 142, in *WJE* 13:298.

[28] "Miscellanies," no. 1062, in *WJE* 20:431.

[29] "Miscellanies," no. 1062, in *WJE* 20:431.

[30]"Miscellanies," no. 1062, in *WJE* 20:431.

[31]Edwards avers, "For God's determining to glorify and communicate himself must be conceived of as flowing from God's nature; or we must look upon God, from the infinite fullness and goodness of his nature, as naturally disposed to cause the beams of his glory to shine forth, and his goodness to flow forth." *WJE* 20:432.

[32]This doxological disposition is consistent with Sany Hyun Lee's thesis of a "dispositional ontology" in the nature of God.

[33]"Miscellanies," no. 1062, in *WJE* 20:431.

[34]Michael J. McClymond and Gerald R. McDermott, *The Theology of Jonathan Edwards* (Oxford: Oxford University Press, 2012), 205.

[35]Herman Bavinck concurred with Edwards when he stated, "Without generation, creation would not be possible. If, in an absolute sense, God could not communicate himself to the Son, he would be even less able, in a relative sense, to communicate himself to his creature." *Reformed Dogmatics,* 2:308.

[36]Robert Caldwell, *Communion in the Spirit: The Holy Spirit as the Bond of Union in the Theology of Jonathan Edwards* (Eugene: Wipf and Stock, 2006), 68–69.

[37]"Miscellanies," no. 1062, in *WJE* 20:432.

[38]Amy Plantinga Pauw, *"The Supreme Harmony of All": The Trinitarian Theology of Jonathan Edwards* (Grand Rapids: Eerdmans, 2002), 107.

[39]"Miscellanies," no. 1062, in *WJE* 20:436.

[40]"Miscellanies," no. 1062, in *WJE* 20:432.

[41]"Miscellanies," no. 1062, in *WJE* 20:434.

[42]"Miscellanies," no. 1062, in *WJE* 20:434.

[43]Michael J. McClymond and Gerald R. McDermott, *The Theology of Jonathan Edwards* (Oxford: Oxford University Press, 2012), 200.

[44]For a critique of this aspect of Warfield's Trinitarianism ad extra, see Scott R. Swain, "B.B. Warfield and the Biblical Doctrine of the Trinity," in *Themelios* 43, Issue 1 (2018), 10–24.

[45]"Miscellanies," no. 1062, in *WJE* 20:437.

[46]"Miscellanies," no. 1062, in *WJE* 20:439.

[47]In 1959, C.C. Goen pejoratively labeled Edwards "America's first major post-millennial thinker." ("Jonathan Edwards: A New Departure in Eschatology," *Church History* 28 [1950], 25–40)

[48]Edwards devotes "Miscellanies" nos. 617, 825, 919, and 1091 to exploring the relationship between the covenant of redemption and the covenant of grace.

[49]"Miscellanies," no. 98, in *WJE* 13:265.

[50]Robert Caldwell, *Communion in the Spirit: The Holy Spirit as the Bond of Union in the Theology of Jonathan Edwards* (Eugene: Wipf and Stock, 2006), 8.

[51]"Miscellanies," no. 1062, in *WJE* 20:437.

[52]"Miscellanies," no. 1062, in *WJE* 20:437.

[53]"Miscellanies," no. 1062, in *WJE* 20:435.

[54]"Miscellanies," no. 1062, in *WJE* 20:435.

[55] "Miscellanies," no. 1062, in *WJE* 20:434.

[56] "Miscellanies," no. 1062, in *WJE* 20:439.

[57] "Miscellanies," no. 1062, in *WJE* 20:440.

[58] Robert Caldwell, *Communion in the Spirit: The Holy Spirit as the Bond of Union in the Theology of Jonathan Edwards* (Eugene: Wipf and Stock, 2006), 97.

[59] "Miscellanies," no. 1062, in *WJE* 20:439.

[60] "Miscellanies," no. 1062, in *WJE* 20:440.

[61] For an extended look into Edwards' thoughts on the doctrine of union with Christ, see Miscellany no. *ff.*

[62] "Miscellanies," no. 1062, in *WJE* 20:441.

[63] This is Augustine's Latin dictum that the "works of the Trinity on the outside are indivisible."

[64] "Miscellanies," no. 1062, in *WJE* 20:443.

[65] "Miscellanies," no. 1062, in *WJE* 20:442.

[66] "Miscellanies," no. 833, in *WJE* 20:45.

[67] Ross Hastings, "Jonathan Edwards and the Trinity: Its Place and Its Rich but Controversial Facets," *JETS* 59 No. 3 (2016): 585–600. Hastings concludes, "Edwards's drive to honor the Spirit may be accounted for by his experience of the power of the Spirit in the Great Awakening. Whatever the reasons, and gains, this results in a relative underplaying of Christology, as compared to pneumatology, in salvation."

[68] "Miscellanies," no. 772, in *WJE* 18:419.

[69] "Miscellanies," no. 181, in *WJE* 13:328.

[70] Michael J. McClymond, *Encounters with God* (Oxford: Oxford University Press, 1998), 29.

[71] See Gilbert Bilezikian, *Community 101: Reclaiming the Local Church as Community of Oneness* (Grand Rapids: Zondervan, 1997), 190-191; Rebecca Merrill Groothius, *Good News for Women: A Biblical Picture of Gender Equality* (Grand Rapids: Baker, 1997), 57; Millard Erickson is a more conservative voice who has also questioned complementarian arguments for EFS in *Who's Tampering with the Trinity? An Assessment of the Subordination Debate* (Grand Rapids: Kregel, 2009).

[72] Philip R. Gons and Andrew David Naselli, "An Examination of Three Recent Philosophical Arguments Against Hierarchy in the Immanent Trinity," in *One God in Three Persons: Unity of Essence, Distinction of Persons, Implications for Life* (Wheaton, IL: Crossway, 2015), 197.

[73] "Miscellanies," no. 1062, in *WJE* 20:430.

[74] "Miscellanies," no. 1062, in *WJE* 20:430.

[75] Bruce A. Ware, *Father, Son, and Holy Spirit: Relationships, Roles, and Relevance* (Wheaton: Crossway, 2005), 162.

[76] Bruce A. Ware and John Starke, "Preface," in *One God in Three Persons* (Wheaton: Crossway, 2015), 11.

Edwards on Reason, Revelation, and Mystery

Jonathan S. Marko

The more persons or beings are in themselves and in their own nature above us, the more are doctrines or truths concerning them mysterious to us, above our comprehension and difficult to our belief, the more do those things that are really true concerning them contain seeming inconsistencies and impossibilities.

— Jonathan Edwards, *Miscellany no. 839*

Introduction of the Topics

THE QUESTION OF THE RELATIONSHIP between reason and revelation and its impact on the acceptance of doctrinal mysteries was a very important point of conversation in the Enlightenment period.[1] While this stage in history is often dubbed the "Age of Reason," in part, for those who would not acknowledge a traditional Protestant understanding of the authority of Scripture and/or who were suspicious of anything typically described as a "mystery," Christian orthodoxy, founded upon God's revelation and numerous so-called mysteries, continued onward.[2] But proper definitions of such terms, like revelation, reason, and mystery, and concomitant relationships were not simply ground-clearing for other discussions or the content of one's prolegomena in this era; rather they frequently were the foci of intense debates—debates to which Jonathan Edwards was no stranger. He evidently saw the importance of these conversations, the subtle snares and opportunities for misunderstanding and misemploying these commonly used terms, and the need to protect God's people from related misconceptions. In the "Miscellanies" and throughout his other works, Edwards demonstrates that he has a fine and incisive grasp on these ideas and their interrelationships.

Revelation is, perhaps, the least nuanced term of the three set upon in this chapter. At the very least, the term will rarely be a cause of confusion for readers. By it he typically means what we, today, commonly refer to as special revelation. In the entries of the "Miscellanies" treated below, Edwards does not use the term in reference to "general revelation." And, in the many instances where he apparently uses the term generically, the context demonstrates that he does not actually give any serious weight to the claims of revelation coming from other faiths. For Edwards, it typically amounts to the revealing of the Trinitarian God's self and will to His people in a supernatural manner and the written record of it. Practically, the term is interchangeable with Scripture in the below entries.

Reason was a term that Edwards was careful in using and wary of when approaching another work using the word. It was used more variously in the era than was the term revelation, and determining what one intended by the use of "reason" was not always readily apparent, or consistent, in the writings of Edwards' interlocutors. In one place he does offer his own definition of the term: "*Definition.* By REASON I mean that power or faculty an intelligent being has to judge of the truth of propositions" by intuition and self-evidence or through the construction of a proof.[3] But he acknowledges elsewhere that it is important to make a distinction between "the *faculty* of reason taken in the whole extent of its exercise," which includes the consideration of alleged divine testimony, human testimony, history and tradition, one's own memory, etc., over and against the faculty considered in a narrower scope.[4] Edwards is adamant "that the evidence or argument which is worthy to influence the faculty of reason . . . comprehends divine testimony as well as other sorts of evidence,"[5] while others will often reference reason taken only in a limited exercise, perhaps devoid of divine revelation.[6] In the latter case, all reason might deliver is "some particular opinions that have appeared rational to us," divine revelation (and, perhaps, other external sources) aside.[7] Moreover, as will be apparent below, Edwards thinks that much of the theological truths that some would often consider as being accessible to our divinely unassisted reasoning faculty (or reason without revelation) is simply scriptural truths passed down through generations and various cultures. This is contrary to, among other things, some histories of philosophy advanced by Christians that commend the unassisted yet impressive reasoning abilities of some of the pagan philosophers thought to be evident from their surprisingly accurate natural theology.

There are other senses he notes that others use that affect the sense in which we should understand their use of related terms. "Sometimes by the word reason, is intended the same as argument, or evidence that the faculty of reason makes use of in judging of truth." This is how people might use the term when asserting that we should not believe something "contrary to reason." He is fine with the use of such a handle as long as people do not intend to assert "reason to be a rule superior to revelation" by it. Since revelation is from God and it is often about supernatural issues, we should expect to learn of and accept propositions and doctrines that are in some way or another beyond our divinely-unassisted faculty of reason (or, again, reason without revelation) but are still "reasonable" in the full scope of the faculty's exercise.[8] In other words, Scripture delivers to us many mysteries that we would have no or little compelling reason to accept other than God told us.

So revelation often contains mysteries. As will be obvious in the discussion of the entries below, mysteries in Edwards' economy are not only found in divine revelation, but also in the natural world. The profundities that arise when speaking of infinity is one example of those that arise from pondering the natural world. But what is more, there are mysteries that are such only in a relative sense. That is, agents of lesser intelligence will often find doctrines, conclusions, or ideas mysterious that are well understood and rational to a more intelligent agent. Such is the case with children and parents or humans and angels. But he does refer to "mysteries in religion" as such doctrines and propositions delivered by Scripture, again, which we would have no or little compelling evidence to accept had we not known it came from God. And, while some of these mysteries will be beyond human comprehension in one or more manners, plenty are sufficiently comprehensible. In summary, so-called mysteries in Edwards' vocabulary are natural or revealed propositions that are incomprehensible or unimaginable or simply those propositions that we could only legitimately believe because God revealed them. But he also allows the term to be ascribed to things that are only relatively incomprehensible or in need of being revealed.

These three terms—reason, revelation, and mystery—are foundational to the entries of the "Miscellanies" that are treated below. The reader must be prepared for subtle and quick shifts of usage of the terms reason and mystery. Conveniently, Edwards often explicitly indicates these shifts.

Overviews & Analyses of the Select Entries of the "Miscellanies" and Interconnections with Edwards' Other Writings

No. 839, "Mysteries in Religion"

No. 839 is a short excursus on doctrinal mysteries, whose points are inferred from (or supported by) an examination of John 3. These are mysteries of the revealed variety and thus not those that we encounter in the natural world. In the entry, he offers a definition of the former:

REASON, REVELATION, AND MYSTERY

things contained in those doctrines that Christ came ... to teach, that are not only so above human comprehension that men can't easily apprehend all that is to be understood concerning them, but that are difficult to the understanding in that sense, that they are difficult to be received by the judgment or belief.[9]

In other words, mysteries are ideas delivered by God that humans would have been unable to discover through their own abilities and, in some cases, even when revealed, are not fully comprehensible. An example of a sufficiently comprehensible revealed mystery might be the resurrection at the end of time. An example of an incomprehensible revealed mystery is that there is only one God, yet He is three persons, each of which are fully God.[10]

There is another important argument that he makes that points to the validity of doctrinal mysteries even amidst their strangeness. He believes that one can infer from the discussion between Jesus and Nicodemus the reasonable principle that "the more persons or beings are in themselves and in their own nature above us, the more are doctrines or truths concerning them mysterious to us, above our comprehension and difficult to our belief, the more do those things that are really true concerning them contain seeming inconsistencies and impossibilities." In short, it should be expected that revelation about beings of a different and superior nature to us should contain mysteries that are rationally difficult, if not impossible to reconcile in our own minds in this life and with these present faculties. Though he does not explicitly say the following, his statement stands to reason since we are trying to envision the supernatural realm using our available ideas that all come from the natural world of colors, shapes, and material things that are apprehended by our natural senses. He concludes 839 by asserting that since we find mysteries in the natural world we should expect, again, there to be more and greater mysteries and seeming impossibilities in God's revelation of Himself.[11] Some of what is argued here is treated at greater length in entry 1340.

No. 1234, "Mysteries"

No. 1234 focuses on the doctrine of the Holy Trinity. More specifically, Edwards' main point is to argue that it is "not absurd and [a] contradiction."[12] Of course, he treats the Trinity with much greater length and detail elsewhere, such as *Discourse of the Trinity,* and numerous other entries of the "Miscellanies," such as 94, 96, 98, 117, 143–46, 151, 154, 157, and 181, just to name a few. In this entry he heavily interacts with a work by Samuel Clarke, *A Demonstration of the Being and Attributes of God,* and Philip Skelton's *Deism Revealed,* volume 2. In fact, the bulk of the entry is from two lengthy quotes from the latter work. Nonetheless, this is a good introduction to his defense of the doctrine and adds to his thoughts on the nature and characteristics of doctrinal mysteries.

The first quotation from Skelton emphasizes our finitude in relation to our understanding of God. When we think of Him we quickly come to the limits of our comprehension: "'We can follow God but one or two steps in his lowest and plainest works, till all becomes mystery, and matter of amazement, to us.'" He follows the lengthy quotation from Skelton's work with an indexing of Samuel Clarke's inconsistency in thinking and concluding about doctrinal mysteries. Edwards thinks that Clarke is a hypocrite because he rejects the orthodox understanding of the Trinity—a great mystery—on the grounds of its seeming inconsistency, while he attempts to avoid God's culpability for evil and hold humans accountable for it by asserting a position on free will that ultimately results in a logical contradiction. In short, he chides Clarke for rejecting a true doctrinal mystery while accepting what yields, in Edwards' mind, a plain contradiction.[13] Moreover, and for Jonathan Edwards neophytes, the notion of free will and numerous related concepts are taken up by Edwards at much greater length in *The Freedom of the Will.*

The rest of the entry is another recorded quotation from Skelton's work. Skelton mentions some of the numerous impossible to reconcile mysteries we run into here in the natural world, such as hyperboles never crossing their asymptotes and profundities involving infinity.

The evident thrust of the lengthy quotation is that mysteries should be expected when faced with supernatural matters, especially God. This is likewise one of Edwards' major messages in the treatment of entries 839 and 1340. The presence of mysteries should not cause doubt.[14]

No. 1340, "Reason and Revelation"

This is Edwards' longest entry of the "Miscellanies" focusing solely on reason and revelation. It is here where he offers the definition of reason already given above. He also defends the relationship of reason and revelation already discussed and the absurdity of rejecting revelation based on its many mysteries. All of this is in response to his reading and study of Matthew Tindal's *Christianity as Old as the Creation,* which earned the moniker of the "Deists' Bible." This is not the only time that Edwards voices his concern with the so-called deists. He does so in a number of sermons and discourses.[15]

After offering the aforementioned definition of reason, he presents Tindal's position on reason and revelation and the *unreasonableness* of it. He understands Tindal to be claiming that reason that is unassisted by revelation is to judge whether or not a particular or specific revelation is truly such. In other words, if natural reason that is undirected or unassisted by divine revelation would not arrive at the same conclusion advanced by a specific, alleged revelation, it cannot be considered such. So, according to Edwards' reading of Tindal, any proposition we understand to be advanced by Scripture cannot be considered to be from God if we could not have concluded that proposition on our own, divinely unassisted reasoning powers. Edwards points out the absurdity of what Tindal is really claiming: the general proposition *that these messages are divinely revealed* will be determined by reason considering first whether or not reason alone will show the truth of a particular proposition.[16]

Edwards argues that if one were to take Tindal's principle to its logical conclusion all reasoning and argumentation must cease. He marshals numerous examples why this would be so. For instance, all testimony about history and tradition is based upon a general proposition that they are to be depended upon under credible circumstances; but, instead, one—again, if one were following Tindal's reasoning consistently to its logical end—would have to judge whether or not one could have come up with each specific historical proposition on one's own; and, if not, then one is being "unreasonable" (in Tindal's sense) to accept any such historical proposition as true. And no human testimony whatsoever could "reasonably" be believed unless the person considering the testimony could have arrived at it on his or her own. In the end, one could only believe self-evident propositions![17] In short, in the mind of Edwards (and according to most thinkers throughout time) we need to be able to argue from general propositions (Scripture is God's word; we can typically trust our senses; we can typically trust historical accounts; etc.) once they have been established. Not doing that, as said earlier, wrongly narrows reason's scope.

After offering his defense of the acceptance of truths not discoverable by one's own unassisted reasoning faculties, he takes up a similar line of argumentation in defense of mysteries, propositions that "appear in themselves not easy and reconcilable to reason, but difficult, incomprehensible, and their agreement with reason not understood."[18] The bulk of his defense is via examples from various fields, especially philosophy. For instance, he points out that no one can explain how an immaterial soul causes a material body to move. But there are not only universal mysteries that humans encounter but also propositions that are relatively mysterious. Regarding the latter, he asserts that there are propositions coming from physics that the mathematician and philosopher understand that are beyond the common person.[19] He continues to offer example after example.

In the midst of the entry, he makes another slight shift and turns his focus solely to divinely revealed mysteries and makes what perhaps are his most interesting points. He reasons that if we have good testimony to receive a divine revelation as such it should not be surprising that we would find it difficult to reconcile to our minds

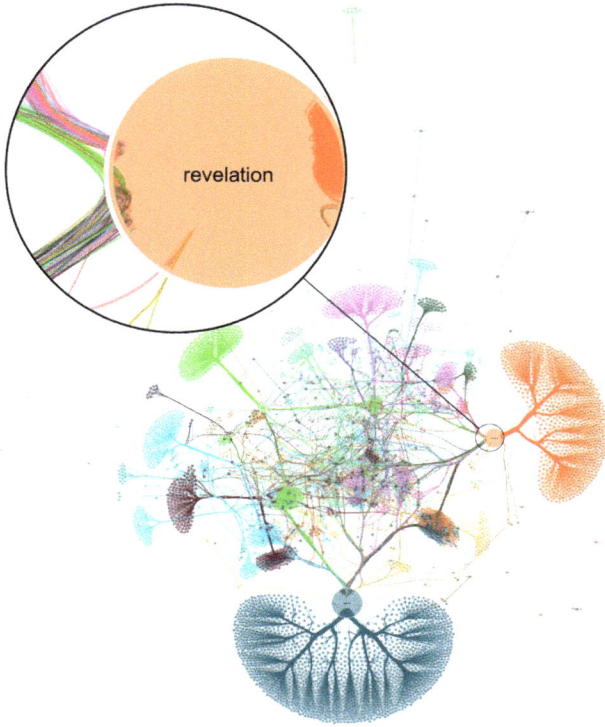

MYSTERY, REASON *and* REVELATION—*a map of mysteries, mysterious, mysteriously, mysteriousness, mystery, reason, reasonable, reasonableness, reasonably, reasoned, reasoner, reasoners, reasoning, reasonings, reasons, reveal, revealed, revealer, revealeth, revealing, reveals, revelation, revelations, unreasonable, unreasonableness, unreasonably, unrevealed with interconnections and page locations in WJE 1–26.*

in a number of different ways because many revealed things would not have been discovered by unassisted reason in the first place. He argues further that if the revelation is not attended with greater difficulties than expected, then these difficulties are not evidence against taking the revelation as such, but, on the contrary, evidence *for* taking the revelation as such! In short, the many difficulties that we find throughout Scripture are confirmations that it is from God.[20]

What comes after these assertions and arguments is an expanded defense of his positions. He argues that it is simply reasonable that we would have difficulties in understanding propositions that by their nature could not be discovered by divinely unassisted human reason. "For certainly whatever is reasonably expect to be found in truth when seeking it, cannot be an objection against its being truth when we have found it."[21] And Edwards argues that we should not expect to fully understand revelation concerning different issues and descriptions of our infinite God or descriptions of the supernatural world beyond our senses and about beings far superior than us. Edwards delivers numerous examples and points of reasoning in support of these claims.[22]

He makes a few concluding points in defense of the often mysterious aspects of divine revelation. He conjectures that divine revelation is actually the original source of the ancient heathen philosophers whose notions about God at times seems to comport surprisingly well with Scripture.[23] In other words, our unassisted reasoning faculties are not as potent as some think. Somewhat similar sentiments are shared elsewhere in the "Miscellanies," like entries 837 and 978, just to name two of many.[24] Also, Edwards notes that one might expect that the many different genres of the books in the Bible, from which we are to cull our theological system, would be the source of many difficulties in our interpretation and understanding. Edwards additionally notes that further difficulties should be expected due to the ancient languages and cultures in which the canonical books were produced. But, Edwards posits, we may unravel many biblical mysteries to a greater degree in the future than we have now.[25]

Observations on the Corresponding Three-Dimensional Visualization

Much can be gleaned from the Dr. Boss's three-dimensional visualization generated with the key words "reason," "revelation," and "mystery." It is evident from viewing the nodes corresponding to "reason" and "revelation" (not to mention the nodes produced by associated terms like "revealed" and "reason and revelation") that these were hardly uncommon themes in Edwards' thought. That fact will probably not come as too much of a surprise to those familiar with him. What is more, there are so many interconnections and pathways for the reader to follow between reason and revelation in the "Miscellanies." These terms, again, not surprisingly, go in tandem. "Mystery" and its closely-related terms also produces an abundance of pathways beyond that revealed in the commentary above. To embark on a comprehensive journey of the interrelationships directly connected to those latter terms would be more manageable than executing a similar study on reason or revelation. Finally, there are some other terms, such as "Scripture," that could be utilized in such a three-dimensional visualization but understandably were not (lest the mapping become too complex). Whatever the case, the visualizations produced give helpful glances into the mind behind the "Miscellanies."

Notes

[1] John Locke, *An Essay Concerning Human Understanding,* ed. Peter H. Nidditch (Oxford: Clarendon, 1979); John Toland, *Christianity Not Mysterious: or, A Treatise Shewing, That There is Nothing in the Gospel Contrary to Reason, Nor Above It: and That No Christian Doctrine Can Be Properly Call'd a Mystery,* 2nd ed. (London: printed for Sam Buckley, 1696); Edward Stillingfleet, *A Discourse in Vindication of the Trinity with an Answer to the Late Socinian Objections against It from Scripture, Antiquity and Reason,* 2nd ed. (London: printed by J. H. for Henry Mortlock, 1697); Edward Stillingfleet, *The Bishop of Worcester's Answer to Mr. Locke's Second Letter; wherein His Notion of Ideas Is Prov'd to Be Inconsistent with It Self, and with the Articles of the Christian Faith* (London: printed by J. H. for Henry Mortlock, 1698); Anthony Collins, *An Essay Concerning the Use of Reason in Propositions, the Evidence*

whereof Depends upon Human Testimony, 2nd ed. (London: 1709); cf. Jonathan S. Marko, *Measuring the Distance Between Locke and Toland: Reason, Revelation, and Rejection during the Locke-Stillingfleet Debate* (Eugene, OR: Pickwick, 2017). George Rust, *A Discourse of the Use of Reason in Matters of Religion: Shewing, That Christianity Contains Nothing Repugnant to Right Reason; Against Enthusiasts and Deists,* trans. and annot. by Hen. Hallywell (London: printed by Hen. Hills, Jun for Walter Kettilby, 1683); John Norris, *An Account of Reason and Faith: In Relation to the Mysteries of Christianity* (London: printed for S. Manship, 1697); Robert Boyle, *Reflections upon a Theological Distinction. According to Which, 'tis Said, That Some Articles Are Above Reason, but Not Against Reason* (London: printed by Edw. Jones, for John Taylor, 1690); cf. Jonathan S. Marko, "Above Reason Propositions and Contradiction in the Religious Thought of Robert Boyle," *Forum Philosophicum: International Journal for Philosophy* 19.2 (Autumn, 2014): 227–39; cf. Jonathan S. Marko, "Supplementing Contemporary Treatments of Doctrinal Mysteries with Largely Forgotten Voices from the Enlightenment," *Trinity Journal* (forthcoming); Francis Turretin, *Institutes of Elenctic Theology,* 3 vols., trans. George Musgrave Giger, ed. James T. Dennison Jr. (Phillipsburg, NJ: P&R, 1992); David Hume, *An Enquiry Concerning Human Understanding,* ed. by Stephen Buckle (New York: Cambridge University Press, 2007); Matthew Tindal, *Christianity as Old as the Creation: Or, The Gospel, a Republication of the Religion of Nature,* volume 1 (London: 1730). This last book is directly responded to in no. 1340 of the "Miscellanies" below.

There are plenty of other works during this period that respond to these questions indirectly. The Trinitarian debates in the late 1600s and early 1700s are good examples of conversations that implicitly treated the issues of the relationships between reason, revelation, and doctrinal mysteries.

[2]E.g., Edward, Lord Herbert of Cherbury, *De Veritate,* trans. Myrick H. Carré (Bristol: J. W. Arrowsmith, Ltd., 1937); cf. Jonathan S. Marko, "Deism," *The Jonathan Edwards Encyclopedia,* ed. by Harry S. Stout (Grand Rapids: Eerdmans, 2017), 136–38.

[3]"Miscellanies," no. 1340, in *WJE* 23:359.

[4]"Mysteries. Concerning Reason's Being Superior to Revelation," *Part IV: Efficacious Grace, WJEO* 27; cf. "Miscellanies," no. 1340, in *WJE* 23: 359–63.

[5]"Mysteries. Concerning Reason's Being Superior to Revelation," *Part IV: Efficacious Grace, WJEO* 27.

[6]John Locke also incorporates a dual use of the term reason in his *An Essay Concerning Human Understanding* that causes no little confusion among Locke scholars up through the present-day. Marko, *Measuring the Distance.*

[7]"Mysteries. Concerning Reason's Being Superior to Revelation," *Part IV: Efficacious Grace, WJEO* 27.

[8]"Mysteries. Concerning Reason's Being Superior to Revelation," *Part IV: Efficacious Grace, WJEO* 27.

[9]"Miscellanies," no. 839, in *WJE* 20:54–55.

[10]There are plenty of incomprehensible aspects of the resurrection. How God will effect it is incomprehensible. There are many such "manner in which" details that assuredly surpass our finite understandings. But the disciples did behold the resurrected Christ with their natural senses. To be alive again but in a new and better body is rather imaginable. Cf. Marko, "Above Reason Propositions;" Marko, "Supplementing Contemporary Treatments."

[11]"Miscellanies," no. 839, in *WJE* 20:55.

[12]"Miscellanies," no. 1234, in *WJE* 23:167.

[13]"Miscellanies," no. 1234, in *WJE* 23:167.

[14]"Miscellanies," no. 1234, in *WJE* 23:168.

[15]E.g., *WJE* 14:499; *WJE* 19:719; sermon on 2 Peter 1:19, no. 443, *WJEO* 52; cf. Marko, "Deism," 137–38.

[16]"Miscellanies," no. 1340, in *WJE* 23:359–60.

[17]"Miscellanies," no. 1340, in *WJE* 23:360–62.

[18]"Miscellanies," no. 1340, in *WJE* 23:362.

[19]"Miscellanies," no. 1340, in *WJE* 23:362–63.

[20]"Miscellanies," no. 1340, in *WJE* 23:366.

[21]"Miscellanies," no. 1340, in *WJE* 23:366–67.

[22]"Miscellanies," no. 1340, in *WJE* 23:367–72.

[23]"Miscellanies," no. 1340, in *WJE* 23:372; cf. Gary L. Finkbeiner, "Revelation," *The Jonathan Edwards Encyclopedia,* ed. by Harry S. Stout (Grand Rapids: Eerdmans, 2017), 498–500.

[24]"Miscellanies," no. 837, in *WJE* 20:52–53.

[25]"Miscellanies," no. 1340, in *WJE* 23:373–76.

Edwards on Reasonable Christianity and Necessary Revelation

Jonathan S. Marko

> *We cannot have any certain, clear and distinct knowledge of these things concerning our restoration and salvation without a revelation. 'Tis said by some that the light of nature and reason is sufficient to teach us that a good God stands ready to forgive sinners on their hearty repentance. But I think it plain that our reason only never, never would give us a clear and evident notice of this.*
>
> — Jonathan Edwards, *Miscellany no. 1304*

Introduction of the Topics[1]

THE REASONABLENESS OF CHRISTIANITY and necessity of revelation are two somewhat well-trod theological topics. Orthodox Christianity has, down through the centuries, argued that our religion is highly "reasonable" in the most appropriate sense of the term and that Scripture is necessary in a variety of ways. For instance, and in relation to Christianity's reasonableness, few Christians have ever affirmed that there are actual contradictions in Scripture; rather they have long spoken of seeming contradictions or the like. Orthodox theologians have long contended that though Scripture will go beyond our present, unassisted reasoning abilities, the doctrines within are commendable by the human reasoning faculty once sufficiently grasped. In the late seventeenth and early eighteenth centuries, a common trend in theological works was to extol Christianity's reasonableness. Though theologians did this to greatly varying degrees, some of the most ardent who are still frequently considered Protestant are those like John Tillotson and John Locke. [2] The latter produced a major theological treatise entitled *The Reasonableness of Christianity,* in which he, like Edwards, as will shown below, argues that while we would not have discovered much of what Scripture promulgates, once understood these doctrines strike people as very reasonable.[3] An issue upon which Edwards tended to lend more clarity than his forbearers on the topic of the reasonableness of Christianity was the necessity of the Holy Spirit in our conviction of Scripture.

Moreover, the Protestant orthodox developed the doctrines of Scripture's attributes—authority, necessity, sufficiency, and clarity—in response to the Roman Catholic declaration that Scripture and its extrapolation, tradition, were both primary authorities. The Protestants would argue that Scripture was necessary in a variety of senses. It appears, however, that Edwards does not so much have the Roman Catholics in mind in his treatment of the necessity of revelation, but rather one or more of the sects that arguably grew out of Protestantism, especially the so-called deists.[4] Interestingly, in the aforementioned book, *The Reasonableness of Christianity,* Locke not only argues for Christianity's reasonableness but also for the necessity of biblical revelation for our redemption against the claims to the contrary of certain deists, proponents of natural religion.[5] Both Locke and Edwards think that along with many doctrines of the Christian faith, much purportedly knowable about God through natural sources and human reasoning unassisted by divine revelation (i.e., natural religion) is at least practically beyond our reasoning abilities, but once revealed is highly reasonable, like the existence of God and human morality.

These terms, the reasonableness of Christianity and the necessity of revelation are foundational to the "Miscellanies" entries treated below. Other vitally important terms, namely reason, revelation, and mystery have been treated by me elsewhere in relation to entries 839, 1234, and 1340. Yet another important term, religion, will be defined below in significant detail.

Overviews & Analyses of the Select Entries of the "Miscellanies" and Interconnections with Edwards' Other Writings

No. 1156, "Observations on the Agreeableness of the Christian Religion"

The primary thrust of entry 1156 is Edwards' indexing of the reasonableness of certain Christian doctrines such as the afterlife, revelation, original sin, the purpose of the church, faith as the instrumental means of justification, God's providence, heavenly beings, and more. All of these topics are treated elsewhere, many of them numerous times in Edwards' "Miscellanies" and often with greater depth. Moreover, a formula of sorts that he employs implicitly throughout 1156 is that assuming such and such revelation is true, he offers the reasons those doctrines or assertions are so agreeable. Furthermore, it is suggested by the editor of *WJE* 23, in which this entry is found, that it is perhaps unfinished, as two thirds of the last page of the original are left blank.

Edwards begins by discussing the agreeableness of the future state, a topic that, again, receives considerable comment elsewhere. It is reasonable to Edwards that good people are rewarded and the bad are punished. What is more, it is rational that the future state would be eternal. If it were not eternal, Edwards argues, people experiencing heavenly felicity would be tormented knowing that the state that they find themselves in would come to an end. Furthermore, considering what is in store for us should reasonably encourage patience under suffering. That is, anything we experience on earth is only temporary. Such is the pattern of his trains of thought throughout the entry.[6]

Likewise, he extols the agreeableness of the doctrine of regeneration and sovereign grace, two topics treated at length elsewhere, especially in *WJEO 37, Documents on the Trinity, Grace, and Faith*. He begins the defense of this assertion pointing out the experience we have supporting the doctrine of original sin (treated at length in *WJE* 3 and *WJEO* 34) and the stupidity of humans and how those show the reasonableness of the doctrines of illumination and the (monergistic) work of the Holy Spirit. Edwards then weaves the broad notion of special revelation in and works in more about the future state. He thinks that it is rational that much of divine revelation is taken up with the topic of justification and reconciliation since the best post-fall, unassisted reasoning (i.e., reason without revelation) is unable to discover it. Moreover, according to Edwards, it is reasonable that the reconciled should be united in one holy society or church because their moral states are considerably distinct from the rest and they share an infinitely important common interest.[7]

Soon after, he argues that the scriptural doctrine of God and his heavenly beings is far more reasonable than the religious position of polytheism that asserts that there is a multiplicity of beings who are "the joint objects of trust, dependence and divine adoration." He asserts that it is evident to reason that there is one eternal, self-existent, independent, infinite Being who is providential over all things. When this is recognized, one cannot look at the angels as assisting him in governing the world (in a manner not unlike that espoused by polytheism with respect to gods giving oversight to particular realms of life), since they are finite.[8] Amidst this portion of the entry, Edwards points out the irrationality of dedicating ourselves to these heavenly beings.[9]

He then offers some space in support of the following statement: "The doctrine of the gospel concerning ANOTHER and INVISIBLE WORLD, to which good men are to be transferred and where they are to have their inheritance and fixed abode, is most rational on this account: 'tis manifest that this visible world is corruptible in its own nature." Thus, he reasons, the world must come to an end. And since it is unlikely that God will let it go gradually, he will at some point "immediately interpose" to destroy it. Those there will either be translated or experience a horrible fate. It is reasonable to suppose he will translate his "favorites" (believers). But if he deals with believers then in such a manner, he would also kindly deal with believers who had already died.[10]

Edwards then slightly shifts his train of thought. He asserts that there is no better way to tell about the invisible world that is humankind's reward than divine revelation. He argues that the general public judgment is reasonable and that it is reasonable that Christ should be appointed judge because the world disregarded him and it is fitting that his friends be acknowledged by him.[11]

He continues on focusing upon doctrines all with the common and broad theme of salvation. He thinks that the doctrine of the resurrection and salvation from sin and Satan are reasonable. And he thinks that Christ's first coming in a low and mean condition is also fitting.

The last major topic Edwards argues for the rationality of is the "doctrine of FAITH as the main condition of salvation." Although, he asserts, virtue is the same between unfallen and fallen men and angels, "the leading exercise of true virtue may differ according to the different nature, state and circumstances of the creature, the different relation it stands in to God," etc. Based on the nature and circumstances of fallen humans under the gospel, the leading virtue is faith. We are sinful, miserable, unworthy, helpless, and lost. It is reasonable, then, that salvation is associated so strongly with faith as our salvation concerns our unseen future.[12] Moreover, faith is treated or commented upon tremendously throughout the "Miscellanies."

No. 1304, "The Necessity of Revelation"

In no. 1304, Edwards focuses on arguing for the necessity of revelation by comparing natural and revealed religion (Christianity). He begins this entry with giving his broad definition of "religion" that serves as the launching point for the entire excursus. He writes, "The religion that is required of us consists in the disposition and affections of mind we ought to have towards God, and our behavior with respect to him."[13] It is incumbent upon us, therefore, to know about God, the concern we have with Him, the concern He has with us, our dependence on Him, the duty we have toward Him, and the like. For instance, if He has no concern with us, we have no foundation for religion. But if He looks upon religion with great importance—and we have proof that he does—it must be extraordinarily important to us.[14] Based upon the manner in which he has equipped humans with intelligence and other gifts, it is clear that we have duties toward him.

Considering the last point, it would be strange if God left us to conjecture how we ought to serve him. Thus, it is agreeable that humans would receive clear and full notice of what He wants from us.[15] The same holds true if there is forgiveness of sins and salvation. Edwards thinks that two claims follow from these truths. And it is these claims that he unpacks throughout the rest of the entry: 1. We stand in a new relation to God as Savior, beyond that of Creator, and thus have a new sort of religion; and 2. "That we cannot have any clear, certain and distinct knowledge of this new relation, etc., any other way than by divine revelation."[16] All of what he says, in what follows, could be made against what could be labeled "deistic" thinking.[17] This is not merely speculative since he addresses his concerns about deists on occasion in his "sermons" and "discourses."[18]

Regarding this new relation we have with God, it is "new" because there is now forgiveness and deliverance, something not required initially from our original parents in their relationship with him. Thus something is added to the requirements of natural religion. Since we deserved to be destroyed, but instead receive forgiveness and restoration, it is as if we were made a new creation out of nothing. What is more, God now stands in relation to believers as savior, which is a relationship infinitely more important than his original one with the human race. If all of these changes were to take place, it only

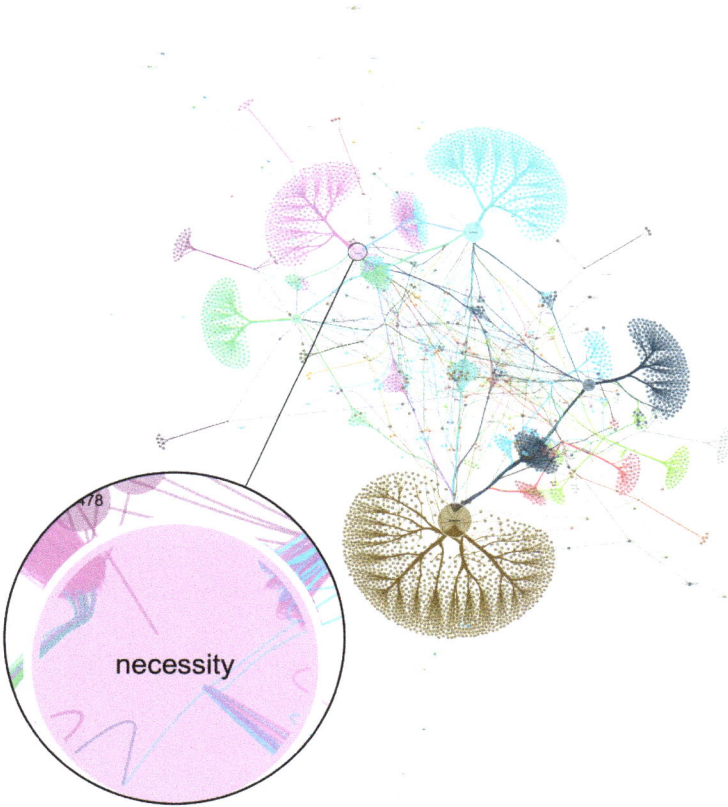

NECESSITY *and* REVELATION—*a map of necessaries, necessarily, necessary, necessitate, necessitated, necessitating, necessities, necessitous, necessity, necessitys, reveal, reveald, revealed, revealer, revealeth, revealing, reveals, revelation, revelations, unnecessary, unrevealed with interconnections and page locations in WJE 1–26.*

stands to reason that he would reveal this new relation and related concerns fully, clearly, and distinctly.[19]

Edwards then explains why revelation is the only way that we could find out about this new relation and religion. He asserts that a good and wise governor is not only influenced by goodness and pity and that wisdom on many accounts may prevent forgiveness. Said more broadly, God has perfections other than goodness and pity and those that come to the fore in emphasis with respect to the sinners and their ends could not be determined. We are finite and to think about God is to ponder an infinite being. How could reason alone determine what might God do for or to sinners? It is reasonable that the answers to such questions would require revelation.[20]

In his pondering, Edwards adds to his human epistemological queries ontological ones. He argues that if we were to take it for granted that God will forgive our sins upon human repentance, it is very difficult to say what repentance might look like for those who have no love or gratitude toward God but only contempt. In other words, how does a being with a bad disposition toward God start to disapprove of its own badness and change in a move towards repentance? Edwards thinks a rebel will not change without God's changing the human heart. We would not know any of this for sure, adds Edwards, without God revealing it.[21] Moreover, there are other related questions that reason has not the ability to discover, such as whether or not a person can repent after a long period of rebellion?[22]

At the end of the entry, he gives a summary comparison of natural and revealed religion. Natural religion is not sufficient for eternal life. Only the revealed religion of the Bible is. And these notions that we learn about God from this provided redemption are more important than the ones we might glean without revelation. This new revealed religion, however, is not contrary to but in agreement with natural religion. His culminating statement of their relationship and the last lines of the entry are: "The light of nature teaches that religion that is necessary to continue in the favor of God that made us. But it cannot teach us that religion that is necessary to our being restored to the favor of God after we have forfeited it."[23]

The necessity of revelation, natural religion, and revealed religion are treated elsewhere. Edwards speaks of the necessity of revelation in relation to our need to be told of our salvation in a number of entries in the "Miscellanies," such as nos. 1230, 1238, and 1346. There are a number of places where Edwards juxtaposes natural and revealed religion. He often stresses post-fall human's inability to access the tenants of even natural religion, often arguing that what some often credit to their unassisted reasoning as actually being sourced in revelation whether they know it or not (e.g., 953, 959, and 969).

Observations on the Corresponding Three-Dimensional Visualization

The three-dimensional visualization associated with these entries was generated focusing on them and three other entries (839, 1234, and 1340) and the key words reason, revelation, and mystery. The reader may want to also read the observations associated with the three other entries in addition to this one. An important observation is the centrality of entry 1156, "Observations on the Agreeableness of the Christian Religion," to the terms reason and revelation. It is yet another angle in approaching Edwards' fascination of the important question of the relationship of reason and revelation. Much of the same could be said about entry 1304. What is more, perhaps unsurprisingly, this latter entry appears to be an important hub in the writings and thoughts of Edwards that connects the idea of the necessity of revelation with other related ideas. It may also be worthwhile to note that 1304 has numerous connections and close proximity to the term "reasons" (plural). This perhaps points to the apologetic weight that this entry held in Edwards' mind and writings.

Notes

[1] This chapter builds upon the foundation laid in my treatment of reason, revelation, and mystery in "Miscellanies" nos. 839, 1234, and 1340.

[2] E.g., Leslie Stephen, *History of English Thought in the Eighteenth Century,* vol. 1, 3rd ed. (London: Harbinger, 1962; 3rd ed. first published, 1902); John Herman Randall, Jr., *The Making of the Modern Mind* (New York: Columbia University Press, 1976; first published, 1926); James C. Livingston, *Modern Christian Thought,* 2nd ed., vol. 1 (Minneapolis: Fortress Press, 2006).

[3] John Locke, *The Reasonableness of Christianity, as Delivered in the Scriptures,* 2nd ed. (London: Awnsham and John Churchil, 1696).

[4] Jonathan S. Marko, "The Brave New World of Discordant Voices into Which Jonathan Edwards Was Born," *A Collection of Essays on Jonathan Edwards* (Fort Worth: JESociety Press, 2017), 85–92; cf. WJE 15:12.

[5] Jonathan S. Marko "The Promulgation of Right Morals: John Locke on the Church and the Christian as the Salvation of Society," *Journal of Markets and Morality* 19, no. 1 (2016): 41–59.

[6] "Miscellanies," no. 1156, in *WJE* 23:61.

[7] "Miscellanies," no. 1156, in *WJE* 23:62–63. For more on the church, see *WJE* 12, *Ecclesiastical Writings.*

[8] "Miscellanies," no. 1156, in *WJE* 23:63.

[9] "Miscellanies," no. 1156, in *WJE* 23:64.

[10] "Miscellanies," no. 1156, in *WJE* 23:65–66.

[11] "Miscellanies," no. 1156, in *WJE* 23:67–70.

[12] "Miscellanies," no. 1156, in *WJE* 23:70–71.

[13] "Miscellanies," no. 1304, in *WJE* 23:253.

[14] "Miscellanies," no. 1304, in *WJE* 23:254–55.

[15] "Miscellanies," no. 1304, in *WJE* 23:256–57.

[16] "Miscellanies," no. 1304, in *WJE* 23:257. The deists and/or some related sect(s) are probably the targets of his thoughts delivered in this entry.

[17] There are a variety of positions regarding the same doctrine (here, the necessity of revelation) that one might hold that can and have been labeled as being "deistic." Cf. Marko, "The Brave New World."

[18] *WJE* 14:498–99; *WJE* 19:719; sermon no. 443, *WJEO* 52; cf. Marko, "Deism."

[19] "Miscellanies," no. 1304, in *WJE* 23:258–59.

[20] "Miscellanies," no. 1304, in *WJE* 23:259–62.

[21] "Miscellanies," no. 1304, in *WJE* 23:262–63.

[22] "Miscellanies," no. 1304, in *WJE* 23:263–64.

[23] Based on Edwards' low view of the natural theological conclusions reasoning humans can make when completely devoid of revelation, it would seem to be the case that this "light of nature" was considerably more evident and helpful to pre-fall Adam and Eve than it is to us.

EDWARDS' COMET: "MISCELLANIES," METEORS, AND THE END OF THE WORLD

Sarah B. Boss

> *Those kinds of heavenly bodies called comets give great evidence that the world is not from eternity and will come to an end.*
>
> — Jonathan Edwards, *Miscellany no. 1038*

A SEARCH THROUGH THE WORKS of Jonathan Edwards for the keyword "comet" yields 34 occurrences, spanning *Religious Affections, Scientific and Philosophical Writings, The Life of David Brainerd, Sermons and Discourses,* and—of course—the "Miscellanies." Throughout these mentions of comets, Edwards repeatedly emphasizes their significance in three primary ways: 1) scientific observations, unsurprisingly in his *Scientific and Philosophical Writings*; 2) illustrations for unsubstantial, transitory faith, contrasted with faith that resembles the "steady lights of heaven," as David Brainerd's did (this kind of mention of meteors is usually paired with a reference to Jude 13: "Raging waves of the sea, foaming out their own shame; wandering stars, to whom is reserved the blackness of darkness for ever"); and 3) associations with or evidence for the apocalypse. In all of these allusions to comets, Edwards views the astronomical bodies as negative entities, which signify a transient faith or foretell cosmic destruction. This essay will focus on how Edwards uses the symbol of the comet in his "Miscellanies" and what greater truth Edwards aims to discover through his astronomical observations. In the "Miscellanies" the comet appears as an apocalyptic symbol, though not in the sense of a modern sci-fi thriller. For Edwards, comets illuminate the edges of time and space and life as we know it. They imprint upon the spectator an understanding that "the world is not from eternity and will come to an end."[1] Edwards' comets are merely one thread in an intricate, cosmic tapestry, but nonetheless one which, when tugged at, can reveal the way in which the world itself will one day be unraveled and destroyed.

Before delving into Edwards' thoughts on comets, it would be helpful to note briefly Edwards' thoughts on astronomy in general. By the seventeenth and eighteenth centuries astronomy had become a more popular and promising endeavour, as astronomers across the world engaged in serious study of the sky. In colonial America, astronomy was also taking root; almanacs were the only American periodical literature in the seventeenth century and, combined with Puritan sermons, comprised the majority of American literature from that century.[2] Although Edwards was not a practiced astronomer himself, he did nevertheless incorporate some consideration of the discipline into his study. He makes note of particular astronomical findings, such as the comet of 1680 and the debates over the shape of the cometary orbit.[3] But he also views the discipline through the distinct lens of the theologian, claiming that astronomy belonged originally to Christianity. In Miscellany no. 962. "Traditions of the Heathen," Edwards retells his own history of astronomy. He extensively quotes Theophilus Gale's mid-seventeenth-century *The Court of the Gentiles,* which attempts to trace all of Greek thought back to Middle Eastern origins. Following these quotations, Edwards concludes,

> That so much is said in ancient tradition and history of Abraham's great skill in astronomy and astrology, and his

teaching the Chaldeans and Egyptians and Phoenicians those sciences, and that this was the original of these sciences among these nations from whom the Greeks received them, is a great confirmation that the ancient astrology had its first rise from the great experience and long observations of the antediluvians, though it soon exceedingly degenerated, and was so mixed and corrupted that at length it became a diabolical art.[4]

He also writes that "human learning and all useful and noble knowledge, and not only knowledge in things divine and spiritual, was originally from the church of God."[5] Astronomy for Edwards, then, was a God-given knowledge which originated from the Christian patriarch Abraham. Although astrology became degenerate and diabolical, as Edwards writes, the first study of the sky was an honorable and truth-giving practice.

Edwards, of course, engages in this practice himself periodically throughout his corpus and in a few select "Miscellanies." In all, only six of the "Miscellanies" mention comets. These are: no. 863 "Conflagration. Misery of the Damned," no. 929 "Hell Torments," no. 931 "Hell Torments. Conflagration," no. 990 "That the World Will Come to an End," no. 1038 "Those kinds of heavenly bodies called comets give great evidence that the world is not from eternity and will come to an end," and no. 1041 "The world is not from eternity and will come to an end." As can be surmised from the titles, half of these entries deal explicitly with hell and damnation, and the other half with the end of the world. Of course, these topics are by no means mutually exclusive. It may be said that, for Edwards, comets are harbingers of the apocalypse and foreshadows of both the cataclysmic end of the world as a whole and the miserable end of lives of sinners individually. As such, comets present didactic reminders of how to live in this life on this earth with an eternal end in mind.

Concerning the first sort of "Miscellanies" on comets, nos. 863, 929, and 931, these entries emphasize the misery of the damned in hell and situate comets in the midst of such torment. For example, in Miscellany no. 863, Edwards writes,

> It looks to me very probable that the time will come, when all the planets and comets shall be cast down into the sun, into that vast fire, there to make that fire the greater, and to add to that ocean of fire; and not altogether unlikely that all the fixed stars shall be thrown together in one, all those many millions of suns be gathered into one great, which, as it will make the fire so many thousand times greater, so it will, in some proportion, [make it] more exceeding fierce and furious. And that thus there shall be a literal accomplishment of those many expressions of Scripture . . . so that the whole visible world shall be destroyed with one great and general destruction.[6]

In this text, comets are not the focal point but rather one item among a list of entities of the cosmos. They are integral to this list, however, because the image Edwards is trying to conjure is one of a catastrophic, burning mass. Comets, with their bright tails burning across the sky, greatly enhance such a picture. Furthermore, they emphasize Edwards' point that the whole of creation will be cast into the sun and consumed in a fiery mass. Comets help communicate this point because, for the eighteenth-century astronomer, they were the outermost known quantity of space. So, then, for Edwards to write that when the "comets shall be cast down into the sun" it will accomplish the biblical prophecy of "the heavens being dissolved and rolled together as a scroll and passing away," he is relying on comets to illustrate that truly the whole universe will cease to exist in this "one great and general destruction."[7]

"Miscellanies" nos. 929 and 931 present similar pictures of mass destruction. Miscellany no. 929 also illustrates the torments of hell:

> When the powers of heaven come to be shaken by the terrible voice of the great judge of the world in pronouncing

the cursed sentence, and his mighty power casts down these globes, and brings 'em together with such a prodigious velocity as to bring 'em all into one heap in a very little, one huge conflagration, and those heavy worlds of liquid fire are sent down in a terrible storm, like burning rain, by thousands and hundreds of thousands, if not millions, with such a prodigious velocity and almighty fury as to bring 'em all together in a very little time, with probably many million times greater celerity than that of lightning; when such infinite bodies of fire, with all the planets and comets belonging to them, thus clash one with another with an immensely forcible collision and infinite rage of their flames, it will probably extremely attenuate their parts and increase their action. These lightnings will be like the breath of the Lord, like a stream of brimstone to kindle the furnace with a witness [Job 41:21].[8]

Edwards' language here is very similar to that of Miscellany no. 863. Perhaps one outstanding difference between the two is that in this entry Edwards offers a biblical reference—Job 41:21—to support his point. The verse reads: "His breath kindleth coals, and a flame goeth out of his mouth." The context for this scriptural reference is God's description of the Leviathan, asking Job whether he can conquer the beast. Interestingly, through this biblical allusion, the Miscellany equates God with the Leviathan and equates comets, by association, with the fiery breath of both the beast and God. In doing so, Edwards extends associations of comets from apocalyptic to even mythic proportions.

Of the three "Miscellanies" which connect comets with hell and the damned, Miscellany no. 931 is notable for its semi-scientific language concerning the constitutions of comets which will be more focal in later "Miscellanies." Edwards writes,

The comets that are sent down blazing from the distant regions of the universe with such a prodigious velocity and fury, so near to the sun as some of them to be as it were involved in its flames, are some presages of this great event; as it is the manner of God, in the works of nature and common providence, to be giving some faint presages of the future grand events that are to come to pass in the natural and moral world. ... The intestine furious commotion and combustion will probably be greatly increased by the heterogeneous particles of the planets and comets. By what is visible in comets, it appears that the matter of which they are constituted, being very heterogeneous, is put as it were into an immense uproar on their near approach to the sun—by what appears in their tails, in which are fumes sent forth in such great quantities, to such prodigious distances.[9]

Here Edwards begins by musing on the connection between comets and the apocalypse, as in the previous "Miscellanies." After this, however, he veers to discuss how this calamity will be magnified by the diverse molecular constitution of the various astronomical objects. He observes that comets must be made of heterogeneous matter and must be greatly affected by their closeness to the sun, as their tails expel great quantities of fumes to prodigious distances. As is typical of Edwards, he relies on detailed observations and logic to support and illustrate strictly biblical truths. In addition to such empirical observations, Edwards' use of the word "presage" also clues the reader into how Edwards conceived of comets and other astronomical phenomena. He writes that it is God's common providence to give "some faint presages of the future grand events."[10] Comets, then, are presages or omens created by God to tell humans of the impending end of the world and the torments of hell. Edwards' idea that comets are such omens is parallel with preceding and peer theologians' opinions.[11] Even scientists like Kepler and Newton wished to maintain "comets as actors in God's eschatological drama."[12] Like Edwards, Increase Mather in his *Kometographia* (1683) asserts the ancient view that comets are connected to catastrophic events on earth. Mather

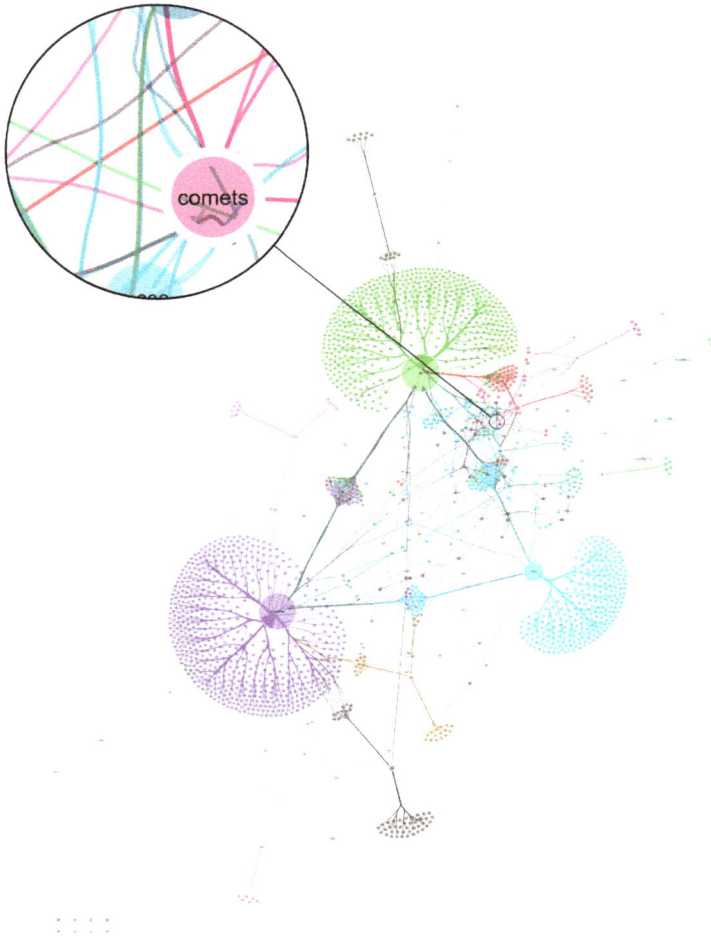

COMET, CONFLAGRATION, PLANET, PROVIDENCE, SUN, UNIVERSE, *and* WORKS OF NATURE*—a map of comet, comets, conflagration, planet, planetary, planets, providence, providences, providential, providentially, sun, sunbeam, sunbeams, sundial, sundown, sunned, sunny, sunrise, sunrising, suns, sunset, sunshine, sunshiny, universe, works of nature with interconnections and page locations in WJE 1–26.*

does not entertain any uncertainty concerning comets' role as divine symbols, He writes,

> There are those who think, that inasmuch as Comets may be supposed to proceed from natural causes, there is no speaking voice of Heaven in them, beyond what is to be said of all other works of God. But certain it is, that many things which may happen according to the course of nature, are portentous signs of divine anger, and prognostics of great evils hastening upon the world.[13]

So then, in Miscellany no. 931, Edwards combines traditional notions of comets as presages of destruction with more modern scientific observations on their composition.

However, perhaps more interesting—and more unique to Edwards—are the entries of the second sort, those which deal more explicitly with the end of the world. These are "Miscellanies" nos. 990, 1038, and 1041. One aspect which makes these entries fascinating is that they raise questions of not only the constitution of the cosmos but also the nature of time itself. In doing so, they simultaneously deal with issues of science and theology.

The first of these, Miscellany no. 990, is an especially delightful entry, in which Edwards unfolds as imaginative and vivid a metaphor of the world as one might find in a work of the Metaphysical poets or among the sketches of da Vinci. He draws a parallel between the human body and the earth to argue that the world will one day end:

> As it is with the body of man—its meat and its clothing perishes and is continually renewed, and at last the body itself perishes . . . —so there is all reason to think it will be with the world. It needs nourishment: the face of the earth continually needs a new supply of rain, and also of nitrous parts by the snow and frost, or by other means gradually drawn in from the atmosphere that it is encompassed with, and of nourishment by falling leaves or rotting plants or

otherwise to feed it; the sea is constantly fed by rain and rivers to maintain it; the earth in all parts has constant new supplies of water to maintain its fountains and streams that are as it were its arteries and veins; the sun itself that nourished the whole planetary system is nourished by comets, by new supplies from time to time communicated from them. And so the world is continually changing its garments as it were. . . . The body of man often lies down and sleeps and rises up again, but at last will lie down and rise no more. So the world every year as it were perishes in the winter, or sinks into an image of death, as sleep is in the body of [man], but it is renewed again in the spring; but at last it will perish and rise no more.[14]

In this lovely Miscellany, Edwards compares the cyclical human consumption of food and use of garments to the earth's diet of rain and clothes of foliage. Such a creative simile is to be expected from Edwards, whose "Images" notebook is full of poetic conceptions of the world order. What concerns this essay, however, is Edwards' inclusion of comets in this entry. Nestled between descriptions of the streams working as veins of the earth and of the earth changing its clothes through the seasons, Edwards also notes a comparison to the solar system's diet of comets, which periodically provide it with "new supplies." Including comets among such a detailed sketch of the cycle of life—both human and earthly—demonstrates the integral role comets play in Edwards' cosmos. They nourish the sun, which in turn nourishes the plants which feed and clothe the earth. Edwards will expand on this idea of cometary nourishment in later "Miscellanies" in more scientific terms. Moreover, mentioning comets in this depiction of the world displays a consideration of the entirety of the universe and so supports Edwards' ultimate conclusion that the world "at last will perish and rise no more."[15]

The final two "Miscellanies" to be discussed, nos. 1038 and 1041, are the most well developed of those dealt with here. In them, Edwards convincingly plays the astronomer and provides thorough, empirically substantiated reasons why comets prove that "the world is not from eternity and will come to an end." [16] First, in Miscellany no. 1038 Edwards enumerates two arguments towards this point. The first of these is that comets, which outnumber planets and have been spotted since the beginning of recorded history, are "coeval with the frame of the universe."[17] That is, they have existed as long as the universe itself has. Yet, Edwards argues, comets cannot exist for an eternity because it can be observed that "they are constantly spending them[selves], sending forth in vast and continual streams parts of themselves clear off from their own bodies and atmospheres … And there is nothing appears of any continual reflux or constant stream of matter to them."[18] Therefore, "they suffer a constant diminution,"[19] and one day they will cease to exist. And if comets, which are "a very considerable part of the frame of the universe, that has hitherto stood through all past ages," can reach a final conclusion, then it follows that so, too, can the world itself.[20]

In the second point of Miscellany no. 1038, Edwards returns to the idea of nourishment expressed in Miscellany no. 990. He educates the reader on the solar diet, which consists of comets. He writes that whatever matter comets constantly expend must be gathered to some place, and, since "the attraction of the sun throughout all parts of these ethereal spaces … is vastly greater than all other bodies," it follows that expended cometary matter must be collected into the sun. This periodic intake of matter is used to "repair the sun's expense, by its constant, immense profusion of beams of light." Yet, seeing as comets are not eternal and must at some point in time be spent, "the sun must want this nourishment and, having no new supplies, must be gradually spent, and so the solar system be destroyed."[21] Thus, relying on speculations concerning the expulsion of cometary matter and straightforward logical processes, Edwards concludes that comets are proof that the world will end.[22]

Lastly, Miscellany no. 1041 adds two more points to his previous entry concerning comets, followed by two answers to a possible objection. Edwards restates his thesis that comets are "evidence that the world is not from eternity," but he offers new support for this claim.[23] He engages in a protracted deliberation on the orbits of comets, concluding that they are elliptical.[24] Such a finely tuned orbital shape and motion, he reasons, necessitates the reliance on a Creator. To this end, he remarks on the comet of 1680 as evidence.[25] This comet, known as Kirch's Comet or Newton's Comet, was the first such astronomical body to be discovered by a telescope. It appeared over North America decades before Edwards' birth, but was written on by many of his Puritan predecessors, such as Increase Mather, and remained close enough to the front of the Puritan mind that Edwards muses on it nearly half a century later.[26] Edwards refers to this particular comet throughout his *Scientific and Philosophical Writings* as well. Additionally, in Miscellany no. 1041 he makes observations concerning sunbeams and their molecular construction, again relying on scientific findings to support his conviction in a divinely operated and non-eternal world.[27]

His second (fourth overall, when added to Miscellany no. 1038) point reiterates that if it were not for "the exact care of a wise Creator and Disposer," comets would have crashed into planets and been destroyed long ago.[28] Again he notes how close the path of the comet of 1680 was to the earth's orbit, remarking that the two bodies should have collided before. In conclusion, Edwards considers an objection which may be made against him. This is that there were once many more planets and comets, which long ago crashed into one another and were destroyed, so that "none are now left but such as can move freely without mutual disturbance."[29] To this, Edwards replies: firstly, that this is not the case, as can be seen from the close course of the comet of 1680, and secondly, that if it were true, it would only support his conclusion, as how else besides divine intervention had all these heavenly bodies not collided sooner?[30] By continuing his previous discussion of comets in the "Miscellanies" with new observations and more empirical details, Edwards creates a compelling case for why comets demonstrate that "the world is not from eternity and will come to an end."

THE MISCELLANIES COMPANION

All of the six "Miscellanies" discussed which mention comets express similar themes of destruction, chaos, a final end (both material and spiritual), and a tone of admonition. As they progress later into Edwards' career, his notes on comets take on a more scientific tenor. He begins to employ a special *modus operandi,* in which he marries contemporary empirical language with more traditional, religious ideas. Even though the shape of a comet's orbit may be ascertained and used to argue why such bodies do not crash into the earth or the molecular constitution of a comet's tail may be hypothetically dissected, such scientific discoveries do not dissuade Edwards from his conviction that the whole cosmos is divinely orchestrated. His writings on comets are not merely empirical observations, but are unions of modern science and ancient didactics. Even if Edwards does not shudder in fear at the approach of a comet, anticipating an immediate apocalypse, he nevertheless uses comets to reflect and teach the impermanence of the world and the catastrophic end which awaits any unregenerate soul.

Edwards' predisposition for moralizing the natural world may have been nothing extraordinary when placed alongside the habits of his Puritan forefathers, but it was nothing short of fantastic when compared to his philosophical contemporaries. Even among the religiously inclined natural philosophers of the Enlightenment, it was becoming more vogue to separate observable, material reality from invisible, spiritual reality.[31] Rene Descartes proposes that the final cause of the universe ("the end for which God created the world," as Edwards might say) could not be discerned through nature or physics. Descartes writes,

> Concerning natural things, we shall not undertake any reasonings from the end which God or nature set Himself in creating these things, and we shall entirely reject from our Philosophy the search for final causes: because we ought not to presume so much of ourselves as to think that we are the confidants of His intentions. But, considering Him as the efficient cause of all things, we shall see what

the natural enlightenment with which He endowed us reveals must be concluded (concerning those of His effects which appear to our senses), from those of His attributes of which He willed that we should have some notion.[32]

Mechanical philosophy presented a one-dimensional, homogeneous world order, which "emptied the created order of teleological purposes, thus stipulating that nature did not manifest the presence of God."[33] Such a perspective is in sharp contrast with Edwards', who writes in Miscellany, no. 42 "Religion,"

> The greatness, distance and motion of this great universe, has almost an omnipotent power upon the imagination; the blood will even be chilled with the vast idea. ...Yea, these are but the shadows of greatness and are worthless, except as they conduce to true and real greatness and excellency, and manifest the power and wisdom of God. When we think of the sweet harmony of the parts of the corporeal world, it fills us with such astonishment that the soul is ready to break. ...That harmony of the world is indeed a very true picture and shadow of the real glories of religion. This great world contains many millions of little worlds vastly greater than it. The glories of astronomy and natural philosophy consist in the harmony of the parts of the corporeal shadow of a world; the glories of religion consist in the sweet harmony of the greater and more real worlds with themselves, with one another, and with the infinite fountain and original of them.[34]

For Edwards, religion and astronomy are not in competition but exist harmoniously. Both the natural and spiritual realms exemplify the excellency of God; therefore, the study of one should inform the study of the other. By reading the Book of Scripture and the Book of Nature in tandem, Edwards considers the heavens—and the comets which populate them—in a multi-faceted, three-dimensional way.

The visualizations which accompany this work—which themselves resemble shooting stars—can likewise rejuvenate Edwards for the twenty first century and herald his messages for a new audience.

Notes

[1] "Miscellanies," no. 1038, in *WJE* 20:378.

[2] Donald K. Yeomans, "The Origin of North American Astronomy—Seventeenth Century," *Isis* 68 no. 3 (1977): 414–15.

[3] In the seventeenth century, the shape of a comet's orbit was hotly debated among astronomers. The strongest contenders were ellipse, parabola, and hyperbola. Delving further into research made by Isaac Newton, Edmond Halley believed the answer to be an extremely elongated ellipse. This meant that comets must reappear and their return could be calculated. For more on this topic, see Jonathan Shectman, *Groundbreaking Scientific Experiments, Inventions, and Discoveries of the 18th Century* (Westport: Greenwood Press, 2003).

[4] "Miscellanies," no. 962, in *WJE* 20:245.

[5] "Miscellanies," no. 962, in *WJE* 20:245.

[6] "Miscellanies," no. 863, in *WJE* 20:94.

[7] "Miscellanies," no. 863, in *WJE* 20:94.

[8] "Miscellanies," no. 929, in *WJE* 20:173.

[9] "Miscellanies," no. 931, in *WJE* 20:182–83, 188.

[10] "Miscellanies," no. 931, in *WJE* 20:182.

[11] Shectman writes, "But more than any single event, comets were supposed to signal the end of the world. In the European Middle Ages, the Church's position was that a comet was a warning shot fired across the bow of Earth by an angry God. This position often led to widespread panics at the mere sight of a comet. So pervasive was this position that, on sighting a comet in 1456, Pope Calixtus II ordered a terrified, xenophobic prayer to be spoken daily, "Lord, save us from the Devil, the Turk, and the Comet!" Shectman, *Groundbreaking Scientific Experiments, Inventions, and Discoveries of the 18th Century,* 55.

[12] Christopher Johnson, "'Periwigged Heralds': Epistemology and Intertextuality in Early American Cometography," *Journal of the History of Ideas* 65, no. 3 (2004): 400.

[13] Quoted in Wallace W. Marshall, *Puritanism and Natural Theology* (Eugene: Pickwick Publications, 2016), 104.

[14] "Miscellanies," no. 990, in *WJE* 20:315.

[15] "Miscellanies," no. 990, in *WJE* 20:315.

[16] "Miscellanies," no. 1038, in *WJE* 20:378.

[17] "Miscellanies," no. 1038, in *WJE* 20:378.

[18] "Miscellanies," no. 1038, in *WJE* 20:378.

[19] "Miscellanies," no. 1038, in *WJE* 20:378.

[20]"Miscellanies," no. 1038, in *WJE* 20:378.

[21]"Miscellanies," no. 1038, in *WJE* 20:378–79.

[22]"Miscellanies," no. 1038, in *WJE* 20:379.

[23]"Miscellanies," no. 1041, in *WJE* 20:380.

[24]"Miscellanies," no. 1041, in *WJE* 20:381.

[25]"Miscellanies," no. 1041, in *WJE* 20:381.

[26]Donald K. Yeomans, "The Origin of North American Astronomy—Seventeenth Century," *Isis* 68 no. 3 (1977): 417–21.

[27]"Miscellanies," no. 1041, in *WJE* 20:381.

[28]"Miscellanies," no. 1041, in *WJE* 20:381.

[29]"Miscellanies," no. 1041, in *WJE* 20:381.

[30]"Miscellanies," no. 1041, in *WJE* 20:381.

[31]Avihu Zakai, "The Rise of Modern Science and the Decline of Theology as the 'Queen of Sciences' in the Early Modern Era," *Reformation and Renaissance Review* 2 (2007): 125.

[32]Quoted in Peter K. Machamer, James E. McGuire & Justin Sytsma, "Knowing Causes: Descartes on the World of Matter," *Philosophica* 76 (2005): 33.

[33]Avihu Zakai, "The Theological Origins of Jonathan Edwards' Philosophy of Nature," *Journal of Ecclesiastical History* 60 no. 4 (2009): 712.

[34]"Miscellanies," no. 42, in *WJE* 13:224.

A World that Excites Devotion

Robert L. Boss

> *As for the other thing that is said, that there may be a degree*
> *of devotion that may hinder one from being useful to the*
> *rest of the universe: I suppose they will not dislike devotion*
> *if it only hinders one for but half a minute, and makes one*
> *much more useful ever after; I mean, if it only makes us*
> *useless during our life upon earth, and much more useful to*
> *eternity afterwards. Not that I believe that a man would be*
> *the less useful even in this world, if his devotion was to that*
> *degree, as to keep him all his lifetime in an ecstasy.*

— Jonathan Edwards, *Miscellany no. tt*

THIS ESSAY WILL BRIEFLY SURVEY the structure of Edwards' world
view and examine the main pillars that support his enchanted
three-storied universe. A reading of "Miscellanies," nos. *tt,* 123, 124,
251, 362, 383, and 408 along with his notebook "Images of Divine
Things" reveals four distinct features which frame Edwards' world—1)
excellent harmony, 2) scriptural regulation, 3) analogies and emblems,
and 4) poetic spirituality. These features serve metaphorically as the
load-bearing columns of Edwards' devotional "reading" of the Book
of Nature.[1]

THE MISCELLANIES COMPANION

Clock, Body, and Soul

Since the Enlightenment, the clock has served as an image of a universe marked by design and regulated by rationality. It is a mechanical metaphor which offers insights into the complex cycles of the created order and evidence of the divine clockmaker. Yet the clock, as a representation of order and rationality, was but a new development in an old quest to explain human correspondence to the universe via microcosm and macrocosm. Jonathan Edwards used metaphors, both new and old, as he reflected on the created order in his "Miscellanies."

Edwards reflects upon the new metaphor—the clock—in "Miscellanies," no. *tt*. DEVOTION to make sense of the world—God is a clockmaker, but according to Edwards the clock's devotional movement is of an entirely different nature and order than that of the Enlightenment's mechanical philosophers. Edwards illustrates the devotional and symbolically communicative nature of the world by comparing it to the inner workings of a clock in which the "immediate communication between one degree of being and the next degree of being (every wheel immediately communicates with the next wheel), but man being the top; so that the next immediate step from him is to God."[2]

As the wheels of the clock, though inferior to the hands, drive the hands to point out the correct time, in the same way, the lower orders of creation are designed to move man beyond himself to a devotion toward God. Edwards believes that the entire creation moves toward the ultimate goal of prompting man to praise God, just as the gears and movements of a clock turn the hands to tell time. In other words, creation has a teleological movement with a devotional purpose. Edwards says that those who term such thinking as enthusiasm "talk very unphilosophically."[3] In a similar way, Edwards embraced the older image of a world alive with God's animating presence. In "Miscellanies," no. 124, he notes:

> There is just the same sort of knowledge of the existence
> of an universal mind in the world from the actions of the

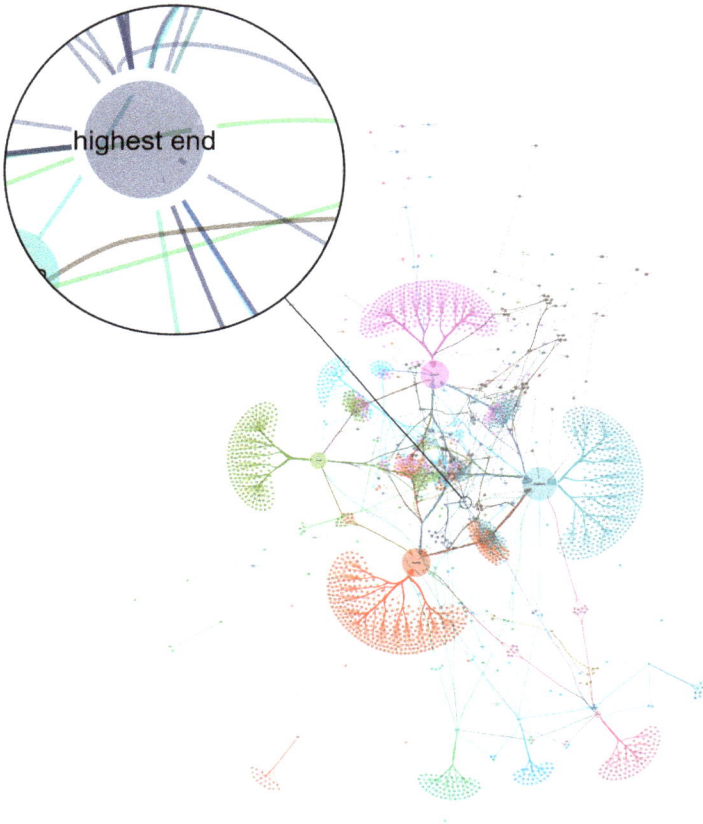

CLOCK, CREATION, CREATURE, DEVOTION, HIGHEST END, and UNIVERSE—
*a map of clock, clocks, clockwork, creation, creations, creature, creatures,
devote, devoted, devotedness, devotees, devotes, devoting, devotion, devotional,
devotions, highest end, universe with interconnections and page locations in
WJE 1–26.*

world, and what is done that is objected to our senses or that is effected by this mind, as there is of the existence of a particular mind in an human body from the observation of the actions of that, in gesture, look and voice.[4]

In "Miscellanies," no. 383, Edwards continues the comparison of God's animating presence in the world to the human soul and body. He concludes that the relationship between the human soul and body is the best shadow of God's relationship with the world. "Man's soul influences the body, continues its nature and powers and constant regular motions and productions, and actuates it, as the supreme principle does the universe."[5]

Edwards observes a universal mind which not only animates the world, but also acts and communicates via "mutual respects and relations."[6] Edwards concludes that this view requires three components—a quick glance without heavy dependence on reason, a comprehensive perspective, and an eye toward relationships.[7] A comprehensive or panoramic perspective and attention to relationships, correspondences, and similitudes are hallmarks of the emblematic world view. A strict focus on the mere outward appearance of the world fails to comprehend the spiritual nature of things.

Edwards' clockwork vision of the world requires a significant step of faith for "reasonable" children of the Enlightenment. Ordinary clocks are easy to understand, yet Edwards' clock is mysterious and anything but mundane. Its gears, wheels, and springs tick, spin, and chime in an otherworldly way, transporting the viewer to spiritual heights.

An Excellent Harmony

In keeping with the clock and the body/soul metaphors, Edwards perceives a general fitness or agreeableness between the spiritual and material constitution of the universe. He alludes to occasional meditation as a way to discover the divine message in the natural order as one goes about everyday life. Divine things will be "excellently represented and held forth, and it will abundantly tend to confirm the Scriptures, for there is an excellent agreement between these things and the Holy Scriptures."[8]

Edwards believes that reflection upon the inhabitants of this world reveals the inhabitants of the spiritual realm and their relative habitations. The physical structure of this world corresponds directly to the structure of the spiritual world:

> There are three sorts of inhabitants of this world inhabiting its three regions, viz. the inhabitants of the earth, and the animals that inhabit the waters under the earth, and the fowls of heaven that inhabit the air or firmament of heaven. In these is some faint shadow of the three different sorts of inhabitants of the three worlds, viz. earth, heaven and hell.[9]

The harmony between the natural and spiritual worlds overlaps with Edwards' perception of excellency. Beauty and excellence are comprised of complicated harmonies of symmetry and correspondence— these are shadows of being. He believes that, as great as harmonies in nature are, spiritual harmonies are much greater and more complicated.

The perception of these equalities and similarities is an acquired skill or taste, much like a developed taste for music. At a basic level, it is not difficult to discern harmony and excellence in simple tunes.[10] The uncomplicated pleasantness in the way notes fit together in their tempo and rhythm is similar to the attractiveness of proportionate bodies and symmetrical faces. Each side of a body or face corresponds to the other side. A lack of symmetry is commonly considered a deformity which destroys the beauty or harmony of the object under consideration, whether person, plant, animal, building, etc. Edwards notes that humans are also wired to seek out patterns, similarities, and correspondences:

> How exceedingly apt are we, when we are sitting still and accidentally casting our eye upon some marks or spots

in the floor or wall, to be ranging of them into regular parcels and figures; and if we see a mark out of its place, to be placing of it right by our imagination—and this even while we are meditating on something else. So we may catch ourselves at observing the rules of harmony and regularity in the careless motions of our heads or feet, and when playing with our hands or walking about the room.[11]

Finding patterns within random spots on the wall can be extended to all types of associations and systems. The need for order and harmony is the driving force for all fields of inquiry, discovery, and invention. Humans expect harmony and order and seek after beauty. A similar bent toward correspondences and relations can be seen in the inescapable use of metaphor in everyday communication. One thing is explained in terms of another. There is an interconnectedness to all communication and reality. The observation of harmony and regularity in the insignificant motions of our human body is easily extended to things outside the body, beyond spots on the floor or wall. Communicative patterns can be discerned in events, providences, and signs.[12]

Edwards understands that harmony, proportion, and excellency require plurality. A single entity cannot be harmonious or proportionate. Likewise, excellence does not occur in solitude, "for there can be no such thing as consent or agreement."[13] For Edwards, true being is spiritual, and material bodies are shadows of being. The more bodies exhibit proportion, similarity, and harmony, the more they shadow or correspond to excellence or true being. In this way there is a consent or agreement between the natural and the spiritual. The more excellent or beautiful something is, the greater its shadow of or correspondence to being itself—God.[14]

The quest for harmony is manifest in Edwards' belief that the Old Testament is full of types and shadows of things which find correspondence and fulfillment in the New Testament. The harmony of the two Testaments is proof of their excellency. The agreement between the two Testaments even overflowed into the created order, resulting in Edwards' "Images." A fitness or consent exists between the shadow and the thing shadowed. As correspondences can be perceived between the two Testaments, the Testaments themselves explicitly point out the correspondence between the created order and the spiritual realm. Man, a created being, is made in the image (shadow, emblem) of God. The incarnate Christ is the express image of the Father. Edwards' philosophical consideration of excellency, founded in proportion, harmony, correspondence, and consent is rooted in the emblematic and representative constitution of the created order. This emblematic world view was recognized by earlier Evangelicals such as John Bunyan. Edwards writes,

> For indeed the whole outward creation, which is but the shadows of beings, is so made as to represent spiritual things. It might be demonstrated by the wonderful agreement in thousands of things, much of the same kind as is between the types of the Old Testament and their antitypes, and by spiritual things being so often and continually compared with them in the Word of God.[15]

Scriptural Regulation

Edwards' devotional world view is founded upon scriptural precedent and subject to its authority. This is especially evident in the "Scriptures" series which follows his two hundred and twelve "Image" entries.[16] He maintains that:

> The book of Scripture is the interpreter of the book of nature two ways, viz., by declaring to us those spiritual mysteries that are indeed signified and typified in the constitution of the natural world; and secondly, in actually making application of the signs and types in the book of nature as representations of those spiritual mysteries in many instances.[17]

In his extensive typology of nature, Edwards remains subject to the authority of the Bible. Though nature receives a measure of exaltation from Edwards, it is nowhere near an autonomous source of revelation. The communicative nature of the created order is constrained by the communication. The purpose of the message is to bring glory to God. Outside the interpretive authority of the Bible, nature has no clear voice.

Analogy and Emblem

Closely related to the agreeableness between the natural world and the spiritual world is the analogous nature of the natural world. Edwards refers to analogy and similitude, which are both markers of the emblematic worldview. "Images," no. 86 is very similar to "Images," no. 82, except no. 82 highlights the three-story structure of the world, whereas no. 86 focuses on similitudes and gradation or chain of being:

> As it is in the analogy that is to be observed in the works of nature, wherein the inferior are images of the superior, and the analogy holds through many ranks of beings, but becomes more and more faint and languid (thus, how many things in brutes are analogous to what is to be observed in men: in some the image is more lively, in others less, till we come to the lowest rank of brutes, in whom it is more faint than others; but if we go from them to plants, still the analogy and similitude holds in many things, and in different degrees in different plants, till we come to metals and some other inanimate things, wherein still is to be seen some very faint representations of things appertaining to mankind); so it is with respect to the representations there are in the external world, of things in the spiritual world.[18]

A dramatic reference to the correspondence between the Spirit and a dove occurs in entry no. 125 of "Images." Edwards highlights love in action—shelter, warmth, heat, brooding, feeding, and nourishment.[19] Another telling example of Edwards' emblematic world view is contained in "Miscellanies," no. 362 on the Trinity, which was written sometime in the latter half of 1728, the same time he began writing "Images of Divine Things." The devotional world of Jonathan Edwards overflows with analogy, emblem, and simile—creation resonates and rhymes with itself on a Great Chain of Being which stretches from Heaven to Hell.

Poetic Spirituality

The perception of correspondences between natural and spiritual excellencies requires poetic discernment and feeling: "And there is really likewise an analogy, or consent, between the beauty of the skies, trees, fields, flowers, etc. and spiritual excellencies; though the agreement be more hid and requires a more discerning, feeling mind to perceive it ... "[20] The agreement between the natural and spiritual is "strange," yet it is "natural in such frames of mind." A poetic spirituality enables one to "discover the beauty of many of those metaphors and similes, which to an unphilosophical person do seem so uncouth."[21]

Edwards notes that such perception requires spiritual knowledge. Written in early 1729 shortly after the commencement of "Images of Divine Things," Edwards notices in "Miscellanies," no. 408 the effect spiritual knowledge has upon one's perception of the natural world. Edwards describes the ability of spiritually enlightened believers to perceive the world and spiritual things in a whole new way, seeing associations and significances that were once obscured or hidden.[22]

Though the act of reading the world like a text requires an incredible shift of perception for modern man, Edwards identifies in "Miscellanies," no. 251 a key to interpreting the world emblematically. He observes that the authors of the Scriptures, in the Psalms and elsewhere, wrote under the influence of a "poetical genius and fire, excited and invigorated by an extraordinary exercise of grace and a holy and evangelical disposition, in which excitations there was the afflatus of God's Spirit."[23] The poetic nature of Scripture, Edwards argues, requires that the reader be poetically disposed or prepared in order to have a clear understanding of the types and shadows intended by the Spirit of God.[24]

A poetic spirituality was not only requisite for composing Scripture, but also hearing it. In a sermon on Matthew 13:23, "Profitable Hearers of the Word," Edwards notes that the reason Scripture often teaches through allegories, parables, and types is that we might have some exercise for our understandings to find out the truth contained in them. Our understandings were given us to be used, and above all to be exercised, in divine things. Therefore God teaches us in such a way that we shall have some exercise of meditation and study. God gives us the gold, but he gives it to us in a mine that we might dig for it and get in a way of our own industry ... and that makes it precious ... This is not only God's method in Scripture, but his method in nature also. The works of God are hard to be understood, that they might be "sought out of all them that have pleasure in them" (Psalms 111:2).[25]

Edwards believes that it should come as no surprise that God takes delight in using the created order to teach humans spiritual things, "representing divine things by his works."[26] God has made the world in such a way that it rhymes with Scripture. This truth was widely accepted in Puritan spirituality.[27] Edwards says that the human mind must be exercised, and spiritual blindness must be healed, in order to perceive and understand the poetic and emblematic nature of Scripture and the world. One must submit to the wisdom of God in creating a world that could be understood by intelligent beings.

In "Miscellanies," no. 123, entitled "Spiritual Sight," Edwards notes that one's eyes must be open in order to see the world in its fullness. Spiritual things "consist in mental motions energies and operations" that defy even the most accurate descriptions.[28]

Experience is an integral aspect of knowledge. Edwards points to the rainbow as an example of something that is hard to explain to someone who has never seen it, but something that is an "easy thing to give a definition of."[29]

A Reinscripturated World

Edwards' clockwork world view is framed by excellency, Scripture, correspondence, poetic spirituality, and what scholar Wilson H. Kimnach called the "doctrinal precision" in Edwards' project of "re-attaching the material and spiritual in accordance with the design of the Creator."[30] This re-attachment of doctrine to the creation can be accurately described as a *reinscripturation* of the world.

If nature's voice speaks of nothing higher than itself, then nature has no purpose beyond itself—nature is for nature's sake, not God's sake. Beyond their bellows and other audible noises, crocodiles and the rest of creation are mute. A truncated understanding of nature highlights the problem which Edwards points out in "Miscellanies" no. *tt* on the devotional purpose of the world.[31] The complex matrices of correspondence between things earthly and spiritual are full of theological content. A spiritually-minded, panoramic first impression of the world was the only thing necessary to see its true character and content.

An Edwardsean world view reveals a creation full of correspondences and similitudes that echo, illustrate, and are governed by the Book of Scripture. The shadowy revelation in nature is full of parables, riddles, and connections—a world illumined by bright shadows. Behind every bush and under every rock and within every tree, creature, and event is a voice of Wisdom crying out to those who have ears to hear and eyes to see.

This imaginative encounter with Scripture and nature is filled with adventure and reward. The pilgrim gains a whole new view of God's creation—an enchanted world without end. An imaginative meditation upon the world and Scripture together is precisely what

Edwards accomplished. He unpacked his quick glance in his notebook "Images of Divine Things" and the "Miscellanies" noted in this essay, yet admitted it was a task impossible to finish:

> I expect by very ridicule and contempt to be called a man of a very fruitful brain and copious fancy, but they are welcome to it. I am not ashamed to own that I believe that the whole universe, heaven and earth, air and seas, and the divine constitution and history of the holy Scriptures, be full of images of divine things, as full as a language is of words; and that the multitude of those things that I have mentioned are but a very small part of what is really intended to be signified and typified by these things: but that there is room for persons to be learning more and more of this language and seeing more of that which is declared in it to the end of the world without discovering all.[32]

Notes

[1] See *God-Haunted World: The Elemental Theology of Jonathan Edwards* (Robert Boss, 2015) and *Bright Shadows of Divine Things: The Devotional World of Jonathan Edwards* (Robert Boss, 2016).

[2] "Miscellanies," no. *tt,* in *WJE* 13:190.

[3] "Miscellanies," no. *tt,* in *WJE* 13:190.

[4] "Miscellanies," no. 124, in *WJE* 13:288.

[5] "Miscellanies," no. 383, in *WJE* 13:451–52.

[6] "Miscellanies," no. 383, in *WJE* 13:451–52.

[7] "Miscellanies," no. 124, in *WJE* 13:288.

[8] "Images," no. 70, in *WJE* 11:74.

[9] "Images," no. 82, in *WJE* 11:84.

[10] *WJE* 6:335–36.

[11] *WJE* 6:336.

[12] "Images," no. 201, in *WJE* 11:125.

[13] *WJE* 6:337.

[14] *WJE* 6:337.

[15] "Miscellanies," no. 362, in *WJE* 13:434–35.

[16] *WJE* 11:131–35.

[17]"Images," no. 156, in *WJE* 11:106.

[18]"Images," no. 86, in *WJE* 11:85–86.

[19]"Images," no. 125, in *WJE* 11:96–97.

[20]*WJE* 12:278.

[21]*WJE* 12:278–80.

[22]"Miscellanies," no. 408, in *WJE* 13:469–70.

[23]"Miscellanies," no. 251, in *WJE* 13:363.

[24]"Miscellanies," no. 251, in *WJE* 13:363–64.

[25]*WJE* 14:246–47.

[26]"Images," no. 57, in *WJE* 11:67.

[27]Charles E. Hambrick-Stowe, *The Practice of Piety: Puritan Devotional Disciplines in Seventeenth-Century New England* (Chapel Hill: University of North Carolina Press, 1982), 163–64, 273.

[28]"Miscellanies," no. 123, in *WJE* 13:286.

[29]"Miscellanies," no. 123, in *WJE* 13:286.

[30]*WJE* 10:45–46.

[31]"Miscellanies," no. *tt,* in *WJE* 13:190.

[32]"Types," in *WJE* 11:152.

EDWARDS ON GOD'S IMMEDIATE AND ARBITRARY OPERATIONS

S. Mark Hamilton

> *The higher we ascend in the scale of created existence, and the nearer we come to the Creator, the more and more and more arbitrary we shall find the divine operations on the creature, or those communications and influences by which he maintains an intercourse with the creature.*
>
> — Jonathan Edwards, *Miscellany no. 1263*

Introduction[1]

No SINGLE MISCELLANY has contributed as much to discussions of Edwards' account of divine action as Miscellany no. 1263.[2] And no single interpretation of Miscellany no. 1263 has appeared that is as technically insightful as that put forward by Oliver Crisp. [3] Before we consider Crisp's account, a slightly amended version of which I shall afterward proffer, let us briefly consider the occasion, substance and structure of Edwards' argument in this otherwise controversial Miscellany entry.

Occasion, Substance, and Structure of the Argument

Composed sometime in late February or early March of 1754—the same month Isaac Hollis made Edwards the sole rector and caretaker of the Indian schools of Stockbridge, Massachusetts, and the same month that the Seven Years War began, putting Edwards and the other residents of Stockbridge under the constant threat of attack—Miscellany no. 1263 bears the somewhat surprising marks of what appears to be an undistracted period of clear reasoning for Edwards. The *occasion* for which this Miscellany appears to have been composed is bound up with Edwards' career-long entanglement with deism.[4] This is evident from the beginning of his entry where he asserts,

> GOD'S IMMEDIATE AND ARBITRARY OPERATION, in all instances of it, at least in this lower world, whether through all ages on men's minds by his Spirit, or at some particular season extraordinarily requiring it in what is called miracles, is that which *there is a strong and strange disposition in many to object against and disbelieve;* but for what reason, unless it be something in the disposition of the heart, is hard to imagine.[5]

The *substance* of Edwards' argument in Miscellany no. 1263 unfolds along the following, rather straightforward line. Summarily speaking, Edwards argues that God's creation of a world that subsists in part by certain divinely constituted laws of nature does not preclude God from acting immediately upon that world in such a way that it appears he is transgressing the fixedness of the very laws according to which he designed the world to be, in part, governed. To this end, Edwards argues,

> There are many who allow a present, continuing, imme-diate operation of God on the creation (and indeed such are the late discoveries and advances which have been

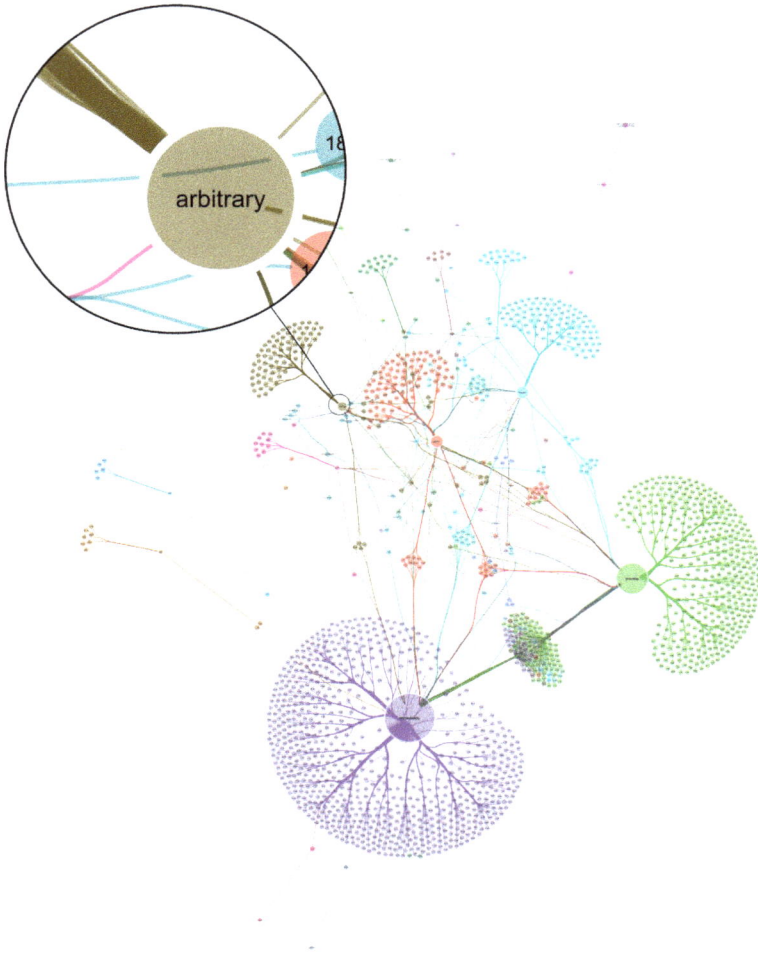

ARBITRARY, IMMEDIATE, OPERATION, and SECOND CAUSES—*a map of arbitrarily, arbitrariness, arbitrary, immediate, immediated, immediately, immediatly, operate, operated, ,operates, operating, operation, operations, operative, operator, second cause, second causes, unoperative with interconnections and page locations in WJE 1–26.*

made in *natural philosophy* that all men of sense, who are also men of learning, are comp[elled] to allow it), but yet, because so many of the constant changes and events in their continued series in the external world come to pass in a certain, exact method, according to certain, fixed, invariable laws, are *averse to allow that God acts any otherwise than as limiting himself by such invariable laws,* fixed from the beginning of the creation.[6]

The *structure* of Edwards' argument unfolds in several main parts. Let us take a moment to unpack the parts with more specificity. In the first part, Edwards considers whether there is anything in either *reason* or *nature* to conclude that *immediate* (i.e., "arbitrary") divine action is incompatible with so-called *mediate* divine action (i.e., laws of nature). In the second part, he grounds the later in the former, stating,

Of the two kinds of divine operation, viz. that which is *arbitrary* and that which is limited by *fixed laws,* the former, viz. arbitrary, is the first and foundation of the other, and that which *all divine operation must finally be resolved into,* and which all events and divine effects whatsoever primarily depend upon. Even the fixing of the method and rules of the other kind of operation is an instance of arbitrary operation.[7]

While this, too, is relatively straightforward, there are several observations worth noting. Chief among these observations is that in distinguishing these two sorts of divine operations, Edwards is careful to point out that one is "finally resolved into" the other. This is not a throw-away comment. By saying that one divine operation is *"finally resolved into"* the other, I take it that Edwards is simply asserting the fact that God is the first cause of all things. This is why he says, "Even the fixing of the method and rules of the other kind of operation is an instance of arbitrary operation." This does not mean, as I will go on to argue, that Edwards did not believe that God assigned causal efficacy to these "method and rules," (i.e., laws of nature). He did, and he did it by degrees. It is the nature of God's causal efficacy and its relationship to these causal fixtures outside himself that is at the heart of the debate around the interpretation of this Miscellany. For, as we shall see, Edwards is often label as an avowed occasionalist. And this is for good reason. For, despite what appears to be his assignment of causal efficacy to certain laws of nature and created minds, elsewhere Edwards says things like, "To find out the reasons of things in *natural philosophy* (i.e., laws of nature) is only to find out the proportion of God's acting."[8] *Prima Facie,* this is fairly strong evidence that Edwards was some sort of occasionalist. For our purposes, however, that God somehow acts in these laws of nature is not so important as *how* God acts. In other words, it is the "proportion" of divine action that is the question. There is more than one form of occasionalism. And with that, two principal question emerge—ones to which we will return in more detail when examining Crisp's claims about Edwards' occasionalism and laws of nature.

The first and perhaps most obvious question is how Edwards can claim that God operates, "mediately," that is, according to certain laws that he himself fixed, by which the universe appears to consistently operate, and yet act "immediately" within that universe of fixed laws without disrupting the order by which these divinely-constituted laws operate. The second and perhaps less obvious question has to do with whether the so-called "fixed laws," by which God designed the universe to be governed, are simply illusory; masquerading, as it were, for God's own handiwork, and thereby eliminating mundane causes. How we answer these questions, as it has been pointed out by Crisp and others, no doubt, has colossal implications for how we understand several aspects of Edwards' philosophical theology. Before we get to Crisp, let us consider a few more features of the structure of Edwards' argument. The more immediate the action, Edwards argues, the more glorious God manifests himself to be. He writes,

Arbitrary operation, being every way the highest, is that wherein God is most glorified. 'Tis the glory of God that he is an arbitrary being, that originally he, in all things, acts as being limited and directed in nothing but his own wisdom, tied to no other rules and laws but the directions of his own infinite understanding.[9]

In other words, if God himself performs a work "immediately," rather than relegating the performance of that same work to a law of nature, God is, according to Edwards, more glorified. This seems to indicate that Edwards thinks that God is willing to be less glorified in certain instances where he is not arbitrarily active. Were God not less active in certain causal circumstances, it would then seem that Edwards would have reason for not making such a distinction as this one. Notice Edwards' assertion that God is "tied to no other rules and laws." As we shall see, caution should at this point be taken. For Edwards is not necessarily saying that laws of nature of have no causal efficacy because God is the sole cause of all things at every moment. He might as easily be understood as suggesting that the laws which God fixes to perform this or that do not preclude divine action over and above what we might call their regular order.

In order to explicate this point, Edwards, rather interestingly, goes on to argue that a similar immediate and mediate causal relationship is represented in human action and the *imago dei.* That Edwards points to humanity as experiencing both primary and secondary causes in a way similar to the manner in which divine operations unfold—immediately and mediately—is not an inconsiderable comparison and one to which we will also return when we look at divine action and created minds. For now, and for Edwards' part, he states,

> So in those that are the highest order of God's creatures, viz. intelligent creatures, that are distinguished from other creatures in their being made in *God's image,* 'tis one thing wherein consists their highest natural dignity, that they have an image of this. *They have a secondary and*

dependent arbitrariness. They are not limited in their operations to the laws of matter and motion, so but that they can do what they please. The members of men's bodies obey the act of their wills without being directed merely by the impulse and attraction of other bodies in all their motions.[10]

"[T]he higher we ascend in the scale of created existence and the nearer we come to the Creator," Edwards concludes, "the more and more arbitrary we shall find the divine operations on the creature, or those communications and influences by which he maintains an intercourse with the creature. And it appears beautiful and every way fit and suitable that it should be so."[11] The question into which we will peer in the final section is whether Edwards thinks that God acts arbitrarily toward those who bear his image in a way that does not subvert the image-bearers moral agency.

In the third part of the structure of Miscellany no. 1263, Edwards defines God's arbitrary operations in terms of three specific categories. These categories will help us determine a suitable answer to the previous questions. For the sake of clarity and brevity, let us call them: *mixed, exceptional,* and *methodological* divine actions. When unpacking these categories, we ought to keep two things in mind. First, and by way of definition, Edwards thinks, "An operation is *absolutely arbitrary* when no use [is] made of any law of nature [and] no respect had to any one [su]ch fixed rule or method."[12] Second, as we just noted, Edwards thinks that the more a divine action is "absolutely arbitrary" the more God is glorified. He goes on to say that "the higher we ascend in the scale or series of created existences, and the nearer in thus ascending we come to the Creator, the more the manner of *divine operation with respect to the creature* approaches to arbitrary in these respects."[13] That Edwards makes reference to divine operations and humanity is once again notable. Apparently, Edwards thinks that there is something quite unique in these divine-human causal operations. So also does he appear to think that there is a uniqueness to the relation of divine action and certain laws of nature. Edwards then ranks his description of these three categories of discriminating divine action as follows:

Mixed Operations

First, a *mixed* operation—the closest causal action in proportion to an absolutely arbitrary divine act—Edwards says, is an act wherein God "makes use" of a law of nature in his acting arbitrarily to bring about this or that end. This suggests that laws of nature are sometimes left to themselves, as it were, to perform this or that divinely appointed thing, and he offers several examples throughout this section to make his point. For instance, Edwards lays out the difference between the creation of Adam, which he refers to as an arbitrary divine action, and the creation of Eve, which he calls a mixed operation (owing to what appears to be fact that Eve's appearance was chronologically subsequent to the first creation, whose origin was also from a source of something that had already existence, namely, the body of Adam).

Think for a moment (at least in terms of a chronology of divine action—creation followed by conservation), of a symphony whose conductor creates an initial alertness throughout an orchestra—signaling they are about to begin—with the first gesture of his baton, a tapping of his music stand, perhaps. This is what Edwards calls an arbitrary action. However, *with* the second gesture of the baton—a raising of his hand, say—the orchestra launches into symphonic harmony with the conductor. Not the least sound from a cello or trumpet is heard with this mixed operation, despite the arbitrary gesture of the conductor. It is notable that Edwards goes on to subdivide this category further in terms of mixed operations that inaugurate actions, like the conductor does with his second gesture, and those that generate new laws of nature themselves. He says,

> The mixing of arbitrary with natural operations was not only in arbitrarily making use of laws already established, as in setting material things in motion, variously compounding them, and the like, but also in establishing new,

more particular laws of nature with respect to particular creatures as they were made, as the laws of magnetism, many laws observable in plants, the laws of instinct in animals and the laws of the operation of the minds of men.[14]

Explaining how Edwards thinks one law of nature causally gives rise to another law of nature, at least on our symphonic analogy, is a bit like trying to show how the sheet music, at such and such a movement, might spontaneously add a few measures to itself while the players play. Unpacking Edwards' claim further need not detain us here. Let us consider the next category of operation.

Exceptional Operations

According to Edwards' next category of divine action—what I am calling exceptional operations—there is some semblance of arbitrary divine action involved when a thing is created and functions as an exception to a fixed rule of a law of nature. Edwards creatively imagines a distant island inhabited by a small number of creatures who for reason of their bodies being created out of a finer material substance, Edwards muses, are able to defy laws of gravity. "This kind of operation," Edwards argues, "would be nearer to arbitrary and miraculous than other divine operations, than those that are limited by the general laws of nature that obtain everywhere through the world."[15] By "general laws," I think Edwards has in mind things like gravity. Notice again that Edwards distinguishes between the causal activity of natural laws "that obtain everywhere throughout the world" and divine arbitrary causes. Were he to think in terms of arbitrary actions alone, it would seem that he would have no need of distinguishing these other causal categories.

Methodological Operations

The final category that Edwards demarcates—what I am calling, *methodological* operations—is comprised of those occurrences where the appearance of a method of supposedly fixed laws fails to achieve a presumably calculable result. Discriminating this category from the previous one, Edwards says, "Another way wherein a manner of operation approaches to arbitrary is when the limitation to a method is not absolute, even in the continued course of that sort of operation, so that the law fails of the nature of a fixed law, as all that are called laws of nature are."[16] However, unlike his descriptions of the two previous categorical distinctions, Edwards supplies no concrete example of how he conceives of methodological operations beyond stating that both God and his laws of nature generally act according to this or that method (whatever that may be) and that God is not bound to uphold such methods. Think, once again, of the law of gravity. Gravity is a law of nature that until the first space flight, say, was thought to be unbreakable. It is true that "whatever goes up must come down," that is, at least until one day when someone reached the mesosphere and the gravitational pull of the earth's mass ceased to require that a spacecraft that had gone up must come down. Something like this (*sans* the spacecraft) might be just what Edwards has in mind with respect to methodological operations. And it is at this point that Edwards' argument pivots toward a rational and then scriptural defense for these propositions. And with that, let us consider Crisp's interpretation of Miscellany no. 1263.

Crisp on Miscellany no. 1263

With one eye on the spectrum of contemporary views about divine action and the other on Edwards' broader metaphysical commitments—his neoplatonism, his immaterialism, his anti-realism,[17] his idealism, his continuous creationism, his four-dimensionalism,[18] his occasionalism, *et cetera*—Crisp discerns three candidate interpretative options for readings of Miscellany no. 1263, ranging from what he labels: *weak* (A1) to *moderated* (A2) to *strong* (A3).[19]

On Crisp's *weak* reading of the Miscellany Edwards appears committed to nothing more than what we might think of as the classical theological distinction between God's initial creation of the world and his subsequent conversation (i.e., provident care) of it. For an example of the classical distinction between creation and conservation (one which notably contains several interesting and controversial assertions and one with which Edwards was undoubtedly familiar and perhaps even influenced by), consider William Ames. [20] According to Ames,

> Conservation is God's making all things, universal and particular, to persist and continue in essence and existence as well as in their powers, Ps. 104:19; Acts 17:28; Heb. 1:3. This is suitably called by the Schoolmen, 'God's holding in his hand,' because by this power God sustains all things as if with his hand. Conservation necessarily comes between creation and the government of things created, because whatever is created is for some end and use to which it ought to be directed and governed. But it cannot reach this end or be directed towards it, unless it be continued and maintained in its being. God's conservation is necessary for the creature because the creature depends in every way upon the creator—not only for its creation, but also for its being, existence, continuance, and operation. Every creature would return to that state of nothing whence it came if God did not uphold it; and the cessation of divine conservation would, without any other operation, immediately reduce every creature to nothing, Ps. 104:29.[21]

Crisp spells out the so-called weak interpretive option as follows. On "(A1) God creates 'arbitrarily;' (i.e., according to his will and fiat), and conservation is God's acting at each successive moment mediately through physical laws has has establishing."[22]

According to what Crisp calls a *moderate* reading of this Miscellany—the interpretive option that he notably assigns to Sang Hyun Lee's interpretation—Edwards appears committed to an account of divine conservation, according to which divine dispositions occasion the activity of this or that law of nature, both of which are "co-dependent" on God's initial creation.[23] According to Crisp, at times, Lee makes the case that Edwards was not an occasionalist (at least in the traditional sense of the term, I suppose), while at other times, he seems committed to the idea that Edwards espoused a "modified" occasionalism of sorts.[24] For example, Lee says things like, "Edwards' view is an occasionalism only in the sense that God moves the world from virtuality to full actuality every moment through an immediate exercise of his power. Edwards' view is not an unqualified occasionalism position, however, since the world has an abiding realism in a virtual mode."[25] Whatever Lee's so-called modified occasionalism works out to be is not entirely clear.[26] Crisp, too, is quite conscious of this. The disparities in Lee's account of Edwards' occasionalism notwithstanding, Crisp assigns the moderate causation thesis of Miscellany no. 1263 to Lee. According to a moderate reading of this Miscellany Crisp reasons that on, "(A2) God creates 'arbitrarily' (i.e., according to his will and fiat), and all conservation takes place according to the immediate occasions of God's activity coupled with 'physical laws' themselves instigated by divine date at the point of actualization, which press through time alongside the creation, and are codependent with creation on God."[27]

Finally, on what Crisp refers to as a *strong* reading of Miscellany no. 1263—the option which he himself thinks best explains Edwards' position and the one that we will spend a little more interrogative capital unpacking—divine conversation is, we might say, reducible to the magician's prestige; to a mere illusion. The cause of all things in conversation, Crisp explains, belongs solely to God. What we call "laws of nature," according to this strong reading, are nothing more than immediate divine actions in clever secondary-cause-like disguise. That Edwards even mentions "laws of nature" is out of mere convention, Crisp argues. In the end, however, because all causal activity is resolved into divine activity, so argues Crisp, Edwards' talk of "laws of nature" is needless. Crisp's reading of this Miscellany goes like this: On "(A3) God creates 'arbitrarily' (i.e., according to his will and fiat), and conversation is an illusion: God recreates all things *ex nihilo* each moment, *including the laws themselves,* which appear to be physical constants at each index merely because God 'arbitrarily' designs that they operate in such a fashion."[28] Let us unpack Crisp's strong reading a little bit further in order that we might see just how he comes to such a conclusion.

Based on several other intimately related and inseparable assumptions about Edwards' metaphysics, the (A3) reading of Edwards' Miscellany reckons that *"all dependent existence"* (as Edwards elsewhere calls it) exists for no more than a moment—given his doctrine of continuous creation and his four-dimensionalism—before it falls altogether out of existence only to be instantaneously replaced with facsimiles or copies of those same created objects, each one possessing all the necessary, perceptible changes that provide the illusion of *every* created object's permanence from this moment to that.[29] Accordingly, Crisp maintains that "[i]n fact, no action that takes time is committed by numerically the same entity."[30] This is because, on (A3), this sort of divine action occurs not only for mundane objects like apples or anacondas or airplanes, but also for humanity (what elsewhere Edwards repeatedly calls "created minds"), or so Crisp's argument goes. Neither created minds nor laws of nature exist long enough—from one moment or temporal stage to the next—to perform any causal act, much less, be assigned responsibility for such an act.[31] For the sake of the ensuing argument we shall limit ourselves to a consideration of this moral agency problem that follows from (A3), which will by some necessity, touch also upon the matter of natural law.

How we resolve the issue of secondary agency hinges on whether we—with Crisp—regard Edwards' notion of "all dependent existence" as inclusive of created minds (and laws of nature) or whether—as I suggest—"all dependent existence" can be resolved phenomenologically into the perceptual or physical (i.e., non-material) world. This is a subtle distinction, but one that I think may well get Edwards off the hook, so to speak. To this end, and now that we are familiar with both Edwards' argument, and Crisp's three-fold interpretation of it,

I want to proffer a fourth interpretative possibility for reading this Miscellany. Let us simply call it (A4). Borrowing a term from Crisp's most recent work on the matter, let us consider what I will call a *mixed mode* (not to be confused with Edwards' so-called mixed divine operation) reading of Miscellany no. 1263 and how it differs from (A3).[32]

Mixed Mode Causation

Like Crisp's (A3) interpretation of Miscellany no. 1263, (A4) is built on some important assumptions about how to interpret Edwards' metaphysics at large. A closer look at three of these assumptions will effectively lead us—similar to how Crisp's assumptions lead him to (A3)—to an assertion of (A4). Let us take each in turn, beginning with realism, followed by created minds, and finally, laws of nature.

Realism and Percepts

Mixed mode causation, as Crisp labels it, assumes Edwards' commitment to a version of occasionalism that maintains the causal efficacy (i.e., moral agency) of created minds and laws of nature. This is not so much a *material* difference with the consensus that Edwards was an occasionalist as it is a *formal* difference. To say that it is a formal difference has to do with how we carve up the occasionalist cake, so to speak. Unlike (A1)-(A3), on the mixed mode causation reading of Edwards' occasionalism, Edwards appears to be able to have his cake and eat it, too. For, if God conserves his creation, as I suggested previously, by merely continuously creating the *ideal* world—that is, the world that is altogether comprised of percepts—then created minds are not falling in and out of existence every moment with the rest of creation (i.e., created minds). Nor are (at least some of) those invisible laws of nature re-created out of nothing each moment. So, where on (A3), Crisp contends, "Edwards' doctrine of continuous creation entails that nothing persists for long enough to constitute a moral or causal agent,"[33] on a mixed mode reading of this Miscellany,

Edwards can still be full blown occasionalist and yet meaningfully preserve human moral agency and the causal efficacy of natural laws. And this is because mixed mode causation relegates such (occasional) divine activity to the creation and re-creation of the *perceptible* world, *not* to created minds nor to laws of nature.[34] That created minds and laws of nature exist in a manner or mode different than their ideas or the ideas they support is precisely why Crisp labels this view *mixed mode* causation. And whether what Crisp calls mixed mode causation is in fact a plausible way to read Edwards' account of divine action in Miscellany no. 1263 depends, in part, on the next two assumptions about Edwards' metaphysics.

Realism and Created Minds

Much is made by those who take Edwards to be an anti-realist of Edwards' assertion that "The substance of bodies at last comes to nothing, or nothing but the Deity acting in that particular manner in those parts of space where he thinks fit. So that, speaking most strictly, there is no proper substance but God himself."[35] On its own, this statement is a not inconsiderable hurdle to the realist reading Edwards' idealism and immaterialism. For, if God is the only "proper substance," it seems that Edwards made no room in his ontology for substances of any other sort. There are several such statements in Edwards' philosophical works that have funded a metaphysical anti-realist reading of Edwards, according to which, *all* that exists outside of the mind of God—laws of nature, created minds and their ideas alike—are in some such way radically dependent upon God's immediate thinking of them for their continued existence. In other words, on the anti-realist reading of Edwardian metaphysics, there is simply no mind-independent existence.

However, if you read some of Edwards' other philosophical note-books, he also, interestingly, says such things as, "*Beings* which have knowledge and consciousness are the only proper and real and sub-stantial beings [because] spirits are the only proper substance."[36] Is this a contradiction to the statement in the previous paragraph? It certainly seems to be, at least at first glance. Edwards' plural use of "beings" is quite curious, though. A moment ago, he asserted that God is the only true substance. Were he to think that God is the only substance, why then does he refer to beings in this passage? I take it that this is not a referent to some trinitarian formula according to which "beings" refers to the persons of the Godhead. Rather, I think he has minds—uncreated and created alike—in mind here (pun intended). So also do I think we can assume that, at least in this instance, by "spirits" he means both uncreated and created "spirits" or minds alike.[37] But there is more. Elsewhere Edwards argues, "When I say, 'The material universe exists only in mind,' I mean that it is absolutely dependent on the conception of the mind for its existence, and does not exist as spirits do, whose existence does not consist in, nor in dependence on, the conception of other minds."[38] Here he goes a step further, differentiating between the existence of "spirits," who (he appears to think) exist independent of mind or thought, and the universe, that exists as both complex sets and simple ideas in the mind. I take it then that Edwards must think that ideas and minds exist quite differently from one another. How they exist differently is the next question.

To this, Edwards offers the following explanation that I think helps us understand what he means by "beings," "spirits," and "substance." He says, "Things *as to* God exist from all eternity alike. That is, the idea is always the same, and after the same mode. The existence of things, therefore, that are not actually created minds, consists only in power, or in the determination of God that such and such ideas shall be raised in created minds upon such conditions."[39] Strictly and categorically speaking, the only things that are "not actually created minds" are, on Edwards' ontology, ideas (or laws of nature). A created mind, then, has the idea of a thing only insofar as that idea—whether simple or complex—is communicated to their minds by God or a law of nature via its sense perception.[40] Notice how Edwards differentiates between the existence of created minds and things that "consist only in power" and notice that he calls those things that consist only in power, "ideas." The implication here is that when Edwards offers up his famous defense for the doctrine of Original Sin, for instance, saying that "*all dependent existence* whatsoever is in a constant flux, ever passing and returning; renewed every moment, as the colours of bodies are every moment renewed by the light that shines upon them; and all is constantly proceeding from God, as light from the sun." What I think he means by "all dependent existence" is, strictly speaking, that which is perceptible to created minds and not created minds themselves.[41] In other words, "all dependent existence" for a created mind is that which is ideal; what is "re-newed every moment" are ideas or percepts, not created minds. Created minds have a moment-to-moment existence that is quite different than ideas. Minds seem to somehow endure across temporal stages, while ideas or percepts are transitory and are renewed moment by moment. The sun is itself not renewed every moment, to borrow Edwards' oft-cited analogy. Rather, it is the beams of the sun's light (and in one sense, the physical human eyes that see them) that are renewed every moment.

Consider how Edwards explains this manner of divine action in some more refined detail elsewhere, when he argues, "[God] causes all changes to arise *as if* all these things had actually existed in such a series in some created mind, and *as if* created minds had comprehended all things perfectly."[42] Notice again that Edwards is not saying that created minds are changed or renewed, but only the mind's perceptions. What this means is that when we read statements where Edwards seems to equate the mind-dependent status of bodies and spirits as anti-real—statements like: "[W]hat we call body is nothing but a particular mode of perception; and what we call spirit is nothing but a composition and series of perceptions, or a universe of coexisting and successive perceptions connected by such wonderful methods and laws"—I think we need to be more discriminating of what I have elsewhere referred to as Edwards' *relative realism*. By relative realism I mean the difference between what I call created-mind-independence and uncreated-mind-independence.[43]

Generally speaking, something is real if that something has mind-independent existence. Relative realism, by contrast, describes something that is created-mind-independent, that is, something that is not contingent on a created minds' perceiving it; something like other created minds.[44] In other words, just because something may be radically dependent for its existence on the uncreated divine mind does not necessarily mean that it has no independent existence from created minds. All things are in some sense mind-dependent, insofar as those things are dependent upon the uncreated mind of God, who is mind or is a mind or has a mind. Relative realism refers to the way things exist (including other minds) in created minds alone.

For Edwards' part, it appears that those objects which are real are reducible to nothing less than two things: created minds and laws of nature. What this means for understanding Edwards' immaterialism in terms of realism rather than anti-realism is that God is really the sole cause of moment-to-moment continuously created percepts. A human body, then, is for Edwards not only a strictly physical phenomenon, but is a complex idea in the divine mind that is immediately and continuously communicated anew (i.e., every moment) to perceiving (created) minds.[45] It is by making this distinction that we can see how Edwards can conclude an extended discussion in "Of Being" on the uncreated-mind-dependence of all things in the absence of a created-minds perceptions, saying, "There is nothing in a room shut up, but only in God's consciousness. How can anything be there any other way?" and yet go on to say a few lines afterward,

> It follows from hence, that those beings which have knowledge and consciousness are the only proper and real and substantial beings, inasmuch as the being of other things is only by these. From hence we may see the gross mistake of those who think material things the most substantial beings, and spirits more like a shadow; whereas spirits only are properly substance.[46]

Elsewhere Edwards carefully explains that in the case of God's communicating divine knowledge to persons (minds), it is paramount in the mind of God to act upon "intelligent creatures" immediately (occasionally), rather than mediately (through some secondary causes). In that now famous sermon, *A Divine and Supernatural Light,* he says that, and here I quote him at length:

> 'Tis strange that men should make any matter of difficulty of it. Why should not he that made all things, still have something immediately to do with the things that he has made? Where lies the great difficulty, if we own the being of a God, and that he *created all things out of nothing,* of *allowing some immediate influence of God on the creation still?* And if it be reasonable to suppose it with respect to any part of the creation, 'tis especially so with respect to reasonable intelligent creatures; who are next to God in the gradation of the different orders of beings, and whose business is most immediately with God; who were made on purpose for those exercises that do respect God, and wherein they have nextly to do with God: for reason teaches that man was made to serve and glorify his Creator. And if it be rational to suppose that God immediately communicates himself to man in any affair, it is in this. 'Tis rational to suppose that God would reserve that knowledge and wisdom, that is of such a divine and excellent nature, to be bestowed immediately by himself, and that it should not be left in the power of *second causes.* Spiritual wisdom and grace is the highest and most excellent gift that ever God bestows on any creature: in this the highest excellency and perfection of a rational creature consists. 'Tis also immensely the most important of all divine gifts: 'tis that wherein man's happiness consists, and on which his everlasting welfare depends. How rational is it to suppose that God, however *he has left meaner goods and lower gifts to second causes,* and *in some sort in their*

power, yet should reserve this most excellent, divine, and important of all divine communications, in his own hands, to be bestowed immediately by himself, as a thing too great for *second causes* to be concerned in? 'Tis rational to suppose that this blessing should be immediately from God; for there is no gift or benefit that is in itself so nearly related to the divine nature, there is nothing the creature receives that is so much of God, of his nature, so much a participation of the Deity: 'tis a kind of emanation of God's beauty, and is related to God as the light is to the sun. 'Tis therefore congruous and fit, that when it is given of God, it should be nextly from himself, and by himself, according to his own sovereign will.[47]

Here he introduces a division of two sorts of continuously creative acts. Let us call them *direct* and *indirect* acts. Direct continuously creative acts appear to be those that Edwards thinks correspond to God's "emanating" communications of himself to "intelligent crea- tures" (i.e., created minds), whereas indirect continuously creative acts are those that Edwards thinks correspond to those laws of nature that are designed by God to occur naturally to perceiving minds. I say "continuously creative acts" because I think that the context of these previous statement warrants as much. What constitutes God acting directly is, as Edwards says, the communication of "knowledge and wisdom, that is of such a divine and excellent nature" and "a participation of the Deity" that results in the creatures glorification of God. What constitutes God acting indirectly through natural causes amounts to what Edwards calls "meaner goods and lower gifts."[48] And with that, let us turn and consider Edwards' account of laws of nature.

Realism and Laws of Nature

How do we make sense of places where Edwards affirms, on the one hand, that it is "certain with me that the world exists anew every moment, that the existence of things every moment ceases and every moment is renewed," and then go on to affirm that "God's constitution that some of our ideas shall be connected with others according to such a settle law and order, so that some ideas shall follow from others as their cause"?[49] The answer to this question is, as we have now see, bound up with both Edwards' immaterial realism and the function of certain laws of nature.

Edwards seems to think that some secondary causes themselves follow laws that are programed, as it were, to perform acts in a way similar to God's performance of them. Whether (for some reason) these secondary causes occur in concert with or altogether without God's immediate causal influence or activity is beside the point. We have already seen that Edwards thinks that at various points, God works in concert with laws of nature that he established. This is, again, what Edwards calls in Miscellany no. 1263, "mixed operations" and what he calls elsewhere, the "course of nature." These are causes that follow from established laws.[50] Edwards explains, "The existence and motion of every atom has influence, more or less, on a motion of all other bodies in the universe, great or small, as is most demonstrable from the laws of gravity."[51] By "influence," I think Edwards means (some degree of) causal influence. So, when Edwards says things like, "All *dependent* existence whatsoever is in a constant flux, ever passing and returning; renewed every moment," I think we ought to work out his meaning according to his own analogue, namely, that "*as the colours of bodies are every moment renewed by the light that shines upon them*; and all is constantly proceeding from God, *as light from the sun*."[52] The big question here is what Edwards means by "*all* is constantly proceeding from God."

Notice that the "sun" is not included among "bodies," "colors," and "light," as something that Edwards thinks is "every moment renewed." According to an immaterial realist reading of Edwards' idealism, "bodies," "colors," and "light" are mere ideas. And according to his four-dimensionalism, these ideas exist for only a moment. If "all" does not include the sun, the next question is whether the sun "ceases" to exist just like the ideas of "bodies," "colors," and "light."[53] On (A3), "bodies," "colors," "light," and "the sun" all come to nought and are continuously re-created out of nothing. In other words, *everything*—ideas, minds, laws of nature—ceases to exists! On (A4) though, the sun is constant. It is not falling in and out of existence. (A3) says that laws of nature are a fiction of true divine agency because God is the first and final cause of all things. Recall that on Crisp's strong reading of Miscellany no. 1263, "conversation is an illusion: God recreates all things *ex nihilo* each moment, *including the laws themselves,* which appear to be physical constants at each index merely because God 'arbitrarily' designs that they operate in such a fashion."[54] In other words, there is nothing *constant* on an (A3) reading of the Miscellany. (A4), on the other hand, says that God has established certain laws of nature with an independent causal efficacy. This, I take it, is precisely what Edwards means when he describes mixed operations.

> The mixing of arbitrary with natural operations was not only in arbitrarily making use of laws already established, as in setting material things in motion, variously com- pounding them, and the like, but also in establishing new, more particular laws of nature with respect to particular creatures as they were made, as the laws of magnetism, many laws observable in plants, the laws of instinct in animals and the laws of the operation of the minds of men.[55]

Again, on (A4), laws of nature perform secondary causes that are programed, so to speak, to perform this or that same sort of con- tinuously creative action. This is why Edwards calls them "mixed operations," including among them, "the laws of the operation of the minds of men," which seems to suggest that God and laws of nature ("at least, the laws of resistance and attraction or adhesion," as Edwards calls them) are charged with the production or publication of (presumably continuously created) perceptible ideas. It seems that Edwards thinks that these secondary causes—like gravity, for instance—have a mechanism that makes them function God-like, in that they are re-creating the very percepts that they are tasked by God with performing. In other words, what is continuously created is that which is strictly phenomenal. Mixed mode causation assumes that Edwards' consistent appeal to mundane causation ought to be taken with metaphysical and theological seriousness; such repeated assertions are more than Edwards simply "speaking with the vulgar." So, following Crisp's (A1-A3) pattern, the mixed mode interpretive option for reading Miscellany no. 1263 might go something like this:

> (A4) God creates "arbitrarily" (i.e., according to his will and fiat), and conversation is God's immediate recreation *of all things phenomenal ex nihilo,* including "laws" of nature which are merely physical (i.e., non-material) constants at each spatio-temporal index because God "arbitrarily" designs that they operate in this continuously creative and causative fashion.

Conclusion

We've covered a lot of ground in this chapter in order to make the modest proposal that there may yet be another way to faithfully interpret Miscellany no. 1263 beyond (A1)-(A3). We first laid out Edwards' argument some detail, after which we considered Crisp's argument in even more detail. And discovering several features of Crisp's reading of Edwards, we worked out several subtle changes to Crisp's account of Edwards' metaphysics that effectively opened the door, as it were, to (A4). Whether these subtle changes to Crisp's account have explanatory power beyond interpretations of Miscellany no. 1263 is a matter that demands more systematic inquiry.

Notes

[1]Several passages of this chapter have been excerpted and adapted from: *A Treatise on Jonathan Edwards, Continuous Creation, and Christology*; foreword by Oliver D. Crisp (Fort Worth, TX: JESociety Press, *A Series of Treatises on Jonathan Edwards,* Vol. 1, 2017).

[2]See e.g.: Jeffrey C. Waddington, "Jonathan Edwards and God's Involvement in Creation: An Examination of 'Miscellanies,' no. 1263" in John M. Frame, Wayne Grudem, and John J. Hughes, eds. *Redeeming the Life of the Mind: Essays in Honor of Vern Poythress* (Wheaton: Crossway, 2017), 203–220; Sang Hyun Lee, *The Philosophical Theology of Jonathan Edwards* (Princeton: Princeton University Press, 1988).

[3]Oliver D. Crisp, "How 'Occasional' was Jonathan Edwards' Occasionalism?" in Paul Helm and Oliver D. Crisp, eds. *Jonathan Edwards: Philosophical Theologians* (Aldershot: Ashgate, 2003), 61–77; idem., *Jonathan Edwards on God and Creation* (Oxford: Oxford University Press, 2012), 23–31. Crisp has mounted a recent defense for his reading of Edwards' occasionalism (based on a lecture given at the *Jonathan Edwards Center* at Trinity Evangelical Divinity School, March 2018) entitled, "Jonathan Edwards on God's Relation to Creation," *Jonathan Edwards Studies* 8:1 (2018): 2–16.

[4]For more on Edwards' entanglement in the deist controversies, as they relate to this Miscellany see: Michael J. McClymond, "God the Measure: Toward a Theocentric Understanding of Jonathan Edwards' Metaphysics," *Scottish Journal of Theology* 47 (1994): 43–59.

[5]"Miscellanies," no. 1263, in *WJE* 23:201 (emphasis added).

[6]"Miscellanies," no. 1263, in *WJE* 23:201–202 (emphasis added).

[7]"Miscellanies," no. 1263, in *WJE* 23:202 (emphasis added).

[8]"The Mind" no. 34, *WJE* 6:353 (emphasis added). I am grateful to Walter Schultz for pointing me to this.

[9]"Miscellanies," no. 1263, in *WJE* 23:202.

[10]Miscellany no. 1263, "Miscellanies," no. 1263, in *WJE* 23:203 (emphasis added).

[11]"Miscellanies," no. 1263, in *WJE* 23:203 (emphasis added). Interestingly, at this point Edwards inserts a reference to Miscellany no. tt, (composed some three decades previous to this point in April 1723), according to which he argues, "In the creation, there is an immediate communication between one degree of being and the next degree of being (every wheel immediately communicates with the next wheel [in a clock]), but *man being the top;* so that the next immediate step from him is to God. Without doubt, there is an immediate communication between the Creator and this highest of creatures, according to the order of being. So that as the intelligent being is exercised immediately about the Creator, so without doubt the Creator immediately influences the intelligent being, immediately influences the soul; for 'tis but one immediate step from the soul to God. Those that call this enthusiasm talk very unphilosophically" (*WJE* 13:190–91 [emphasis added]).

[12]"Miscellanies," no. 1263, in *WJE* 23:203 (emphasis added).

[13]"Miscellanies," no. 1263, in *WJE* 23:204.

[14]"Miscellanies," no. 1263, in *WJE* 23:205.

[15]"Miscellanies," no. 1263, in *WJE* 23:204.

[16]"Miscellanies," no. 1263, in *WJE* 23:204.

[17]It is a matter of some recent debate whether Edwards actually articulated his immaterialism in anti-realist or realist terms. Crisp argues that Edwards was avowedly committed to *anti-realism,* according to which, created things are utterly, ontologically dependent on the divine mind for their existence. The slightly amended reading of Miscellany no. 1263 to which this chapter points hinges in large part on reading Edwards' immaterialism on a *realist* line, that is, along the lines that created minds do exist in some sense as independent of the divine mind, that God is continuously creating the *perceptible* world, *not* created minds, and that mundane causes follow laws that are in some sense programed to perform this or that same sort of continuously creative divine action.

[18]Four-dimensionalism is idea that ordinary objects like apples, anacondas or airplanes persist through time in a way similar to how they extend through space. There are several species of Four-Dimensionalism such as, growing-block theory, shrinking-tree theory, and stage theory. See: Michael Rea, "Four-Dimensionalism," in Michael J. Loux and Dean W. Zimmerman, eds. *The Oxford Handbook of Metaphysics,* (New York: Oxford University, 2003), 246–280. While it is certainly not the consensus among scholars, there is a recent trend in the literature that explains Edwards' four-dimensionalism in terms of stage theory. Stage theorists think that created objects are divisible into spatial and temporal "stages" rather than, as some had supposed to this point, spatial and temporal "parts." The technical difference between persistence as "stages" and persistence as "parts" amounts to a distinction between an individuated time and space slices of a thing versus a thing that has, as the stage theorist argues, temporal and spatial *counterparts.* For a detailed and interesting argument for stage theory, see: Katherine Hawley, *How Things Persist* (Oxford: Oxford University, 2001), pp. 189-91. For a more recent and additionally helpful, though brief account of stage theory, see: Bradford Skow, *Objective Becoming* (Oxford: Oxford University Press, 2015), 216–21.

[19]Walter Schultz's recent work notably dissents from several popular opinions about Edwardsian metaphysics; see: "Is Jonathan Edwards a Neoplatonist? The Concept of Emanation in *End of Creation*" *Jonathan Edwards Studies* 8:1 (2018): 17–36.

[20]There are a host of interesting parallels (logical and linguistic alike) between Ames' and Edwards' accounts of God's creation and conservation, a full outworking of which has yet to appear. Some initial ground work to this end appears in: Hamilton, "Jonathan Edwards, Anselmic Satisfaction, and God's Moral Government," *International Journal of Systematic Theology* 17:1 (January 2015): 1–22.

[21] Interestingly, Ames goes on to argue—echoing Edwards—that "some things—subject only to God—are conserved directly. This conservation is the same as creation, except that creation has a certain newness which conservation lacks and creation lacks a preceding existence which conservation implies. Conservation is nothing else than a *continued creation,* so to speak, and therefore it is joined with creation," in *The Marrow of Theology,* ed. by John Dykstra Eisden (Grand Rapids: Baker, 1968), 1.9.14–18, 108–9. Notice Ames' subtle claim that "some things—subject only to God—are conserved directly," after which he distinguishes between what he calls God's common and special governance. By "some things," Ames seems to have in mind, God's special governance and moral agents. This distinction is similar in part to Edwards' notion of *natural* and *moral* [i.e, creaturely] governance (see e.g.: "Miscellanies," no. 1196, in *WJE* 23:118), about which he says a great deal, much of which warrants further inquiry, particularly as it relates to Edwards' philosophical commitments.

[22] Crisp, *Jonathan Edwards on God and Creation,* 28.

[23] Crisp, "Jonathan Edwards on God's Relation to Creation," 28–9. See also: "Jonathan Edwards' Ontology: A Critique of Sang Hyun Lee's Dispositional Account of Edwardsian Metaphysics," *Religious Studies* 46 (2010), p. 11. I find it interesting that Crisp points out that the sources Lee uses to make the case against Edwards' occasionalism are often those also used to prop up Lee's widely influential interpretation of Edwards' supposed development of a Dispositional Ontology.

[24] Crisp, "Jonathan Edwards on God's Relation to Creation," 28, n. 49. For an insightful comparison of Crisp and Lee on the matter of Edwards' occasionalism, see: Stephen H. Daniel, "Edwards' Occasionalism" in Donald Schweitzer, ed., *Jonathan Edwards as Contemporary: Essays in Honor of Sang Hyun Lee* (New York: Peter Lang, 2010), 1–14. While Daniel's work is succinct and to the point, it is, I think, indicative of a much more extensive comparison of Lee and Crisp's findings about divine action that warrants further research.

[25] Sang Hyun Lee, *The Philosophical Theology of Jonathan Edwards* (Princeton, NJ: Princeton University Press, 1988), 63 (hereafter, *PTJE*). Crisp rightly points out that Lee later suggests that 'Edwards avoids deism as well as occasionalism,' *PTJE,* 107 (cited in Crisp, *Jonathan Edwards on God and Creation,* 201, n. 49).

[26] There are several species of occasional causation. For more on these distinctions, see: Steven Nadler, *Occasionalism: Causation Among the Cartesians* (New York: Oxford University Press, 2011).

[27] Crisp, *Jonathan Edwards on God and Creation,* 28.

[28] Crisp, *Jonathan Edwards on God and Creation,* 28 (emphasis added).

[29] Edwards' full quotation reads: "*All dependent existence* whatsoever is in a constant flux, ever passing and returning; renewed every moment, as the colours of bodies are every moment renewed by the light that shines upon them; and all is constantly proceeding from God, as light from the sun," "Original Sin," *WJE* 3:401.

[30] Crisp, "Jonathan Edwards on God's Relation to Creation," 10 (emphasis added).

[31] The Christological implications of this view are wildly problematic. For, if no human agent has causal powers of any kind, and human agency is requisite to any orthodox Christology, then on Crisp's reading of these matter, Edwards is flatly unorthodox. I have argued to the contrary and at length in Hamilton, *A Treatise on Continuous Creation and Christology* (Fort Worth, TX: JESociety Press, 2017).

[32] I am borrowing the term *mixed mode causation* from Crisp's "Jonathan Edwards on God's Relation to Creation," *Jonathan Edwards Studies,* 8.1 (2018): 9. According to Crisp, "[On] Hamilton's reading of Edwards, God creates creaturely minds, which are independent of God in some sense, and may act as causal agents in their own right. But he communicates to them all the percepts of the world around them immediately. In this way Hamilton suggests a kind of *mixed modes* account of causation in Edwards. God creates us to be causal agents. But the same is not true of the ideal world in which he places us" (emphasis added; used with permission of the author).

[33] Crisp, "Jonathan Edwards on God's Relation to Creation," 10.

[34] In fact, this sounds quite similar to Berkeley, who argues, "A proper active efficient cause I can conceive none but Spirit; not any action, strictly speaking, but where there is a Will. But this doth not hinder the allowing occasional causes *(which are in truth but signs);* and more is not requisite in the best physics, i.e., the mechanical philosophy. Neither doth it hinder the admitting other causes besides God; such as spirits of different orders, which may be termed active causes, as acting indeed, thought by limited and derivative powers. But for an unthinking agent, no point of physics is explained by it, nor is it conceivable," *Philosophical Correspondence with Johnson,* "II. Berkeley to Johnson [November 25, 1729]," *WGB* 2:280-1 (emphasis added).

[35] "Of Atoms," *WJE* 6:215.

[36] "Of Being," *WJE* 6:206 (emphasis added).

[37] This is perhaps similar again to Bishop Berkeley, Edwards often employs the terms "spirit" and "mind" interchangeably. For some helpful discussion of "Berkeleyan Spirits," see John Russell Roberts' seminal work: *Metaphysics for the Mob: The Philosophy of George Berkeley* (Oxford: Oxford University Press, 2007).

[38] "The Mind," *WJE* 6:368.

[39] "The Mind," n. 35, *WJE* 6:355 (emphasis added).

[40] It is interesting that Edwards distinguishes between complex and simple ideas in terms of "substances" and what he calls "modes." He argues, "The distribution of the objects of our thoughts into substances and modes may be proper, if by substance we understand a complexion of such ideas which we conceive of as subsisting together and by themselves; and by modes, those simple ideas which cannot be themselves, or subsist in our mind alone,' "The Mind," *WJE* 6:350 (According to Anderson, Edwards' distinction of complex and simple ideas and their attached meanings follows the Cartesianism reflected in Arnauld's, *Art of Thinking*; see: *WJE* 6:350, n. 3).

[41] Ibid., *WJE* 3:404 (emphasis added). Edwards remarks similarly elsewhere, "Since, as has been shewn, body is nothing but an infinite resistance in some part of space caused by the immediate exercise of divine power, it follows that as great and as wonderful a power is every moment exerted to the upholding of the world, as at first was to the creation of it; the first creation being only the first exertion of this power to cause such resistance, the preservation only the continuation or the repetition of this power every moment to cause this resistance. So that the universe is created out of nothing every moment; and if it were not for our imaginations, which hinder us, we might see that wonderful work performed continually, which was seen by the morning stars when they sang together," *WJE* 6:241–2.

[42] "The Mind," *WJE* 6:354 (emphasis added).

[43] "Notes on Knowledge and Existence," *WJE* 6:398 See also: "The existence and motion of every atom has influence, more or less, on a motion of all other bodies in the universe, great or small, as is most demonstrable from the laws of gravity. God's constitution that some of our ideas shall be connected with others according to such a settle law and order, so that some ideas shall follow from others as their cause," "The Mind," *WJE* 6:358. (Compare with: "The Mind," n. 13, *WJE* 6:344).

[44] I am grateful to Greg Trickett, who pointed out a similar distinction in Berkeley's idealism, about which he wrote in some detail in his "Realist Conception of Truth," in Jim Spiegel and Steve Cowan, eds., *Idealism and Christianity: Idealism and Christian Philosophy,* Vol. 2 (New York: Bloomsbury Academic, 2016), pp. 29–50.

[45] "The Mind," entry n. 62, *WJE* 6:377-80 (Edwards calls things like gravity and laws of nature, "shadows of excellency," a category often curiously also attributed to his descriptions of the divine).

[46] "Of Atoms," *WJE* 6:204, 207.

[47] "A Divine and Supernatural Light," *WJE* 17:421–2.

[48] This is not the only place Edwards makes this distinction. Compare with "Miscellanies," no. 1263, in *WJE* 23:201–212. There may also be something to this distinction as it pertains to Edwards' soteriology, particularly his account of regenerate and unregenerate knowledge. For more on this distinction see: Norman Fiering, *Jonathan Edwards' Moral Thought and It's British Context* (Chapel Hill, NC: University of North Carolina Press, 1981), ch. 2.

[49] "The Mind," *WJE* 6:359; Compare with: Miscellany no. 125a, *WJE* 13:288.

[50] "Miscellanies," no. 1263, in *WJE* 23:201–212.

[51] "The Mind," *WJE* 6:358. Compare with: "God's constitution that some of our ideas shall be connected with others according to such a settle law and order, so that some ideas shall follow from others as their cause," *WJE* 6:359. This is also a clue into how we ought to understand the function of Edwards' doctrine of occasionalism, namely, that divine causes are limited to perceptions.

[52] "Original Sin," *WJE* 3:404 (emphasis added).

[53] Part of what characterizes the supposed incoherence of Edwards' account of temporal persistence is the idea that Edwards thought temporal stages, upon being

re-created, were destroyed. For Edwards says, 'Tis certain with me that the world exists anew every moment, that the existence of things every moment ceases and every moment is renewed," "Miscellanies," no. 125a, in *WJE* 13:288. Some have taken this to mean that "past" temporal stages (or temporal parts, depending on the model of four-dimensionalism used to explain Edwards account of persistence), fall out of existence. The implication here, were Edwards an anti-realist, like Crisp suggests he is, and God were re-creating minds every moment, that persons are destroyed every moment. This is a problem in general and sheds some lights of the issues related to moral responsibility that have populated the literate related to this subject to this point.

[54]Crisp, *Jonathan Edwards on God and Creation,* 28.
[55]Miscellany no. 1263, *WJE* 23:205.

Preparationism in Edwards' Theology of Evangelism and Missions

Adam G. Cavalier

That argument to prove that God's usual method is to make sinners very sensible of their misery, and bring them to a despair of help from themselves or any other creature before he converts them, viz. that 'tis agreeable to his wisdom to bestow his blessings and grace in that way as makes it most seen and admired, and received with the greatest thankfulness, has certainly some force in it.

— Jonathan Edwards, *Miscellany no. 255*

IN THE SECOND-GENERATION of Puritan New England, an acute problem developed around the salvation of settlers within the colonies. The children of the colonists who made the transatlantic voyage to flee religious persecution did not always have the same spiritual convictions of their parents. Combined with other contributing factors, a need for spiritual awakening within the colonies arose. Additionally, since their arrival in the New World, the colonists made contact with a host of different Native American peoples. By the middle of the eighteenth century, the new immigrants established numerous missionary outposts. These settlements began to push English interests further westward into the frontier regions. Encroaching into Native American territory, these outposts were cohabited settlements established by colonial missionaries and businessmen. The economic, political, military, and religious interests of the English served as the purpose of these outposts. All while considering the conversion of the next generation of Puritans, the colonial clergy began to consider the scope of the divine redemption as they interacted with indigenous people. Taken together, the need for a more robust theology of evangelism came to the forefront. In short, they began to ask the follow question: How would these two groups be grafted into the covenant promises of God?

Recent suggestions claim that Jonathan Edwards should be considered the Grandfather of the Modern Missions Movement. This claim is due in part to his inspiring generations of missionaries, pastors, and theologians to consider God's global purposes of redemption.[1] Scholars are beginning see the impact that Edwards has made on those pioneers of cross-cultural evangelism. Those who were shaped by Edwards' theology have been considered the vanguard of that nineteenth-century movement. Edwards' inspiration can be seen as he modeled missionary living by undertaking service in the missionary outpost in Stockbridge, Massachusetts for seven years. His editing and publication of the wildly popular journal of David Brainerd catapulted him to fame in this regard. His calling on others to an international prayer movement—in his treatise *An Humble Attempt*—exemplifies his desire to advance Christ's kingdom on earth. Summarizing his missionary spirit, one scholar writes, "Virtually every well-known Protestant missionary and mission society of the nineteenth century considered Edwards' writings indispensable, and regarded his example as paramount . . . [Edwards] both inspired future missionary practice and brought missiology to the center of Protestant theology."[2]

Why did Edwards' theology make such an impact on missions? Why were generations of ministers inspired to go from their country and kindred to a foreign land due to Edwards' ministry? Recently, scholars have begun to outline Edwards' theology from a missional standpoint. Attention has been directed towards missional themes within his *Dissertation Concerning the End for Which God Created the World,* public reports of revivals, his publication of David Brainerd's journals, and other widely-distributed works. This focus is due largely in part to the impact Edwards made on later generations. Again, those writings that were publicly consumed deeply influenced later generations of missionaries, pastors, and laypeople. Thus, much of that scholarly analysis has focused on Edwards' public ministry and writings.[3] Yet, little attention has been given to his private writings. These private writings constitute many of the themes that play out in these public writings. Furthermore, Edwards was a voracious reader and a student of other world religions.

Gerald McDermott summarizes, "Like some of the better-known thinkers of the Enlightenment, [Edwards] was mesmerized by non-European religions and scoured New England for books on unfamiliar faiths."[4] Edwards was greatly interested in other cultures not his own and made great attempts to learn their cultures, religions, practices, and traditions. This interest inspired a missionary zeal that played out in his theology and practice. Edwards' private writings reveal a widow into the theologian's understanding of peoples outside Christendom. This neglected issue will be addressed in the latter half of this chapter. Yet, the issue must be located within a larger framework of evangelism. That broad approach will give greater context to his evangelistic methodology and philosophy of ministry.

This chapter will show that in his private theological journal, the "Miscellanies," Jonathan Edwards articulated a theology that incorporated a preparatory element to evangelism to people within and outside of Christendom. Moreover, the present chapter will argue that the doctrine played out differently in the conversion of the unbeliever and their place vis-à-vis Christendom. The following questions will be addressed throughout the course of this chapter: What is Edwards' theology of preparation in evangelism and missions, as it is found in his "Miscellanies"? How did he view the preliminary stages in evangelism to the unconverted? Additionally, how how did Edwards apply this view to the heathen—that is, people outside Christendom? Thus, this chapter will answer these questions in two parts. The first part of this chapter will engage Edwards' preparationism for those within Christendom. This aspect of Edwards' preparation, stresses the divine role played. Yet it also incorporates an active creaturely participation in the process. The second part of the chapter will look at the doctrine as it relates to those heathen outside of Christian society. Alternatively, this aspect has the overwhelming emphasis on the divine role, while the creature's role is more passive throughout. In short, this chapter will analyze the doctrine as it develops in these two vastly different contexts.

To offer a definition, preparationism is "the view that God's usual way of bringing His elect to the place of being willing to believe on the Lord Jesus Christ is by means of a 'law work,' that is, the use of His law to produce conviction of sin and a sense of need for Christ."[5] While this term is sometimes used to describe a view that the unregenerate can conjure up the unassisted will to prepare themselves to receive divine grace, that perspective is not in view here. The view Edwards espouses is in line with the *Westminster Confession,* John Calvin's teaching, as well as the Puritan tradition. Jonathan Edwards believed that the unregenerate were spiritually dead and could do nothing to awaken their own hearts to spiritual truths. As will be outlined in this chapter, Edwards' unique contribution is that he builds on this tradition. Edwards broadens this definition by communicating it into contexts outside Christendom. In short, the heathen nations are being divinely prepared to receive the gospel.

Edwards believed the contemporary church had a duty to proclaim the gospel to the unconverted. This duty necessarily led to cross-cultural evangelism that reached those outside of polite Western society. If God's redemptive purposes included all of history and those within it, then God's redeemed people are inevitably called to preach the gospel to every creature. In sum, this chapter will argue that Edwards' "Miscellanies" contain a theology that includes both a philosophy and practice of evangelism. His theology emphasized the work of God in conversion, as will be evidenced in the research that follows. Nevertheless, the human agents, who received and/or proclaimed that gospel message, had a necessary role to play in the conversion event.

Creaturely Preparation

Edwards' Preparationism Explained

Jonathan Edwards held to the Reformed concept of gospel preparation. This idea flourished in Puritan New England. It described the distinguishable steps towards conversion. Preparationism explained the process of a person's activity in seeking salvation. In most cases, non-believers could go through a period of stages that prepared one's heart for conversion. These works did not bring about salvation, yet they served to make ready the individual for salvation. Edwards believed that conversion was instantaneous.[6] Once a person trusted in Christ alone for salvation, they were immediately forgiven of their sins and declared righteous based on the merits of Christ. However, there were successive events or stages that a person normally experienced beforehand that prepared the soul for that salvation experience. George Marsden aptly describes the Puritan tradition of preparationism:

> Unable to control God's grace, one could at best prepare oneself to be in a position to receive it. So the steps leading through the gradual process of conversion were steps of "preparation." The irony of the rigorous discipline was one could not take any pride in successfully following it. One sign of being on the road to conversion was to strive fervently to keep God's law, but it was only when sinners came to realize their total inability to succeed in keeping that law that they would be prepared truly to depend on God's grace. Seldom has their been a spiritual

discipline where so much effort was put into recognizing the worthlessness of one's own efforts.[7]

Edwards writes, "As to preparatory work before conversion, there is undoubtedly always, except very extraordinary cases, such a thing."[8] A person seeking divine favor would take steps towards God by renouncing sins, practicing Christian morality, reading Holy Scripture, prayerfully asking God for mercy, and fellowshipping with faithful Christians. Peoples could use the means of grace to draw nearer to God. One of the key elements in this process was the awareness of personal sin and its devastating consequences. God would cause the person to have a "dreadful idea and notion of the punishment."[9] The individual would develop a God-given sense of grief and remorse over their sins. Additionally, Edwards thought the depth of sorrow should be somewhat relative to the grievousness of the offence. He writes, "It don't seem congruous . . . for God quite to pass over sin rebellion and treachery, and receive the offender into his entire favor, either without a repentance and sorrow and detestation of his fault adequate to the aggravation of it."[10] He quickly clarifies saying that no amount or degree of repentance will ever equal the true weight of guilt. Edwards' point here is simply to say that one should be profoundly struck to the heart over their sins.

This sense of anguish would make them ready for salvation. Edwards notes that this is typical of God's working salvation: "God's usual method is to make sinners very sensible of their misery, and bring them to a despair of help from themselves or any other creature before he converts them."[11]

Edwards believed a person could perform preparatory work that ultimately led to salvation; however, they would not ultimately receive the glory for those works because God initiated and sustained the work. He says, "Tis the Spirit's ordinary method, first to make them concerned about it."[12] Also, Edwards says, "God's ordinary way is thus first to convince them."[13] God causes the sinner to be concerned in the first place. He influences and shapes their desires. So, while from the observer's standpoint the subject prepares himself by developing

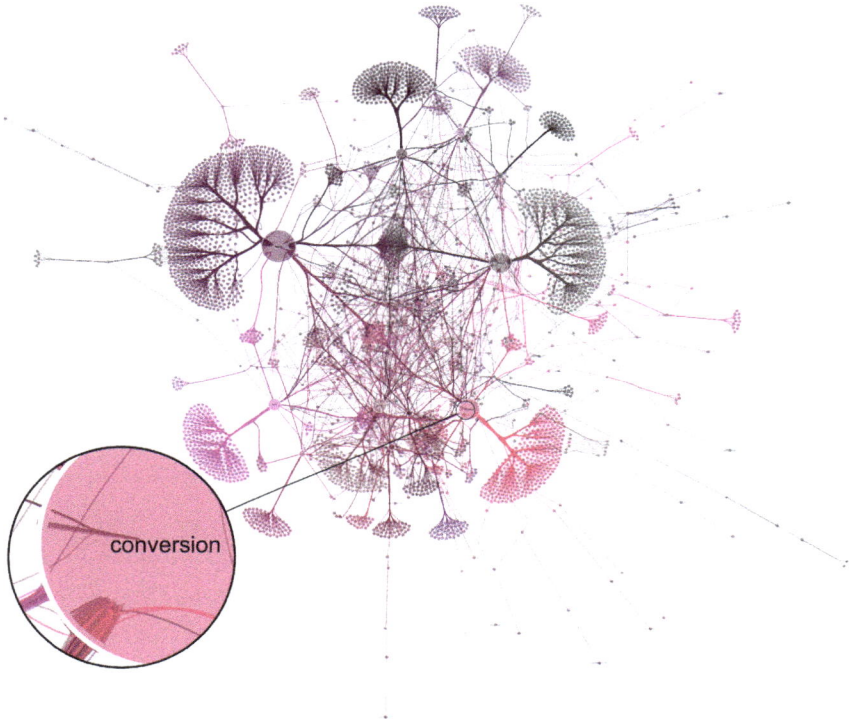

CONVERSION, DESPAIR, MERCY, METHOD, MISERY, *and* PREPARATION—*a map of conversion, conversions, convert, converted, converter, converteth, converting, converts, despair, despaired, despairing, despairs, immethodical, mercy, mercys, method, methodical, methodically, methodicalness, methodize, methods, misery, preparation, preparations, preparative, preparatives, preparatories, preparatory, prepare, prepared, preparedness, prepares, preparest, prepareth, preparing, unconverted, unprepared with interconnections and page locations in WJE 1–26.*

a hatred and rejection of sin, God is the source of that inner longing. God's grace is the harbinger to the event of conversion. In other words, sinner's work is not the primary cause of God's saving graces to be dispensed upon him. Therefore, he is sovereign over the entire conversion experience, even the preparatory work that precedes it.

Furthermore, this sorrow would overwhelm them to the point that they would begin to sense the need for divine forgiveness. A natural conviction in the heart would necessarily lead to an awareness that one needed to be pardoned of that sin. This feeling would cause them to cry out for the grace of God to graciously come upon them. Thus, fear of punishment would normally be the catalyst for salvation, not the blessings of fellowship with God and all that it entailed. The thoughts of the rewards of salvation would typically come later. In all, these events happened over a period of "considerable time."[14]

God can act however he chooses. Thus, he can dispense grace on whomever he pleases. Saving grace is wrought "by his free and most arbitrary motions."[15] However, the means by which God normally operates is to give his grace to "those that are much concerned about it."[16] Thus, the subjects of salvation would prepare themselves for receiving divine grace by performing outward acts that accorded with Christian practice.

Edwards held to a broadly Reformed *ordo salutis*. In short, he believed that regeneration preceded the act of conversion. God inwardly transformed the soul of the believer, and then the recipient later expressed the outward signs of saving faith in Christ. Edwards gave no indication of what length of time that was between these two events. However, Edwards held that the two could appear in the same outward act. The two events could "be as quick as one thought can follow another."[17] Edwards gives no indication if it were possible that any intervening gap or significant time could appear between the events, though in normal cases they appear together. Ultimately, Edwards believed that the two necessarily fell in a logical sequence of events. This belief was against the position of some within the broadly Reformed tradition. Edwards' own grandfather,

Solomon Stoddard, held that there was no work of sanctification before the explicit outward sign of conversion. As is typical of Edwards' theological conclusions, he starts with a philosophical principle. He writes, "There must be the principle before there can be the action."[18] From this premise, he brings it to bear on the person's reception of divine grace. He continues the logical sequence: "There must be an alteration made in the heart of the sinner before there can be action consequent upon this alteration; yea, there must be a principle of holiness before holiness is in exercise." A person cannot behold the beauty of Christ in the mind until that person's soul is made ready to receive it properly. Again, this person must necessarily come to a personal hatred of indwelling sin in order that they may be able to receive Christ as Savior and Lord. Only divine grace can bring about that type of inward transformation. The creature cannot will that conversion into existence due to their innate sinful nature. Yet God in his mercy changes the sinner's heart.

All human beings are born in Adam, and thus, by nature, are children of wrath. They are "altogether depraved and corrupted, and without the least grain of true holiness."[19] Grace is "infused" to the individual and is according to God's "arbitrary, efficacious operation."[20] This saving grace is immediately imparted to the believer. Far behind the infamous sermon "Sinners in the Hands of an Angry God," quite possibly his most famous sermon is "A Divine and Supernatural Light Immediately Imparted to the Soul by the Spirit of God." The title of this publicly delivered message—as well as its subsequent content—bears evidence to this fact. Edwards believed that a person, upon conversion, was immediately forgiven, imputed with the righteousness of Christ, and declared righteous by the Father. His private writings also buttress this fact. To clarify, Edwards held that the individual can do nothing to will salvation into existence, nor can they perform any meritorious work to earn this divine grace.[21] The grace that is infused to the believer is the sustaining mercy of God on the regenerate which confirms the place of the believer. Ultimately, God bestows his grace on whomever he chooses, whenever he chooses, and in whatever manner he chooses.

God could convert anyone without any preparatory work, yet in most cases, he chooses to do so. Edwards looks to the biblical narrative as an example for this principle. He says that much was done to prepare Joseph before he ascended the ranks of the Egyptian government. This preparation was seen similarly in the life of Moses.[22] In the case of the nation of Israel, they were prepared before they received the law on Mount Sinai. They were also divinely prepared in the wilderness before receiving the blessing of entering the Promised Land. David underwent a long period of preparation before he was anointed king. John the Baptist was sent to prepare the nation of the coming of Christ. As the most supreme example, Christ was prepared in numerous ways. He prepared himself in the wilderness before his public ministry. Paul was prepared in Arabia before he could enter into his ministry to the Gentiles. Edwards summarizes that the entire Old Testament served to prepare the church for the coming of Christ. He surmises, "If the wisdom of God did not see it meet that there should be preparation for that spiritual good that he bestows on his church and people, there would be no use at all of means of grace, and prayer to God for the blessings we need would be of no benefit."[23] In other words, there are means by which a person can be prepared to receive the blessings of the gospel. God uses certain means to prepare the hearts of the unconverted to properly shape their hearts. When the saving mercy of God arrives, the person is ready to suitably embrace it.

Once that work of preparation set it and was consummated at conversion, the new believer could never fall away from God's sustaining grace. In other words, Edwards held to the doctrine of persevering grace. David Barbee says that Edwards' doctrine of preparationism "can only be understood properly within a staunchly Trinitarian and predestinarian theology."[24] Thus, the subject of this divine grace would inevitably continue on in that grace because they were divinely chosen by the Triune God. The Father had chosen them; the Son secured the salvation; the Holy Spirit applies the work. Their persevering in the faith will necessarily endure because they are among the elect. God has sovereignly predestined that they would meet their sure end in glory. They can be assured of this grace by their endurance through suffering and the evidence of good works. Edwards writes, "We must determine that good fruits, or good works and keeping Christ's commandments, are the evidences by which we are chiefly and most safely and surely to be determined, not only concerning the godliness of others, but also concerning our own godliness."[25]

The Limitations of Preparationsim

Jonathan Edwards' predecessor to his Northampton pulpit was Solomon Stoddard. He was the most well-known and respected preacher in the entire region in the early eighteenth century. Stoddard would receive the epitaph "Pope of the Connecticut River Valley." When he arrived to pastor this Congregationalist church, the town was only a small town. As the town grew, so did Stoddard's reputation as an able pastor. By the 1720s, this church would grow to be the largest congregation in New England outside of Boston. During his forty-seven-year pastorate, he oversaw several periods in which many people came to saving faith in Christ.[26] The central piece of these "harvests" was Stoddard's charismatic preaching. He would exhort sinners to repent of their sins and turn to Christ for forgiveness. Additionally, one essential element of his revival ministry was the idea of preparation. He held that progressive steps towards conversion were fundamental to the sinner's conversion. The most controversial step in that process was the use of the Lord's Supper as a converting ordinance.

Rhys Bezzant offers a helpful summarization of Stoddard's practice:

> [Stoddard] upheld the remarkable position that the Lord's Supper should function not merely as an affirmation and seal of conversion already won, but also as an opportunity to receive grace at the beginning of the Christian walk.

During the period of preparation for salvation, the sacra-
ments ought to be open to any who shunned a scandalous
life and were credally sound. Stoddard privileged the *pursuit of conversion* over the provisions for *purity of church
membership.*[27]

Although controversial, this approach would be effective in seeing
the numbers of converts within the town soar. This evangelistic practice would come to be known as Stoddardeanism. The methodology
was rooted in a desire to reach the unconverted and it stemmed from
a broader belief in preparationism. This philosophy of evangelism was
outlined in his works *The Safety of Appearing at the Day of Judgment,
The Efficacy of the Fear of Hell, and A Treatise Concerning Conversion.*
The practice would put him at odds with other colonial ministers
such as Edward Taylor and Increase Mather. Stoddard vigorously
defended the practice in a series of pamphlets and treatises. However,
Stoddardeanism was popular, especially in western Massachusetts.[28]

Early in his ministry, Edwards would affirm this evangelistic strategy. In one entry in the "Miscellanies" on church order, Edwards
affirms Stoddard's position. He said that if the minister was to demand a credible profession of faith from persons, a great number of
"truly upright ones would be excluded [from the table]."[29] So, in an
effort to preserve the unity of the church and civil order of the community, Edwards continued to treat this means of grace as a converting
ordinance. However, Edwards would later develop the conviction
that the Lord's Supper should not be used in such a manner. In short,
Edwards reversed his position. This fact is evident in the events that
would unfold later in his life. The more he considered 1 Corinthians
11:29 and the implications of the practice on ecclesiastical matters,
Edwards altered his position. He began to teach that the Lord's Supper was a means of grace that was unavailable to the unconverted. It
was limited to those members who could give a credible profession
of faith. So, Edwards would distance himself in this respect from
his predecessor. Although it was not the only factor, this conviction
would put strife between Edwards and his Northampton congregation.

It would ultimately lead to Edwards' dismissal from the pastorate in 1750. Edwards' convictions on the Lord's Supper would bring him to a point where he was willing to lose his job over this evangelistic strategy.

The Creator's Preparation

Edwards was careful to delineate what creatures are capable of doing. Creatures are unable to convert themselves. They simply cannot will themselves into a state of grace or favor with God. This explanation of creaturely capability is articulated in his *Freedom of the Will*.[30] However, Edwards began the groundwork for this famous work in his "Miscellanies."[31] His insights into the realm of theological anthropology had implications for all of humanity, not simply those within Christendom. He makes several entries in the "Miscellanies" on the nature and conversion of the heathen.

Locating the Doctrine

The eighteenth century Enlightenment tended to interpret all forms of religious expressions as culturally conceived. The movement stressed the notion that natural and unassisted reason could lead to truth. The world was based on immutable, ordered, and natural laws that could be observed and interpreted by all. Intellectuals were wholly optimistic about the innate human ability to make progress in society. Medicine, law, politics, science, and religion were all spheres where human flourishing could occur in this new intellectual and cultural milieu. Thus, there are natural laws which govern human attempts at discovering spiritual truth. Religion was seen as just an expression of one's own natural properties. Unassisted reason alone could lead to spiritual truths. This method of discovering truth was available to anyone. Therefore, any claim to special revelation from God was to be rejected. Particular ways to salvation were seen as archaic and fundamentally opposed to all sense of fairness and goodness. Broadly speaking, orthodox religion was under heavy assault from proponents of Deism.

One estimate concludes that nearly twenty-five percent of all the "Miscellanies" are dedicated to combating Deism (357 of 1412).[32] This fact shows that for much of his adult life, Edwards engaged the Deists claims on both unassisted reason and divine revelation. McDermott points out, "Deism stimulated [Edwards'] thinking on the relationship of reason to revelation."[33] However, Edwards emphatic rejection of Deism was not simply dogmatic refutations of the standard order. Edwards was nuanced in his argumentation and sensitive to the methodology of the Deists.

In several entries in the "Miscellanies," Edwards considered the possibility that there were underlying elements within a heathen tradition. These underlying themes might ignite and intensify gospel proclamation for that particular people group. In other words, there might be some sort of philosophy, tradition, or practice embedded in the heathen culture that could prepare the nation to receive the gospel. Gerald McDermott was the first to connect Edwards' teaching with the concept of *prisca theologia* in his book *Jonathan Edwards Confronts the Gods*. Broadly defined, this teaching sees non-Christian traditions paralleling and complementing Christian doctrine.[34] This corresponding structure exists because all cultures around the globe, regardless of race or religion, derive from a singular point in human history. At that point, Christian truth was known and preached to everyone. Thus, every human culture derives its being and practices from an earlier point where God was known in truth. The doctrine posits that at one point in human history all human beings were given unalloyed Christian doctrine. This truth was not communicated in its fully realized form. In other words, divine truth was communicated in an embryonic form. It could be that the Noah's good sons or some other antediluvian person was the source of that knowledge. Just like the child's game telephone, where one passes a secret down the line, it is most likely that the original message is corrupted, yet it has some semblance of the original idea. When the game is completed and the truth is revealed in light of the the distorted message, the differences can be clearly seen. McDermott sees Edwards as being greatly intrigued with this teaching and developing it to his theological context.

It is the insightful work of Gerald McDermott to locate Edwards' aforementioned doctrine within the doctrinal theory of the *prisca theologia* and polemics against Deists.[35] It is the argument of this chapter to place it within the methodology of evangelistic preparationism in colonial America. This placement should not be seen as countering McDermott's claim. His argument stems from a rubric of theological anthropology. The present connection to the Reformed doctrine of preparationism adds another layer, placing it within the matrix of colonial polemics of natural and divine revelation.

In one particular entry, Edwards says that divine inspiration was not limited to the nation of Israel.[36] He points to Balaam's prophecy as evidence of this theory. He also notes dreams given by God to heathens outside of God's people. He says that the wise men who came from the east were under divine inspiration when they received word to visit the infant Jesus. Additionally, he looks to the Exodus narrative. He says that Pharaoh, the cupbearer, and the baker were subjects of revelatory dreams, all of a divine origin. He also says Nebuchadnezzar, although a wicked and idolatrous ruler, received visions that prepared the way for God to act. Looking outside Scripture, Edwards says that pagan philosophers such as Socrates and Plato may have been subjects of direct inspiration of God. Surely, this revelation was not of a salvific nature, yet it prepared the way for divine action.

Certain truths revealed to them through their analysis of reason, tradition, providence, nature, logic, etc., could be a way that God has made them ready to accept the gospel whenever it does arrive. So, when these people come into direct contact with the gospel, they would be more likely to accept the things of God because they have been divinely prepared for it. Edwards writes, "[These revelations] might prepare the Gentile nations . . . to receive the gospel when God's time came for its promulgation among these nations, by disposing them the more diligently and impartially to attend to it."[37] The reason for such revelation given to the philosophers was so that these people could better understand the gospel when it arrived. It would also give them a sense of God's beauty and excellency when they fully understood both the gospel and the means by which God revealed himself in the preparatory work.

Moreover, Edwards believed these revelatory acts would confirm the truthfulness of the Christian religion. Thus, they had an apologetic effect. There were signs before, during, and after the time of Christ that point the nations to God. For example, Edwards notes the Roman historians, Suetonius and Tacitus, recorded that many eastern nations expected a person would arise out of Judea who would govern the whole world.[38] He proceeds to give other numerous examples where those located outside God's chosen people acknowledge something that attest to the beauty and excellency of God. The eclipse of the sun at Christ's passion was also a sign to the nations. All these signs would go towards verifying the authenticity of the message, thus enlightening the subjects, making them ready for gospel proclamation.

The Possibility of Salvation for Those Who Have Not Heard

Some had supposed that God would save only the heathen who were sincere. Surely, God would extend his saving mercies on those heathen who did good to others and were sincere in their own faith. However, Edwards says, "There is nothing appears in the reason and nature of things... that can justly lead us to determine that God will certainly reveal Christ and give the necessary means of grace, or ... saving grace, and so eternal salvation, to those heathen that are sincere."[39] God was under no obligation to save anyone. Moreover, there is no one who is sincere in his desire to please God. Edwards believed that all persons, including the heathen, are complicit in the Fall; the are in Adam, as evidenced by continuing in their sin and disbelief.

Gerald McDermott notes that Edwards held a "curious tension" between two seemingly opposing realities.[40] First, Edwards joined the chorus of innumerable Reformed theologians who believed that there was no salvation outside of conscious faith in Jesus Christ as savior and Lord. Although there were some that were wise and astute, Edwards largely saw the heathen as uncouth and immoral. They were idolaters who were lost in their sin. However, McDermott believes Edwards quite possibly could have prepared the way "for a more hopeful view of the salvation of the heathen."[41] Edwards' interest and development of the *prisca theologia* played an important role in making way for a more "expansive view of salvation."[42]

Synthesis of Edwards' Preparationism Within and Without Christendom

Although it may appear contradictory to hold to both total depravity and an evangelistic methodology that incorporates steps of preparation performed by an unregenerate person to draw nearer to salvation, Jonathan Edwards held both in tension with each other. It has been shown from the "Miscellanies" that Edwards' doctrine of preparation played out differently in diverse contexts. Within Christendom, the unregenerate could use certain means of grace to seek salvation. While this did not ensure that a person would necessarily arrive at saving faith, it did ensure they would be more likely to be saved by God. Again, it must be said that this teaching did not create dissonance between total depravity and God's unmitigated and complete sovereignty. God could choose whomever he wished. Moreover, it was not considered a form of Arminianism or semi-Pelagianism whereby a sinner could soften their own heart and achieve salvation by their own efforts. Divine grace initiates this movement. For the elect, grace overcomes their hardness of heart. For the reprobate, their hearts are further hardened and all their use of means is considered increasing judgment that will come down on a future day of reckoning. Outside of Christendom, preparationism is manifested differently. The heathen is not judged for their open rejection of Christ, but for their sins. Thus, they stand condemned before a holy God. Yet God in his mercy extends grace to prepare the nations for salvation. He does this by various means. He might prepare a nation by sending dreams or visions to particular persons. A nation might have certain traditions, practices, or rituals that have gospel themes embedded into them. So, whenever that nation comes into contact with the Christian message, they are softened to receive it. These embedded institutions might serve to catalyze a movement that sparks mass conversations and inflames Christian devotion. Taken together, these two practices constitute a widened view of preparationism. Edwards played a key role in the development of this doctrine as he expanded the teaching to include nations outside Christendom. Additionally, he shifted the divine methodology employed in the process. Subjects inside Christendom are actively seeking salvation. They are aware of their pursuit. However, those heathen outside Christendom are wholly unaware and passive with regards to their preparation. Their culturally embedded institutions will serve to fuel a future movement. Yet currently, they are ignorant of the future part those practices will play in the greater history of redemption.

Conclusion

In summary, Jonathan Edwards held to the Puritan concept of preparationism, whereby the sinner could use the means of grace to take preliminary steps towards conversion. Yet Edwards' immediate context was somewhat of a retrieval of the Reformed practice. His grandfather and predecessor had altered the schema of the process for evangelistic purposes. Edwards was not convinced of the Scriptural basis for that alteration, for it had detrimental implications on his ecclesiology. Edwards would be ejected from his pulpit as a result. This crisis served as a catalyst to the theologian's expansive work on the doctrine. As Edwards began to rethink through this practice, he decided to return the original Puritan practice, that is, not using the Lord's Supper as a converting ordinance. Yet he expanded the scope of the original doctrine to incorporate heathen nations in this practice. Because he does not have knowledge or access to the means of grace, the heathen could not use them to prepare himself. Nevertheless, God would sovereignly prepare them by embedding certain practices within their culture, language, or tradition that would ready them for gospel proclamation. Regardless of one's ethnic or cultural background, God would prepare them for salvation.

Notes

[1] Michael McClymond and Gerald McDermott, *The Theology of Jonathan Edwards,* (New York: Oxford University Press, 2012), 565.

[2] Brian Russell Franklin, "Missions and Missiology." In *The Jonathan Edwards Encyclopedia.* Eds. Harry S. Stout, Kenneth P. Minkema, and Adriaan C. Neele. (Grand Rapids, MI.: Eerdmans, 2017), 385.

[3] Nathan Finn and Jeremy Kimble, eds. *A Reader's Guide to the Major Writings of Jonathan Edwards,* (Wheaton, IL: Crossway, 2017).

[4] Gerald McDermott, *Jonathan Edwards Confronts the Gods: Christian Theology, Enlightenment Religion, and Non-Christian Faiths,* (New York: Oxford University Press, 2000), 3.

[5] Alan Cairns, in *Dictionary of Theological Terms,* (Belfast; Greenville, SC: Ambassador Emerald International, 2002), 337.

[6] "Miscellanies," no. 2, in *WJE* 13:197.

[7] George Marsden, *Jonathan Edwards: A Life* (New Haven: Yale University Press, 2003), 28.

[8] "Miscellanies," no. r, in *WJE* 13:173.

[9] "Miscellanies," no. 116b, in *WJE* 13:283.

[10] "Miscellanies," no. 244, in *WJE* 13:359.

[11] "Miscellanies," no. 255, in *WJE* 13:365.

[12] "Miscellanies," no. 255, in *WJE* 13:365.

[13] "Miscellanies," no. 255, in *WJE* 13:365.

[14] "Miscellanies," no. 255, in *WJE* 13:365.

[15] "Miscellanies," no. 255, in *WJE* 13:365.

[16] "Miscellanies," no. 255, in *WJE* 13:365.

[17] "Miscellanies," no. 77, in *WJE* 13:245.

[18] "Miscellanies," no. 77, in *WJE* 13:245.

[19] "Miscellanies," no. 77, in *WJE* 13:245.

[20] "Miscellanies," no. 1029, in *WJE* 20:366.

[21] William L. Hawkins, "Infusion of Grace," *In The Jonathan Edwards Encyclopedia,* eds. Harry S. Stout, Kenneth P. Minkema, and Adriaan C. Neele. (Grand Rapids, MI.: Eerdmans, 2017), 334.

[22] "Miscellanies," no. 1053, in *WJE* 20:393.

[23] "Miscellanies," no. 1053, in *WJE* 20:393.

[24] "David M. Barbee, in *The Jonathan Edwards Encyclopedia,* eds. Harry S. Stout, Kenneth P. Minkema, and Adriaan C. Neele. (Grand Rapids, MI.: Eerdmans, 2017), 461–3.

[25] "Miscellanies," no. 790, in *WJE* 18:474–76.

[26] Stoddard was pastor from 1672–1729.

[27] Rhys Bezzant, "Orderly But Not Ordinary: Jonathan Edwards' Evangelical Ecclesiology" (Th.D. Thesis, Australian School of Theology, Melbourne, 2010), 29–30.

[28] Michael A.G. Haykin, "Solomon Stoddard," in *Biographical Dictionary of Evangelicals,* eds. Timothy Larsen, David Bebbington, and Mark Noll (Downers Grove, IL: Intervarsity Press, 2003).

[29] "Miscellanies," no. 462, in *WJE* 13:504.

[30] *Freedom of the Will,* in *WJE* 1.

[31] For example, Edwards' entry 1153 is largely replicated in *Freedom of the Will,* Pt. II, Sec. 5.

[32] McDermott, *Jonathan Edwards Confronts the Gods,* 5.

[33] McDermott, *Jonathan Edwards Confronts the Gods,* 51.

[34] *Prisca theologia* is a Latin term meaning "ancient theology."

[35] McDermott, *Jonathan Edwards Confronts the Gods,* 93–109.

[36] "Miscellanies," no. 1162, in *WJE* 23:84–85.

[37] "Miscellanies," no. 1162, in *WJE* 23:85.

[38] "Miscellanies," no. 981, in *WJE* 20:299–301.

[39] "Miscellanies," no. 840a, in *WJE* 20:56.

[40] McDermott, *Jonathan Edwards Confronts the Gods,* 143.

[41] McDermott, *Jonathan Edwards Confronts the Gods,* 143.

[42] McDermott, *Jonathan Edwards Confronts the Gods,* 143.

EDWARDS ON CHINA

Victor Zhu

> *I am of the mind that mankind would have been like a parcel*
> *of beasts with respect to their knowledge in all important*
> *truths, if there never had been any such thing as revelation*
> *in the world, and that they never would have rose out of their*
> *brutality. We see that those that live at the greatest distance*
> *from revelation, as to time and place, are far the most*
> *brutish ... China probably, being from the people that Noah,*
> *that holy man, immediately ruled over for many hundred*
> *years, and being much separated from other nations, have*
> *held more by tradition from Noah than other nations, and*
> *so were a more civilized people.*
>
> — Jonathan Edwards, *Miscellany no. 350*

Edwards' Fascination with China

FROM HIS EARLY CAREER, Edwards held a rather favorable view of China. In this essay, his awareness on China is presented according to his Miscellany entries 350, 1181, 1236, 1350 and 1351.

In his discussion of "Christian religion" (Miscellany no. 350), Edwards claimed that peoples living in America and most parts of Asia and Africa were "the heathens" who were "far more barbarous than those [who] lived at Rome, Greece, Egypt, Syria and Chaldea formerly,"[1] because these people were "more distant from places enlightened with revelation."[2] The people of China, however, "were a *more civilized* people." [3] Edwards kept this favorable view of China until the end of his life. In one of his "Miscellanies" drafted in the 1750s, Edwards quoted *Ophiomaches,* or *Deism Revealed* (1749) by Philip Skelton (1707–1787) to highlight that China was a unique nation. Skelton argued that while the art of reasoning was flourishing from Syria to Egypt, Greece, and Italy and to the rest of Europe, "all the other nations of the earth" had not made any advance in knowledge, "lying without the verge of right religious instruction" and thus "remained profoundly ignorant."[4] Yet he went on to assert that China was the only exception among all these non-Mediterranean and European countries. Edwards agreed with Skelton that China was an exceptional nation. In his interpretation of Genesis 8:4, he reinforced this position by quoting Samuel Shuckford (1694–1754).[5] For Edwards, the Chinese are so unique that their language, learning and social order are all kept intact, in spite of the world-wide impact of sin.[6]

Deists' Idealization of China

Edwards was not the first to hold a positive view of China. In the late seventeenth and early eighteenth centuries, the Qing empire (1644-1912) that known as "China" became a fashionable topic among European intellectuals.[7] China's popularity emerged from late Ming (1368-1644) and early Qing dynasties, thanks to the Jesuits' favorable introduction of Confucianism and claim that China actually had embraced Christianity from ancient times.

Consequently, Chinese culture and philosophy based on the teachings of "Confucius" (孔子, 551–479 BC) attracted increasing attention among the eighteenth century intellectuals in the European Enlightenment. Gottfried Wilhelm Leibniz (1646–1716) declared, "We need missionaries from the Chinese who might teach us the use and practice of natural religion, just as we have sent them teachers of revealed theology."[8] Similarly, Christian Wolff (1679–1754), promoted that this Chinese social system would promise a prosperous and perfect political, economic and administrative order for any governmental system that would follow it.[9] In this "idealized image of China," Wolff argued that for Confucius and the ancient Chinese emperors, the source of their social ethics and morality was not divine revelation, but human nature.[10]

Edwards Versus the Deists' Fervency on China

While holding a positive view of China, Edwards did not think that western European nations should learn from the Chinese in ethics and social order. On the contrary, for him China was such a remote and alien nation that their views were rather irrelevant to him or his congregation.

First of all, while Edwards was fascinated with the Chinese language and culture, the written Chinese remained for him something foreign and incomprehensible. At times, when he wanted to emphasize that some biblical texts could be obscure and difficult for some Christians, he would describe them "as if [they] were written in the Chinese . . . of which we know not one word."[11]

Secondly, lives of the Chinese people were not relevant to Christians living in the new colonies in North America. In the sermons of early 1730s and his "Miscellanies" passages of the 1750s, Edwards took the Chinese people as an example in illustrating what it would be like if Christians would not follow his advice that they should have a relationship with God and take their responsibilities before Him. He wrote,

> Not only is it necessary that we should know that God is, and what he is, in order to know what that religion which our duty is, but also 'tis requisite that we should know those other things mentioned, viz. what concern we have with him, etc. *Whatever we hear of the excellencies of a person in China . . . yet if we have no concern with him, nor he with us, no service from us to him is properly our duty.*

There can be no intercourse, nothing to excite the exercises and services of friendship according to the human nature ...According to the human [nature], such distance and exclusion from all concern is, as to influence on the heart, much like exclusion from reality of existence.[12]

Thirdly, in his early career, Edwards thought that the Chinese people were so distant and irrelevant to local life in the American colonies that they could not even have an emotional impact on his own life. In his "Miscellanies" entry No. 232 Edwards wrote, "If some man in China were very angry with me, I should not regard it so much as the displeasure of one that lived near me ..."[13]

Fourthly, during his later years, Edwards maintained that the Chinese were too distant to be often remembered in his prayers. In his *Some Thoughts* (1743), Edwards argued that "our near friends are more committed to our care than others ...than those that live at a great distance; and the people of our land and nation are more in some sense, committed to our care *than the people of China* ..."[14]

China in Edwards' Account of God's Redemptive and Eschatological Scheme

The Realm of Elite Chinese Person's Knowledge of Christian Doctrines

Edwards assumed, on the basis of report made by the Jesuits using figurist methods in their seventeenth and eighteenth-century works, that traditionally the ancient Chinese had the notion of some fundamental Christian doctrines. In several of his "Miscellanies" he extensively quoted Chinese understandings of many theological loci, ranging from the nature of God to the Messiah and His redemption.[15]

Being strongly interested in what the Deists called natural religion, during his Stockbridge years, Edwards spent much time on two works by Chevalier Ramsay (1686-1743) and quoted sixteen thousand words, amounting to ten percent of all the material constituting

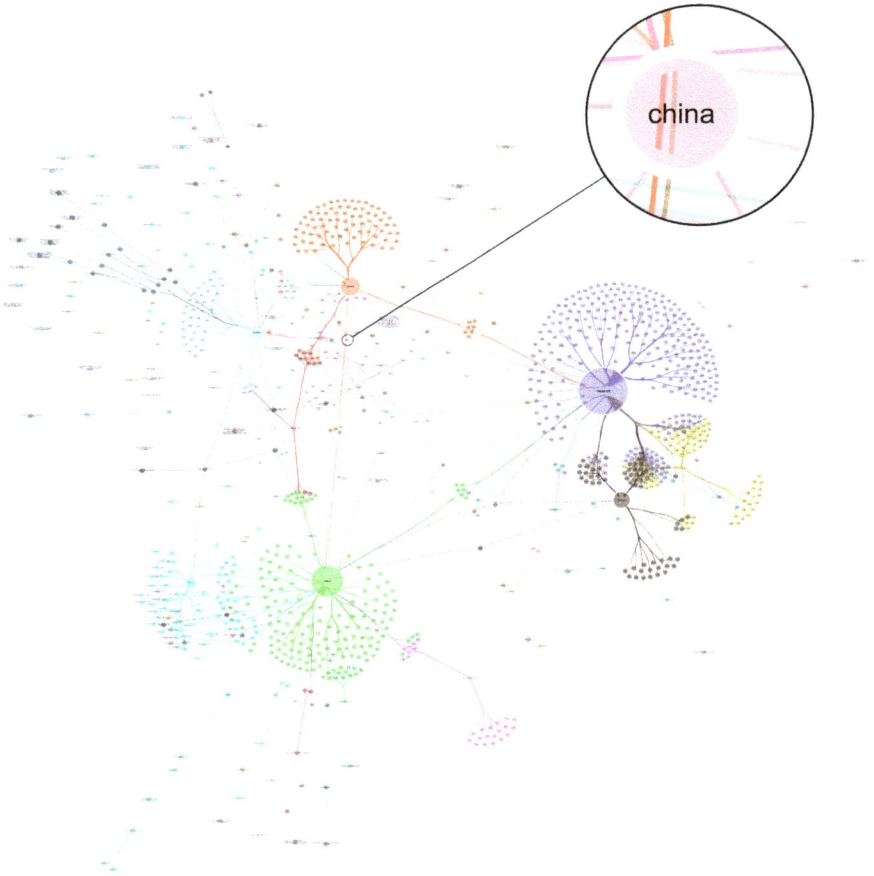

CHINA, CONFUCIUS, MESSIAH, TRADITION, *and* TRINITY—*a map of china, chinese, confucius, messiah, messiahs, messiahship, tradition, traditional, traditionally, traditionary, traditions, trinity with interconnections and page locations in WJE 1–26.*

his "Miscellanies" during this period.[16] Most of Edwards' quotations from Ramsay's posthumous magnum opus, *Philosophical Principles,* are found in his "Miscellanies" entry no. 1181 that covers many theological topics, including "the Trinity, the nature of the Deity, the paradisiacal state, the Fall, the redemption of the Messiah, the fall of angels, [and] the nature of true religion."[17] A few examples of the materials cited and assessed by Edwards should suffice in revealing the significance of those claims.

Above all, from his study of the Daoist canonical book of the Laozi (also known as *Daodejing,* 道德经) and other passages from ancient Ruist (Confucian) scriptures, Ramsay suggested that some ancient Chinese writers potentially depicted God as a self-existent, eternal Creator of the ultimate truth. According to Ramsay,

> God is called Chang-Ti [Shangdi, 上帝], or the sovereign emperor, and Tien [Tian, 天], the supreme heaven, the intelligent heaven, the self-existent unity, who is present everywhere, and who produced all things by his power … The same books of *King* call God Tao, which signifies reason, law, eternal code; Yen, word or speech; Tching-Che [Jing, 经], sovereign truth.[18]

Moreover, from Laozi's passage of *Tonchu* (*Tai Chu,* 太初, in the beginning), Ramsay thought that these ancient Chinese even had a notion of the Trinity. At least, Ramsay claimed, Laozi (老子, ?–?) seemed to be aware that "in the beginning the supreme reason subsisted in a triple unity, and that this unity created the heavens and the earth, separated them from each other, and will at last convert and perfect all things."[19] Edwards seemed to agree with Ramsay and added in front of this paragraph the following: "Our author proceeds to examine the hints and shadows of this doctrine preserved among the pagans, beginning with the Chinese, in whose canonical books he says the following surprising passages are to be found."[20] Edwards was obviously sensitive to the unusual character of Ramsay's argument. In another "Miscellanies" passage (Miscellany no. 1236), he quoted

Skelton's *Deism Revealed* to restate that Laozi (or Laokun, as spelled by Edwards) knew about the Trinity.

> And Laokun [Laojun, 老君], who lived before Confucius, was as remarkable for another saying, which seems to point at the Trinity: 'Eternal Reason produced one, one produced two, two produced three, and three produced all things.'[21]

Next, in his research of the I-King (Yi Jing, 易经, *The Book of Changes*) and other classics, Ramsay claimed that Confucius, Laozi and Mencius (372–289 BC or 385–303 or 302 BC) had abundant knowledge about the Messiah. Edwards was fascinated and carefully copied it down. Certain elite ancient Chinese masters regarded the Messiah, as Edwards quoted from Ramsay, as "a minister of the supreme God" and addressed him with various names, including "Holy or the Saint by excellence," "Wen-wang [文王], or the prince of peace; Chin-gin [Shen Ren 神人], the divine man; Chang-gin [Sheng Ren 圣人], God-man [probably misunderstood]; Tient-see [Tian Zi 天子], son of the sovereign lord; Kiunt-see [Jun Zi 君子], son of the king [a mistranslation]; Kigen [Ji Ren 至人], son of heaven [probably misspelled and mistranslated]."[22] Edwards believed that these three ancient Chinese wrote many hints about the theology of life and work of the coming Messiah: he "created the universe" as a Creator; he would govern the whole universe and teaches people with "the instructions of ldots the supreme God himself;" he would be incarnate and undertake severe suffering; and in his triumph he would reestablish the world "in the ways of righteousness," banishing sin and sufferings and restoring "all things to their primitive perfection and felicity."[23] On the basis of what he heard from Ramsay, Edwards adopted these "hints" and assumed that Ramsay's theory was reliable at least for those who wrote the above texts on Messiah. During this same period of Edwards' life, in order to demonstrate certain Chinese teachings and claims concerning the Messiah, he quoted the English clergyman John Jackson's (1686-1763) *Chronological Antiquities,* found in *The*

Monthly Review for August 1752.[24] According to Jackson, Confucius had a rich knowledge of the coming Messiah. The holy one who would appear in the west, Edwards copied, is "the supreme truth and reason, or the fountain from whence truth and reason are communicated unto men . . ."[25] Confucius' Messiah is "one, supremely holy, supremely intelligent and invisible," but he "produced and sustains all things" and "is expected to come upon earth; even though an hundred ages should pass before his coming."[26]

Lastly, Edwards was impressed by Ramsay's interpretation of the Chinese knowledge about human's fall.

> In the book *Chi-king* [*Shijing,* 诗经], it is said, "Heaven placed mankind upon a high mountain, but Taiwang made it fruitless by his fault. Wen-wang [文王], or the king of peace, endeavored to render to the mountain its primitive beauty, but Taiwang contradicted, and opposed his will."[27]

Quoting Ramsay's interpretation of Confucius' writings, Edwards said that the Chinese claimed that they would be restored in "primitive light and purity, which the soul received from heaven, upon its first creation, which it has lost by sin, and which heaven alone can render to it, by its internal irradiations and influences."[28] To Edwards and Ramsay, the Chinese were even aware of the "three necessary means of reuniting the soul to God: by contemplation or prayer; by the sacrifice of the passions, or mortification; by humility, or self-denial . . ."[29] Edwards also seemed to agree with Ramsay that the ancient Chinese had a tremendous understanding about repentance and restoration of sinners.

> The canonical books of China, and the most ancient commentators upon them, who lived long before the Christian era, are full of such passages, in commendation of internal prayer, purity and humility, inward recollection, and continual vigilance and true self-denial.[30]

From the above three cases, it seems that Edwards followed both Ramsay and Jackson in believing that most fundamental Christian doctrines can be traced in the ancient Chinese philosophical classics. These doctrines potentially cover some hints or similarities to many orthodox teachings such as God's nature and His creation, the Messiah's person and His work, as well as humanity's fall and regeneration.

The Realm of the Necessity of Divine Revelation and Redemption

In contrast to Leibniz and Wolff who asserted that human beings could live properly alone with reason and according to their human nature, Edwards firmly defended the reality of human sinfulness and proved the necessity of God's revelation and salvation. This applied to the "China" discussed and promoted by Jesuits and Deists. Instead of being a people group typified by rational self-sufficiency, Edwards asserted that China would be hopeless without divine special revelation and Jesus Christ's redemption.

He held this belief from his early years. In a sermon preached in the late 1720s, Edwards maintained that the Chinese were still in "great darkness and blindness," just like any person of American or European origin who had not been redeemed by God.[31] He went further and stated that these Chinese persons were of no greater value than any other sinners who would perish without divine revelation and salvation. Even with their impressive civilization, the Chinese people were still no less under the domain of Satan, until the gospel arrives.[32] Edwards kept repeating this observation even in his later years. In the 1750s, in his "Miscellanies" entry entitled "The Necessity of Revelation," Edwards quoted Philip Skelton's *Deism Revealed* at length to prove the necessity of God's revelation and to demolish the Deist theory of "complete" human self-sufficiency. According to Edwards, despite being more civilized than many other "heathen" nations, contemporary China (being the Qing empire) had *not* been able to show any development towards "true religion."

The doctrine of St. Paul concerning the blindness into which the Gentiles fell, is so confirmed by the state of religion in Africa, America, and even China, where, to this day, *no advances towards the true religion have been made,* that we can no longer be at a loss to judge [. . .] of the insufficiency of unassisted reason to dissipate the prejudices of the heathen world, and open their eyes to religious truths.[33]

Edwards continued to demonstrate that human beings tended to employ philosophy, reason and science for idolatry rather than for worshiping the Creator. This remained true for both the Chinese and Western peoples, as Edwards commented on the first chapter of Romans:

But St. Paul gives us quite another history of the business: he says, that 'from the Creation, απο κτισεως, the invisible things of God are clearly seen' [Rom. 1:20]; and afterwards, *through philosophy, and the boasted wisdom of man, almost wholly lost, or changed into idolatry, worse in itself than even total ignorance.*[34]

So he insisted again: "Our knowledge of God did not take its rise from mere reason, but from revelation."[35]

It is clear that, in contrast to the Deist natural theology, Edwards had offered strong insistence for the necessity of revelation and redemption, because human reason and philosophy is insufficient even for human knowledge of the physical world, and they are defective or even useless in knowing God and the way toward redemption. This is a universal principle and applied in Edwards' theology to ancient and contemporary China as well as to all the other nations, whether they are "civilized" or not.

The Realm of God's Progressive Revelation in Chinese Classics

It seems that Edwards accepted two seemingly opposite facts. On the one hand, ancient Chinese philosophical classics, particularly the Ruist and Daoist scriptures, were enriched with a clear awareness of the fundamental Christian doctrines. On the other hand, Edwards had argued that the ancient Chinese worldview was unsustainable without God's revelation and salvation. How did Edwards resolve the tension between these two claims? His strategy was to prove that God's progressive revelation in these Chinese philosophical classics involved identifying "hints and subtleties" of divine work within those ancient volumes.

Firstly, Edwards was convinced that there was an apparent correlation between Noah and Fu Xi (伏羲), the founder of ancient Chinese civilization. In his early career, Edwards advocated that that the reason why the Chinese were more civilized is that they probably were "from the people that Noah . . . immediately ruled over for many hundred years," and so "held more by tradition from Noah than other nations."[36] In 1747, Edwards found support in Shuckford's *Sacred and Prophane History of the World Connected* and agreed to the hypothesis that Fu Xi and Noah were probably just one and the same person.[37]

Secondly, Edwards was confident that the ancient Chinese inherited many of their notions from the Jewish patriarchs. In the entry entitled "Tradition of the Chinese Concerning the Messiah and the Trinity" (Miscellany no. 1236), Edwards quoted from Skelton's *Deism Revealed* and observed that it was possibly from the Israelites, or the patriarchs specifically, that the ancient Chinese people inherited their knowledge about God and Christian doctrines. Edwards suggested that many years before the Christian era, it was possible that some Israelites had been brought to the mainland of China as captives and educated Chinese people with biblical teachings. That could be the reason why many notions prevalent in ancient China appeared similar to those of the Jews. In particular, he argued this might be the reason why Confucius and Laozi had some vague understandings of Christianity. Living five hundred years before Christ, Confucius predicted that a "true saint," the Messiah, would be born in the West. And Laozi, Edwards believed, knew about the Trinity before Confucius.[38] One Chinese emperor who reigned for about sixty years after Christ, Edwards was convinced, was informed by Heaven that this saint was in the West and sent ambassadors to search out for him.[39]

Edwards' conviction that these Christian notions found in the ancient Chinese texts were the legacy of Jewish patriarchs was reinforced by Ramsay's work. In quoting Ramsay in two "Miscellanies" entries, no. 1255 and no. 1351, Edwards evidently accepted the theory that the founders of ancient China actually received divine revelation containing Christian truths from the patriarchs.[40] For Edwards, this was a significant piece of the historical and theological puzzle of how the ancient Chinese sages gained some knowledge of certain Christian doctrines. It is noteworthy that Edwards copied into his notebook many portions of Ramsay's "Discourse upon the Theology and Mythology of the Pagans."[41] In his Miscellany entry no. 1351, Edwards echoed Ramsay's observation with this heading to his quotation: "The first religion of mankind [proved] agreeable to the religion of the Holy Scriptures."[42] He concluded, "We see then that the doctrines of the primitive perfection of nature, its fall and its restoration by a divine hero, are equally manifest in the mythologies of the Greeks, Egyptians, Persians, Indians and *Chinese.*"[43]

Finally, Edwards believed that the scheduled nature of the development of Chinese civilization would be finally merged within the flow of God's eschatological scheme. In commenting on Revelation 16:13–21, Edwards maintained that the final consummation of God's kingdom cannot be accomplished without the conversion and involvement of the gigantic heathen countries like China. As he wrote,

The event that the church has been laboring and in travail for, is that event that is accomplished by the sounding of the seventh trumpet. Rev. 11:15, "And the seventh angel sounded: and there were great voices in heaven, saying, "The kingdoms of this world are become the kingdoms of our Lord, and of his Christ; and he shall reign forever and ever." ... But we must suppose, that this will be accomplished in a greater extent at the sounding of the seventh trumpet than ever before, because 'tis spoken of as a new thing, that shall first be accomplished then. And by this world must be meant a much bigger world than the Roman world that became Christian in Constantine's time. *And this event can't be looked upon to be accomplished, as long as such mighty empires as that of the Turks, and of the Chinese, and great Mogul, etc., remain in opposition to Christ's kingdom.*[44]

To conclude, Edwards was confident that it is from God's revelation that the ancient Chinese sages obtained some notions of Christian doctrines. In this way, Edwards attempted to resolve the dilemma between the ancient Chinese persons' knowledge of Christian doctrines and their current spiritual darkness. For Edwards, China had always been in God's scheme as He kept expanding His divine kingdom. The ancient and current Chinese civilization and philosophical classics were the legacies of God's progressive revelations in that part of the world. Through these, China would gradually emerge into the eschatological blueprint of God's kingdom.

Edwards' fascination with China and the anticipation of Chinese people's involvement in the divine kingdom has not been well documented in Edwardsean scholarship until the end of the twentieth century, but it in fact marks a significant and clear thematic departure from many of his Reformed forefathers and Puritan colleagues. To the best of our knowledge, Edwards appears to be the only Puritan theologian who has carefully and attentively studied what he considered to be China and her eschatological end. Most of the reformers including John Calvin, Martin Luther and John Knox, did not write anything about Chinese culture and philosophy, let alone associating this nation with God's redemptive work or His kingdom. Similarly, most of Edwards' contemporaries would not share his enthusiasm for the Chinese philosophical classics.

We note however, that Edwards was not always consistent or effective in his debate with the Deists. At the best of his knowledge in his era, Edwards' view on Chinese philosophical classics and God's revelation seems problematic and not as convincing in a number of ways. For instance, the Israelite influence on ancient Chinese culture is difficult to justify and is unable to be developed. More seriously, in his search for Christian notions in the Chinese classics, Edwards was misled by the resources he used. At a fundamental level, Edwards, as well as his Jesuit and Deist contemporaries, held a simplified and over-generalized understanding of Chinese philosophy. For one thing, Edwards seemed has no awareness of dynastic changes in Chinese history and thus was convinced that Confucianism was consistently ruling the ideological system in "China." For another, Edwards did not realize that he was actually aligned with the Jesuits' and Deists' idealization of Confucianism.

Notes

[1]"Miscellanies," no. 350, in *WJE* 13:424.

[2]"Miscellanies," no. 350, in *WJE* 13:424.

[3]"Miscellanies," no. 350, in *WJE* 13:424. Emphasis added.

[4]"Miscellanies," no. 1350, in *WJE* 23:437–38.

[5]Samuel Shuckford, *The Sacred and Prophane History of the World Connected: From the Creation of the World to the Dissolution of the Assyrian Empire at the Death of Sardanapalus, and to the Declension of the Kingdoms of Judah and Israel, under the Reigns of Ahaz and Pekah* (London: Printed for J. and R. Tonson, 1740). See also *WJE* 26:215.

[6]*WJE* 15:535–36.

[7]Walter W. Davis, "China, the Confucian Ideal, and the European Age of Enlightenment," in *Discovering China: European Interpretations in the Enlightenment*, ed. Julia Ching and Willard Gurdon Oxtoby, 1–26 (Rochester, N.Y.: University of Rochester Press, 1992), 1.

[8]G. W. Leibniz, Preface to the *Novissima Sinica* (1697) in G. W. Leibniz, *Writings on China*, ed. and trans. Daniel J. Cook and Henry Rosemont, Jr. (Chicago: Open Court, 1994), 51.

[9]For Wolff's idealization of China, see Stefan Gaarsmand Jacobsen, "Limits to Despotism: Idealizations of Chinese Governance and Legitimizations of Absolutist Europe," *Journal of Early Modern History* 17 (2013): 347–89.

[10] Jacobsen, "Limits to Despotism," 353; Mark Larrimore, "Orientalism and Antivoluntarism in the History of Ethics: On Christian Wolff's *Oratio De Sinarum Philosophia Practica," The Journal of Religious Ethics* 28, no. 2 (2000): 197.

[11] *WJE* 22:88.

[12] "Miscellanies," no. 1304, in *WJE* 23:253–54. Emphasis added.

[13] "Miscellanies," no. 232, in *WJE* 13:349.

[14] *WJE* 4:470–471. Emphasis added.

[15] *WJE* 13:147.

[16] The two works are *Philosophical Principles of Natural and Revealed Religion* (1748-1749) and *Travels of Cyrus* (1727). For the details of Ramsay, see Douglas A. Sweeney, "Editor's Introduction," *WJE* 23:13. For Edwards' quotation from Ramsay, see Peter J. Thuesen, "Editor's Introduction," *WJE* 26:48; Gerald McDermott, *Jonathan Edwards Confronts the Gods* (New York: Oxford University Press, 2000), 213.

[17] "Miscellanies," no. 1181, in *WJE* 23:95.

[18] "Miscellanies," no. 1181, in *WJE* 23:97.

[19] "Miscellanies," no. 1181, in *WJE* 23:98.

[20] "Miscellanies," no. 1181, in *WJE* 23:98.

[21] "Miscellanies," no. 1236, in *WJE* 23:171.

[22] "Miscellanies," no 1181, in *WJE* 23:98–99. The Chinese pronunciation and translation are corrected and confirmed by Prof. Lauren Frederick Pfister in a private correspondence on 2 February 2018.

[23] "Miscellanies," no. 1181, in *WJE* 23:99–100.

[24] "Miscellanies," no. 1200, in *WJE* 23:123.

[25] "Miscellanies," no. 1200, in *WJE* 23:123.

[26] "Miscellanies," no. 1200, in *WJE* 23:123.

[27] "Miscellanies," no. 1181, in *WJE* 23:101.

[28] "Miscellanies," no. 1181, in *WJE* 23:104.

[29] "Miscellanies," no. 1181, in *WJE* 23:103.

[30] "Miscellanies," no. 1181, in *WJE* 23:104. Additionally, Edwards was impressed by the Chinese understanding of paradise and the Fall of the angels and recorded all these attentively in this "Miscellanies" passage. See "Miscellanies," no. 1181, in *WJE* 23:101–103.

[31] *WJEO* 43.

[32] *WJEO* 43.

[33] "Miscellanies," no. 1350, in *WJE* 23:454. Emphasis added.

[34] "Miscellanies," no. 1350, in *WJE* 23:454. Emphasis added.

[35] "Miscellanies," no. 1350, in *WJE* 23:454.

[36] "Miscellanies," no. 350, in *WJE* 13:424. Emphasis added.

[37] *WJE* 15:535–36.

[38] "Miscellanies," no. 1236, in *WJE* 23:171.

[39] "Miscellanies," no. 1236, in *WJE* 23:171.

[40] See "Miscellanies," no. 1255, in *WJE* 23:190–91; "Miscellanies," no. 1236, in *WJE* 23:461–81. See also McDermott, *Jonathan Edwards Confronts the Gods,* 211–12.

[41] "Miscellanies," no. 1351, in *WJE* 23:461–81. This is a lengthy appendix to Ramsay's *Travels of Cyrus* (1728). See *WJE* 23:461, n. 1.

[42] "Miscellanies," no. 1351, in *WJE* 23:461.

[43] "Miscellanies," no. 1351, in *WJE* 23:480. Emphasis added.

[44] *WJE* 5:182–83.

Edwards on Covenant Theology

David Mark Rathel

God often speaks in his Word of the covenant he has made with his people, comparing it to the covenant between husband and wife. By this covenant is intended the covenant between Christ and his people.

— Jonathan Edwards, *Miscellany no. 617*

Introduction

COVENANT THEOLOGY EMPHASIZES the divine covenants found in Scripture and portrays the relationship between God and humans primarily in covenantal terms. This approach to biblical interpretation features many notable exponents. David Dickson, Johannes Cocceius, and Hermann Witsius are among its most important advocates.[1]

A former generation of scholars incorrectly promoted the belief that Edwards rejected covenant theology. Perry Miller famously exulted that Edwards "threw over the whole covenant scheme" so that he might declare "God unfettered by any agreement or obligation."[2] The influence that Miller exercised over the early years of modern Edwards research ensured this judgment received wide acceptance. Peter

DeJong built on Miller's thesis and presented Edwards as removing from New England theology any emphasis on divine covenants.[3]

Recent scholarship has provided a necessary corrective. Contemporary researchers demonstrate that Edwards possessed a great interest in covenant theology and openly made use of it in his theological reflection.[4] He employed covenantal language when describing relationships between human persons, often writing about the national covenant, as well as the covenantal obligations that exist in an ecclesial context. He also employed covenant theology when constructing his soteriology, a fact that has until recently received little attention.[5]

Edwards' "Miscellanies" feature some of his most substantive considerations of how covenantal theology might relate to soteriology. There he engaged with concepts prominent in covenant theology and at times engaged with leading covenant theologians.

In this essay, I survey Edwards' covenant theology as found in his "Miscellanies," demonstrating that he refined his convictions over time. I argue that Edwards developed a sophisticated covenant structure that attempted to balance divine grace with the need for human action. His approach would carry great significance for other aspects of his theology; most notably, it would inform how he understood justification by faith.

Introducing Covenant Theology

Traditional accounts of covenant theology distinguish between three covenants—the covenant of works, the covenant of grace, and the covenant of redemption. The covenant of works, the *foedus operum,* represents a divinely initiated compact between God and prelapsarian Adam. This covenant was conditional in that it required Adam's obedience; Adam was to avoid fruit from the forbidden tree. Should Adam obey this commandment, he and his posterity would enjoy life with God. Should Adam fail to meet this requirement, he would experience death.[6]

The covenant of grace, the *foedus gratiae,* serves as a New Testament counterpart to the covenant of works. This covenant occurs between Christ and the elect. Having fulfilled the duties of the law through a sinless life on earth, Christ provides redemption for those who trust in him. The elect then procure Christ's unmerited favor not by obeying commandments but by accepting Christ's work on their behalf.

Most versions of covenant theology present faith in Christ as a condition of the covenant of grace. This approach allows the covenant of grace to mirror the covenant of works. As the covenant of works obligated Adam to fulfill the condition of obedience, so now the covenant of grace obligates people to fulfill the condition of placing faith in Christ. The Westminster Confession of Faith summarized this issue by explaining that while the Lord through the covenant of grace "freely offers unto sinners life and salvation by Jesus," in the covenant he is also "requiring of them faith in him."[7]

Though faith remains a condition of this covenant, the exercise of faith is a non-meritorious act. Divine grace assists the elect to trust in Christ. Faith, therefore, does not constitute a work that earns righteousness. Faith is merely instrumental; it is the means by which the elect receive Christ and his benefits.

The covenant of redemption, the *pactum salutis,* "rests in the cradle of the federal theology of the Reformed tradition," between the covenant of works and the covenant of grace. This covenant details a pre-temporal, intra-trinitarian agreement between Father and Son. In this agreement, the Father and Son agreed before the creation of the world to enact the plan of redemption in human history. The Father proposed that the Son should obtain salvation for humanity through his death and resurrection. The Son agreed to this proposal and received the promise of glorification as a reward for his obedience.[8]

Edwards' Early Covenant Theology in the "Miscellanies"

Edwards provided his first substantial reflection on covenant theology in Miscellany no. 2. In a partly autobiographical entry, he admitted he experienced "difficulties" over the way many theologians constructed their understanding of the covenants.[9] He sought an alternative.

His primary concern was with the use of conditional language in relation to the covenant of grace. While he acknowledged that theologians had a right to present faith as a condition of the covenant, he found this rhetoric unhelpful and chastised those who used it as "speaking so wrong." He feared that when attached to the reception of salvation, references to conditions may display "the foundation of Arminianism" or even mark a return to Richard Baxter's Neonomianism. They might "make men value themselves for their own righteousness."[10]

Edwards speculated that a willingness on the part of some theologians to distinguish the covenant of works and the covenant of grace accounted for this focus on conditions. Rather than separating these two covenants, he suggested the existence of a single covenant—the covenant of works. In his scheme, Adam failed to uphold the terms of the covenant by disobeying the Father, but Christ obeyed the Father perfectly. Christ in this way fulfilled all of the covenant of works' conditions.

The elect enter into no direct covenant with the God as they would in the covenant of grace; instead, Christ serves as their representative in the covenant of works. As representative, Christ shares with them the blessings of covenantal obedience. Edwards wrote, "By Christ's performing the condition of the covenant, the condition is as if it were performed by them."[11]

This move left no conditions for the elect to fulfill. Edwards championed, "Salvation is not offered to us upon any condition, but free and for nothing. We are to do nothing for it, we are only to take it." Elsewhere he claimed, "Faith can't be called the condition of receiving, for it is the receiving itself; Christ holds out and believers receive."[12]

Early entries in the "Miscellanies" developed this proposal further. Edwards wrote that the covenant of works and the covenant of grace are synonymous. Though some theologians may divide them, the two terms refer to the same covenant (nos. 30, 35). The New Testament presents God as covenanting with Christ—not with the elect (no. 35). Christ serves as a delegate on behalf of the elect to ensure free salvation and the preservation of justification by faith (no. 33). The elect should receive the benefits that Christ has obtained for them and not seek to fulfill certain conditions (nos. 171, 498).

While Edwards' remarks reveal a departure from more typical presentations of covenant theology, his argument is not necessarily new. Several prominent theologians took issue with the language of conditions in the reception of salvation—Thomas Boston the most notable.[13] They possessed the same concerns that Edwards expressed; they feared that conditional language might portray salvation as a work. Even so, these theologians like Edwards did not reject the significance of personal faith. They only objected to framing faith as a condition that the elect must fulfill.[14]

Edwards' proposal to restructure covenant theology with a focus on Christ as the fulfiller of a covenant's conditions was also not unusual. Other theologians from his time and after—Thomas Boston, Samuel Petto, and A. H. Strong, for example—sought a similar approach.[15]

Interestingly, Edwards' views evolved as he composed subsequent "Miscellanies." Later entries reveal that he began to acknowledge some distinctions between the covenant of works and covenant of grace. This admission coincided with his developing interest in the relationship between the Old and New Testaments. In Miscellany no. 250, he admitted to differences in the way the Old Testament and New Testament present the covenant of works. By Miscellany no. 439, he conceded that dissimilarities exist between these two covenants. Most significant, Edwards slowly introduced conditional language when describing the importance of human faith. In Miscellany no. 299, he emphasized human responsibility by noting that the elect must offer their consent to enter a covenantal relationship with Christ. He changed this rhetoric in no. 439, openly describing faith as "primarily the condition of the covenant of grace."[16]

These changes reveal tensions in Edwards' thought but at this stage mark no explicit rejection of the claims found in Miscellany no. 2. As he experimented with his theology in his (mostly private) notebook, Edwards considered potential avenues for improvement. However, more extensive modifications would in forthcoming "Miscellanies."

Edwards' Mature Covenant Theology in the "Miscellanies"

Edwards developed a more sophisticated framework for his covenant theology in Miscellany no. 617.[17] He offered complex arguments for God's covenantal arrangements, addressing the covenant of redemption with a considerable degree of interest. He also frequently used conditional language when discussing the covenant of grace.

Knijff accounts for these developments by noting that Edwards' concerns changed by 1733, near the time that he composed Miscellany no. 617. No longer fearing just Arminianism or Neonomianism, he now dreaded the rise of Antinomianism. Sensing this new threat, he sought a covenant theology that could account for human responsibility so that he might promote a commitment to personal holiness.[18]

Edwards' more refined covenant theology appears scattered throughout various entries in his latter "Miscellanies," but his position can receive easy systematization by examining its most significant feature—the covenant of redemption.

A focus on the covenant of redemption allowed Edwards to smooth the tensions that emerged in his thought when he began to employ conditional language. The covenant of redemption provided him a theological backdrop on which he could build a more intricate version of the covenant of grace that could account for his growing acceptance of conditionality. Edwards expressed hope that his method might "reconcile the difference between those divines that [think] the covenant of grace is not conditional as to us ... and those that think that faith is the proper condition of the covenant of grace."[19] In making this statement, he perhaps had his own thought in mind as well as the thought of his contemporaries.

He depicted the covenant of redemption and the covenant of grace as distinct covenants that function closely together. While both covenants pertain to redemption, the covenant of grace remains "properly a different covenant" from the covenant of redemption.[20] It involves a compact between believers and Christ and does not technically include the father.

In Miscellany no. 617, Edwards explained, "There is doubtless a difference between the covenant that God makes with Christ and his people [the covenant of redemption], considered as one, and the covenant of Christ and his people between themselves [the covenant of grace]."[21] In the covenant of redemption, the Father only covenants with Christ; the elect are included in this interaction in virtue of the fact that Christ stands as their representative. In the covenant of grace, Christ only covenants with his people; the Father does not directly involve himself directly.

This division allowed Edwards to envision salvation as simultaneously unconditional and conditional while avoiding contradiction. The covenant of redemption presents the procurement of salvation as contingent solely on Christ's obedience to the Father and not on humanity's ability to meet the condition of faith. Edwards explained, "Faith is not properly the condition of this covenant, but the righteousness of Christ."[22] The covenant of grace, by contrast, "is conditional to us: the proper condition of it, which is a yielding to Christ's wooings and accepting his offers and closing with him as a redeemer and spiritual husband, is to be performed by us."[23]

Miscellany no. 1091 outlined how these two covenant perspectives may overlap in the economy of salvation. Discussing the covenant of redemption, Edwards argued that the Father not only proposed

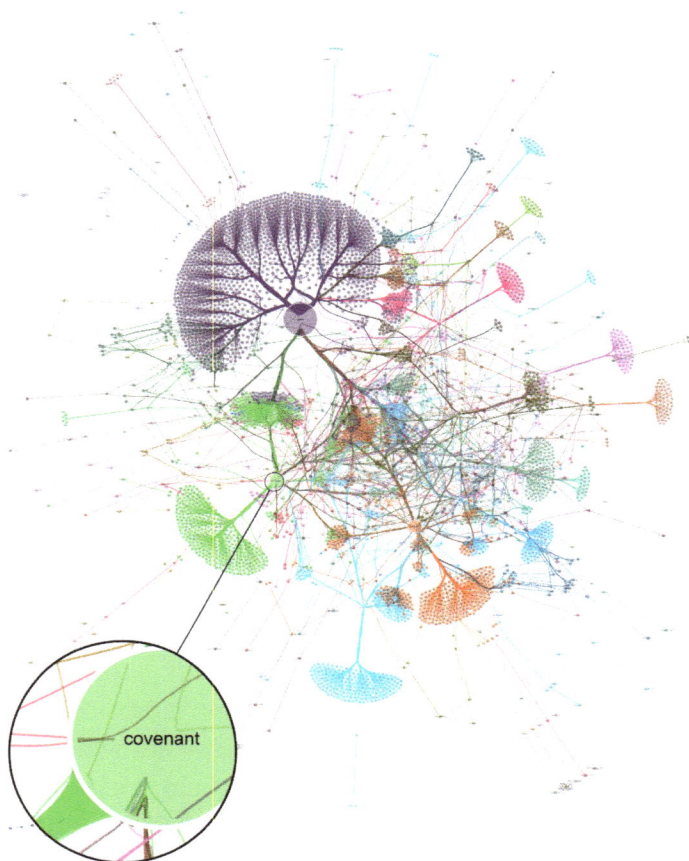

COVENANT, GRACE, MARRIAGE, and REDEMPTION—*a map of covenant, covenanted, covenanting, covenantings, covenants, disgrace, disgraced, disgraceful, disgraces, grace, gracefulness, graceless, graces, intermarriages, intermarried, marriage, marriageable, marriages, married, marries, marrieth, redeem, redeemed, redeemeds, redeemedst, redeemer, redeemers, redeemership, redeeming, redeems, redemption, redemptions, uncovenanted, unmarried with interconnections and page locations in WJE 1–26.*

that Christ live a righteous life and die a sacrificial death to fulfill the covenant of works. The Father also promised to Christ blessings related to salvation—justification, eternal life, and entrance into God's kingdom. Interestingly, because Christ represented the elect in this covenant, Edwards claimed that the Father could make these promises not to Christ only but also to "Christ mystical," the church.

These promises were significant, even though at that this stage the elect did not yet exist. Edwards alleged that the Father's promises "were made to the whole mystical Christ," though "the whole of Christ mystical was not yet in being" and its human members only existed "in God's decrees." Nevertheless, given the elect's non-existence, the Father could only make these promises "virtually."[24] The promises were latent and not yet effectual.

The covenant of grace serves as the means by which the elect actualize these promises. This covenant between Christ and his church—a covenant that Edwards often described as a marriage—is the way that Christ's church "is united to him, is interested [in] him, and becomes his spouse and mystical body."[25]

Faith is this covenant's condition. Through divinely enabled faith, the elect consent to enter the covenant of grace and receive its benefits, just as the partners in a marriage ceremony consent to join in matrimony. Finding the illustration of marriage suitable for his purposes, Edwards used it often. The concept of a marriage featured prominently in such "Miscellanies" as nos. 617, 825, and 919.[26]

With this construction of covenant theology, Edwards attempted to synthesize the competing theological interests present in his system. The covenant of redemption allowed him to preserve salvation as a free and gracious gift promised and obtained by God. The covenant of grace allowed him to present the elect as receiving this gift through the instrumentality of human faith. Edwards' Gospel message could, therefore, address both divine grace and the need for human response.

Conclusion

The covenant theology found in Edwards' early "Miscellanies" sought to highlight divine grace. Edwards highlighted Christ as the one who fulfilled the covenant of works, and he rejected rhetoric that might make salvation appear too contingent on human response. This approach departed from more typical accounts of covenant theology by dismissing conditional language and by formulating a modest covenant structure that focused exclusively on Christ as the fulfiller of the covenant of works. Nevertheless, it did not represent a radical break from the tradition.

Edwards' later covenant theology displayed a more nuanced perspective. In post-1733 entries, Edwards sought to maintain attention to divine grace while leaving room for human action. He made use of the covenant of redemption to describe salvation as a free and unilateral work of God, and he refined his understanding of the covenant of grace to account for faith as a condition for salvation.

The structure of Edwards' more mature covenant theology comes closer to that formulated by many of his theological contemporaries. His willingness to accept a three-covenant structure—the covenant of works, the covenant of redemption, and the covenant of grace—as well as his use of conditional language in the reception of salvation, placed him more in line with the covenant theology found in such confessional standards as the Westminster Confession of Faith.

Nevertheless, the changes he brought to his theology might have been more formal and structural than substantive.[27] His earlier version of covenant theology did not wholly reject the importance of faith; it only dismissed conditional language when attached to the covenant of works. The more settled covenant theology displayed in his later writings prioritized the covenant of redemption but did not explicitly reject Christ's fulfillment of the covenant of works—an essential feature of his earlier publications. In both versions of his covenant theology, he sought to find the right balance between divine grace and human action.

Examinations of Edwards' covenant theology have relevance for modern scholarship. The digital exploration of Edwards' "Miscellanies" led by Robert Boss reveals that Edwards connected his remarks about divine covenants to his understanding of justification by faith, an aspect of his thought that generates considerable debate.[28] A survey of Edwards' covenant theology in relation to his views on justification by faith falls outside of the purview of this chapter, but modern considerations of Edwards' views on faith and justification would do well to give attention to his covenant theology.

Notes

[1] See, for example, the introductory chapter found in Michael Horton, *Introducing Covenant Theology* (Grand Rapids: Baker, 2006).

[2] See Perry Miller, *Errand into the Wilderness* (Cambridge: Belknap Press, 1956), 98. Also idem., *The New England Mind: The Seventeenth Century* (Cambridge: Belknap, 1983), 395.

[3] Peter DeJong, *The Covenant Idea in New England Theology, 1620–1847* (Grand Rapids: Eerdmans, 1945).

[4] An important article in starting this correction was C. Conrad Cherry, "The Puritan Notion of the Covenant in Jonathan Edwards' Doctrine of Faith," *Church History* 34, no. 3 (1965): 328–41.

[5] Bogue's work helped to start new conversations about the relationship between Edwards' covenant theology and his soteriology: Carl W. Bogue, *Jonathan Edwards and the Covenant of Grace* (Eugene: Pickwick, 2009; repr. Cherry Hill: Mack Publishing Company, 1975).

[6] For historical development of the covenant of works, see Robert Letham, "The Foedus Operum: Some Factors Accounting For Its Development," *The Sixteenth Century Journal* 14, no. 4 (1983): 457–467.

[7] Westminster Confession of Faith, 7.3. For relevant resources on the covenant of grace, consider John von Rohr, *The Covenant of Grace in Puritan Thought* (Atlanta: Scholars Press, 1986), 53–86.

[8] Perhaps Edwards' most detailed remarks about the covenant of redemption appear in Miscellany no. 1062. Space constraints preclude a detailed examination of his statements, but see the helpful survey provided in Sang Hyun Lee, "Editor's Introduction," in *WJE* 21: 28–34. Consider also Reita Yazawa, "Covenant of Redemption in the Theology of Jonathan Edwards: The Nexus Between the Immanent and the Economic Trinity" (PhD diss., Calvin Theological Seminary, 2013). Interestingly, Edwards introduced the concept of the covenant of redemption in his earlier writings—specifically Miscellany 222—but did not develop it until much later.

[9]"Miscellanies," no. 2 in *WJE* 13:197.

[10]"Miscellanies," no. 2 in *WJE* 13:198–99.

[11]"Miscellanies," no. 2 in *WJE* 13:198–99.

[12]"Miscellanies," no. 2 in *WJE* 13:198–99.

[13]E.g., Thomas Boston, *The Whole Works of Thomas Boston,* ed. Samuel M'Millan (Aberdeen: George and Robert King, 1850), 8:398.

[14]Lachman rightly notes that the disagreement between theologians who empha-sized conditionality and the theologians who rejected this terminology was "largely verbal" and that there was often "no significant doctrinal difference" between the positions. See David C. Lachman, *The Marrow Controversy* (Edinburgh: Rutherford House, 1988), 37. Nevertheless, some thinkers did take denial of conditions too far by minimizing human agency. Consider the controversial work Tobias Crisp. E.g., David Parnham, "The Covenantal Quietism of Tobias Crisp," *Church History* 75, no. 3 (2006): 511–543.

[15]Three-fold and two-fold approaches to covenant theology exist in the tradition. Three-fold approaches posit a covenant of works, covenant of grace, and a covenant of redemption. Two-fold approaches posit a covenant of works and then place the covenant of grace and redemption closely together—often doing so to demonstrate Christ's fulfillment of the covenant of works. Edwards' proposal comes closest to the latter category. For the distinction between three-fold and two-fold approaches, see J. V. Fesko, *The Covenant of Redemption: Origins, Development, and Reception* (Göttingen: Vandenhoeck & Ruprecht, 2016), 72.

[16]"Miscellanies," no. 439 in *WJE* 13:489.

[17]The first contemporary researchers to examine Edwards' covenant theology in a detailed way gave the impression that Edwards' convictions remained consistent. See, for example, Bogue, *Jonathan Edwards and the Covenant of Grace.* Recent surveys, however, demonstrate that Edwards' covenant theology developed over time. McClymond and McDermott argue this development occurred in three stages in Michael J. McClymond and Gerald R. McDermott, *The Theology of Jonathan Edwards* (Oxford: Oxford University Press, 2011), 324–327. Knijff more persuasively argues for two stages of development. I assume his approach here. See Cornelis van der Knijff, "The Development in Jonathan Edwards' Covenant View," *Jonathan Edwards Studies* 3, no. 2 (2013): 269–281. Consider also the helpful Cornelis van der Knijff and Willem van Vlastuin, "Why Edwards Did Not Understand Thomas Boston: A Comparison of Their Views on the Covenants," *Jonathan Edwards Studies* 5, no. 1 (2015): 44–57.

[18]Knijff, "The Development in Jonathan Edwards' Covenant View," 270.

[19]"Miscellanies," no. 1091, in *WJE* 20:478.

[20]"Miscellanies," no. 1091, in *WJE* 20:478. For a passage in which Edwards closely connects the covenant of redemption and the covenant of grace in the economy of salvation, consider Miscellany no. 919. In that entry, Edwards makes a distinction between these two covenants but also notes that because the covenant of grace

emerges from the covenant of redemption the covenants are related. Consider similar remarks that appear in "Miscellanies," nos. 617 and 1039.

[21]"Miscellanies," no. 617, in *WJE* 18:148.

[22]"Miscellanies," no. 1091, in *WJE* 20:478.

[23]"Miscellanies," no. 1091, in *WJE* 20:478.

[24]"Miscellanies," no. 1091, in *WJE* 20:475–76.

[25]"Miscellanies," no. 1091, in *WJE* 20:477.

[26]The illustration of a human marriage appears so often in Edwards' remarks about the covenant of grace that McClymond and McDermott conclude that Edwards proposed four covenants: the covenant of works, the covenant of redemption, the covenant of grace, and a marriage covenant between Christ and believers. Edwards' willingness to place these covenants together and occasional even use their various titles almost synonymously can create confusion. However, I maintain that Edwards only intended three covenants: a covenant of works that Christ fulfilled, a covenant of redemption between the Father and Christ as the representative of the elect, and a covenant of grace that Edwards sometimes referred to as a marriage covenant. C.f., McClymond and McDermott, *The Theology of Jonathan Edwards,* 326.

[27]See footnotes thirteen and fourteen above. The differences between the type of covenant theology promoted in Edwards' earlier writings and more traditional outlines of covenant theology were not considerable.

[28]For "Miscellanies" that connect covenant theology with justification by faith, consider 36, 315, 412, 415, 416, 474, 504, 847. For an overview of modern debates over Edwards' views on justification by faith, consider Fesko, *Covenant of Redemption,* 127–39.

EDWARDS' VISION OF THE MILLENNIUM

Victor Zhu

Christ's exaltation and ascension to heaven is spoken of as cause of exceeding joy to his church. It was an instating him in his throne in his people's name. 'Tis a glorious privilege to the church to have their Mediator in heaven, in the holy of holies, at the right hand of God; it tends to strengthen their faith, and greatly to encourage and comfort them. No saint that considers things aright will desire that he should leave heaven.

— Jonathan Edwards, *Miscellany no. 827*

DURING THE PERIOD BETWEEN the Reformation and Post-Reformation (sixteenth to eighteenth centuries), the history of millennial thought witnessed a dramatic transformation in both hermeneutical interpretation and theological awareness. While there were several hundred treatments of Revelation flourishing in European countries in the sixteenth and seventeenth centuries,[1] the mainstream interpretation of the millennium was moving from the symbolic to the literal. Consequently, while many reformers in the early 16th century turned away from the future and earthly millennium, it enjoyed a renaissance from the late sixteenth century and flourished among the Puritans in the seventeenth and eighteenth centuries. As a typical example of this paradigm shift, Edwards was expecting an earthly and future millennium that had a specified duration. In this essay, his millennial vision is presented according to his Miscellany entries 26, 356, 740, 756, 776, 827, 1131 and 1224.

In contrast to Calvin and other early reformers who firmly rejected the view of the terrestrial millennium, Edwards advocated a millennium that would definitely be inaugurated on earth. In the millennium, "the *whole earth* may be as one community, one body in Christ," he asserted.[2] And it would be in *"this lower world"* that the saints would spend significantly more time on spiritual business than their ordinary things.[3] And the divine knowledge will be "diffused *all over the world*," including "the most barbarous nations" and the "ignorant heathen lands."[4] Edwards wrote,

> How happy will that state be, when neither divine nor human learning shall be confined and imprisoned within only two or three nations of Europe, but shall be diffused *all over the world,* and *this lower world* shall be all over covered with light, the various parts of it mutually enlightening each other; when the most barbarous nations shall become as bright and polite as England...[5]

Secondly, Edwards saw the millennium as being an actual period in a future timeline. It is a significant fact that Edwards insisted that the phrase "a thousand years" in Revelation (Rev. 20:2) should be "literally understood."[6] In this sense, for him the duration of the millennium would be approximately one thousand years. In his "Miscellanies" entry 1224, "MILLENNIUM, or sabbatism of the world," Edwards observed that it would *not* be much more than a thousand years. Otherwise, in a prolonged millennium, God's mighty work and his glory will not be so manifest. Edwards made the following four assertions:

1. Humankind would forget the corruption of nature, would be insensible of the dreadful ruin sin has brought on the nature

of man, would not be so sensible of the great benefit of the redemption of Christ.

2. The curse of God on this world, consisting in the calamities of it, would not be very sensible. The world would scarcely appear as a great wilderness in the way to a land of rest. God's people would be under great temptation not to behave themselves as pilgrims and strangers on earth, forget to live as not of the world and to lay up treasure in heaven.

3. 'Tis not probable that so much of the Scripture would have been calculated for the church in a suffering state, and both for the church and the world in a state of so great pollution, temptation and danger.

4. The distinguishing grace of God in election would grow much out of sight.[7]

In another entry to the "Miscellanies," numbered 836, Edwards offered more reasons why he thought the millennium should be around one thousand years. In short, he maintained that it is by God's wisdom that the millennium would be set to an actual one thousand years. In this way, the earth will be more appropriately preserved for its created residents. More importantly, God's glory and his grace in creation and redemption will be more evidently manifested to forgetful humankind.[8]

Nevertheless, Edwards was aware that the duration of the millennium would not necessary be exactly one thousand years. In this sense, it would be even more difficult to predicate the historical point of its beginning and ending. He wrote,

When the duration of the glorious times of the church on earth after the fall of Antichrist is spoken of in the twentieth chapter of Revelation as being a thousand years, the words are to be literally understood that it will be about that space of time, though perhaps it will not be so precisely; and if [it] be so precisely, *it will probably be difficult precisely to fix the beginning, and so the end of it.*[9]

Despite this, in his notes on Revelation 20 in "Notes on the Apocalypse" (1748), Edwards assumed that the millennium would start in the year 2000 and revealed how he calculated that.[10] In so doing, Edwards departed from his Puritan colleagues, including John Cotton (1585–1652), Samuel Willard (1640–1707), Increase Mather (1639–1723), Cotton Mather (1663–1728) and Benjamin Coleman (1673–1747), who upheld the view of the imminent millennium.

Thirdly, Edwards believed that in the millennium, Christ would reign on earth by His Spirit while His body would remain in heaven.[11] Edwards' standpoint can be seen as his response to one of the millennial controversies among the Puritans. There was a dispute over whether Christ would, in the millennium, reign in his physical presence or in a spiritual form. Some believed that Christ would reign in his spiritual presence in the church. These include Cotton Mather, Daniel Whitby (1638–1725), John Eliot (1604–1690) and Thomas Shepard (1605–1649). For instance, Cotton Mather insisted that the millennium would emerge from the faithful preaching by the Spirit-filled ministers rather than from Christ's personal and physical presence.[12] However, their opponents such as John Davenport (1597—1670) argued that Christ, in his physical and visible presence, would appear at the beginning of the millennium and reign together with the saints.[13]

In his Miscellany entry on "Millennium" (no. 827), Edwards clearly presented his view of Christ's spiritual reign on earth. He started by claiming: "It is a greater privilege to the church on earth to have Christ, her head and Redeemer, in heaven at the right hand of God, than for him to be in this lower world."[14] Edwards sought to justify this position from the perspective of the divine glorification. He argued that God's glory would be more effectively manifested by Christ's spiritual presence in His churches. If, on the other hand, Christ comes down and physically dwells on earth during the millennium, it would be "a second humiliation, a descending from a higher glory to a lower."[15] Furthermore, Christ's spiritual reign will be more beneficial for the church, because that would be a "greater privilege to the church on earth to have Christ, her head and Redeemer, in heaven at the right hand of God," and because it would "strengthen their faith, and greatly to encourage and comfort them."[16] Thus God will be greatly glorified in the church. "Christ's reigning on earth by his Spirit," Edwards asserted, "is more *glorious* and *happy* for his church than his human presence would be."[17] By insisting on Christ's spiritual reign in the millennium, Edwards rejected John Davenport's view and followed that of John Cotton, Daniel Whitby and Cotton Mather. In fact, Edwards was very confident in his stand on Christ's spiritual reign and went further by saying that there should be *no* Christian who "considers things aright will desire that he [Christ] should leave heaven" before the close of the millennium.[18]

Furthermore, Edwards was actually expecting an inchoate, or an imperfect millennium. For Edwards, the millennium would be "a mixture of the saints in heaven ruling through their spiritual successors over their mortal and sinful counterparts on earth."[19] It should be noted, however, that Edwards was not the only one who held this view. Many Puritan divines in the seventeenth century, including Joseph Mede (1586–1639), John Cotton, Thomas Shepard and Cotton Mather expected an inchoate millennium.[20] For them, before the second resurrection at the end of the millennium, the saved nations were not free from imperfection of the fallen world. Instead, saints and sinners would still suffer from mortality, sin, disease and death. However, Edwards had a much more promising perspective on the millennium. in his other sermons and in his "Miscellanies," he defined this period as "the glorious millennium."[21] It will be the "prosperous, glorious state of the church,"[22] ushering in the "eternal state of the church's consummate rest and glory" in heaven.[23] While there is sin and death, the inhabitants on the earth will enjoy a life of abundant material and spiritual blessings. As Edwards said, they will live "under such great universal and uninterrupted prosperity, health and long life."[24] More importantly, in his view, this will be a long time for

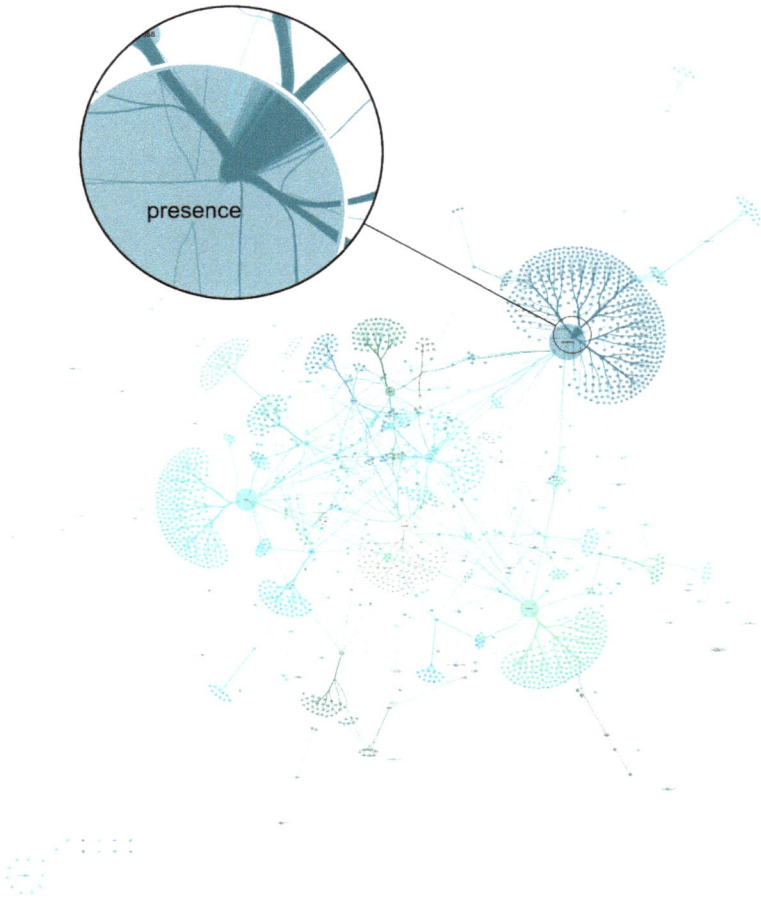

ASCENSION, MEDIATOR, MILLENNIUM, PRESENCE, *and* REIGN—*a map of ascend, ascendance, ascendancy, ascendant, ascended, ascendent, ascendeth, ascending, ascends, ascension, ascent, intermediation, mediate, mediates, mediating, mediation, mediations, mediator, mediatorial, mediators, millennial, millennium, millenniums, omnipresence, presence, reascended, reign, reigned, reigners, reigneth, reigning, reigns with interconnections and page locations in WJE 1–26.*

several generations, and those living on earth will live in a world freed from both natural and man-made catastrophes. They will not be "diminished with wars, pestilences and other desolating calamities which now waste humankind."[25]

Fourthly, believing Christ would reign in His spiritual presence, Edwards was convinced that the millennium would start before Christ's future physical return. Again, this is how he responded to the controversy over the millennial chronology in his time. While the future millennium became prevalent among the Puritans, there were evident disagreements. Some Puritan divines still insisted on the *preterist* system of Augustine. This camp includes Thomas Parker (1595–1677), who followed John Bale (1495–1563), and Thomas Brightman (1562–1607). These authors asserted that the events recorded in Revelation 20 had already taken place at certain times in history; therefore, Satan's binding was a past event. For them, Satan's binding probably began when Constantine was crowned as the first Christian emperor of Rome (ca. 306) and ended with Wycliffe's reformation (ca. 1300). Thus, Christ's millennial reign in his spiritual presence started from the year 1300 and was already in progress in the lifetime of these preterists.[26]

The followers of the *futurist* system, however, would not accept this assertion. They all expected a millennium arriving in the future, but fell into at least two camps. Some like Cotton Mather in his mature eschatology represented in his *Threefold Paradise* (1727) may be regarded as pre-millennialists if we categorize them with nineteenth-century labels. According to Cotton Mather, Christ will physically appear at the beginning of the millennium to inaugurate this golden age, and he will come at the end of the millennium for the Final Judgment.[27] Others, including Daniel Whitby, Joseph Bellamy (1719–1790) and Samuel Hopkins (1721–1803) were post-millennialists. They believed that Christ would not appear *until* the end of the millennium. For them, with the church's effort in her spiritual improvement and social reform, the millennium will be ushered in *before* Christ finally descends for the final judgment.[28] Undoubtedly, Edwards belonged to this camp.

Nevertheless, while Edwards preferred post-millennialism, his millennialism is not exactly in accordance with what is believed by the modern post-millennialists. For one thing, he did not accept the strict futurist interpretation of Revelation. In fact, he often took the preterist approach in interpreting certain prophecies as the symbolic representation of actual historical events. For instance, he viewed the martyrdom of the two witnesses in Revelation 11 as the persecution that fell upon the church during the Reformation, and their resurrection as Antichrist's failure to reverse the Reformation.[29] For another, he argued in *A History of the Work of Redemption,* that the millennium would be the *third* coming of Christ to set up his kingdom "at the destruction of Antichrist."[30] As for the other comings, the first is "Christ's appearing . . . in the apostles' days," the second is "that which was accomplished in Constantine's time in the destruction of the heathen Roman empire," and the fourth is Christ's coming to the last judgment at the end of the millennium.[31] Edwards' assertion of Christ's four comings actually ensures that the distinction between premillennialism and post-millennialism loses most of its pertinence, as Michael McClymond observes.[32]

Finally, Edwards stressed the eschatological restoration of Israel in his anticipation of the millennium. For him, in the gospel time, the Christian church inherited all the promises and prophecies to the people of Israel. These promises are mainly "concerning their future prosperity and glory."[33] However, this is only God's temporary arrangement during the gospel time. God would fulfill His promises to the Jews more conspicuously and remarkably when they are Christianized, Edwards claimed.[34] In this sense, the seeming rejection of Jews actually is God's way to bring them closer to Him. Edwards stated,

> God has not cast off the seed of Abraham and Israel now in the gospel times in no wise, but hath brought them *nearer* to himself, and hath, according to frequent

prophecies of gospel times, abundantly increased their blessings and the manifestations of his favor to them.[35]

Therefore, Edwards was confident that Israel would be restored after the restoration of the Christian church. This restoration will be a national conversion and reparation of the people of Israel. "When the greater part of the nation of the Jews were broken off by unbelief," he insisted, "the seed of Israel were no more cast off then than in the time of the captivity of Israel and Judah into Assyria and Babylon."[36]

Notes

[1]Douglas A. Sweeney, *Edwards the Exegete: Biblical Interpretation and Anglo-Protestant Culture on the Edge of the Enlightenment* (New York: Oxford University Press, 2016), 164. See also Bernd Engler et al, "Transformation of Millennial Thought in America, 1630-1860," in *Millennial Thought in America: Historical and Intellectual Contexts, 1630-1860,* eds. Bernd Engler et al., 9-37 (Trier: WVT Wissenschaftlicher Verlag Trier, 2002), 11.

[2]"Miscellanies," no. 262, in *WJE* 13:369. Emphasis added.

[3]"Miscellanies," no. 26, in *WJE* 13:212. Emphasis added.

[4]"Miscellanies," no. 26, in *WJE* 13:212. Emphasis added.

[5]"Miscellanies," no. 26, in *WJE* 13:212. Emphasis added.

[6]"Miscellanies," no. 836, in *WJE* 20:50.

[7]*WJE* 23:156.

[8]See "Miscellanies," no. 836, in *WJE* 20:50–52.

[9]"Miscellanies," no. 836, in *WJE* 20:50. Emphasis added.

[10]Edwards wrote, "There are these remarkable periods of time: when Abraham was called, in the year of the world 2000; Solomon's glorious kingdom settled, and temple finished, in the year of the world 3000; Christ born in the year 4000; and the millennium to begin in the year 6000." See *WJE* 5:135.

[11]"Miscellanies," no. 827, in *WJE* 18:537.

[12]J. F. Maclear, "New England and the Fifth Monarchy: The Quest for the Millennium in Early American Puritanism," *The William and Mary Quarterly* 32, no. 2 (1975): 233. See also Joel R. Beeke and Mark Jones *A Puritan Theology: Doctrine for Life* (Grand Rapids, MI: Reformation Heritage Books, 2012), 780–81.

[13]Reiner Smolinski, "Apocalypticism in Colonial North America," in Apocalypticism in the Modern Period and the Contemporary Age, *The Encyclopedia of Apocalypticism,* 36–71 (New York: Continuum, 1999), 44, 49.

[14]"Miscellanies," no. 827, in *WJE* 18:537.

[15]"Miscellanies," no. 827, in *WJE* 18:537.

[16]"Miscellanies," no. 827, in *WJE* 18:537.

[17]"Miscellanies," no. 827, in *WJE* 18:537. Emphasis added.

[18]"Miscellanies," no. 827, in *WJE* 18:537.

[19]Smolinski, "Apocalypticism in Colonial North America," 59.

[20]Smolinski, "Apocalypticism in Colonial North America," 41–50.

[21]"Miscellanies," no. 702, in *WJE* 18:289.

[22]*WJE* 22:369.

[23]"Miscellanies," no. 702, in *WJE* 18:289. See also *WJE* 9:509.

[24]"Miscellanies," no. 836, in *WJE* 20:51.

[25]"Miscellanies," no. 836, in *WJE* 20:51.

[26]Smolinski, "Apocalypticism in Colonial North America," 38–39, 45.

[27]Smolinski, "Apocalypticism in Colonial North America," 39, 49.

[28]Smolinski, "Apocalypticism in Colonial North America," 39–40. See also, Sweeney, *Edwards the Exegete,* 350, n. 4.

[29]*WJE* 5:105. See also "Miscellanies," no. uu, *WJE* 13:191.

[30]*WJE* 9:351.

[31]*WJE* 9:351.

[32]Michael J. McClymond, *Encounters with God: An Approach to the Theology of Jonathan Edwards* (New York: Oxford University Press, 1998) 73.

[33]"Miscellanies," no. 597, in *WJE* 18:131.

[34]"Miscellanies," no. 658, in *WJE* 18:198.

[35]"Miscellanies," no. 649, in *WJE* 18:189.

[36]"Miscellanies," no. 649, in *WJE* 18:189.

A Millennial Vision of One Glorious and Amiable Society

Bonghyun Yoo

'Tis probable that this world shall be more like heaven in the millennium in this respect, that contemplative and spiritual employments, and those things that more directly concern the mind and religion, will be more the saints' ordinary business than now.

— Jonathan Edwards, *Miscellany no. 262*

THIS ESSAY IS DESIGNED to provide a brief overview of Jonathan Edwards' postmillennialism, especially its elementary parts, so as to help readers clarify his postmillennial thought scattered throughout a number of his miscellaneous notebooks. After looking at the ideas from which Edwards developed his millennial theology and its impact on American society later, the essay focuses on the exegesis of "Miscellanies" no. 262, cross-referencing it with one of his well-known sermon "Heaven is a World of Love." This study offers readers a helpful introduction to his vision of the millennial society as an earthly mirror of the heavenly realities.

Eschatology never played a peripheral role in the theology of Jonathan Edwards (1703–1758), an eighteenth-century New England

Puritan pastor and revivalist.[1] Like many of his Puritan forefathers and successors, Edwards was significantly interested in the millennium (Rev 20).[2] Indeed, Edwards believed in a millennial society for a literal period of one thousand years, anticipating that it would be more glorious and more beautiful than ever before in history. For him, the society would be ushered in through a gradual and global expansion of the gospel throughout the whole globe. Edwards held an optimistic view with regard to the church, believing that she would be in a time of peace and prosperity during the period ("the Sabbatism, or the time of her rest") after her long premillennial tribulations ("a state of warfare, or her militant state").[3] Finally, Christ would return to bring the last judgment and consummate the work of redemption after the millennium.

The belief may seem to fit conventionally into what we today call postmillennialism. Modern scholars interpret him as a leading pioneer of postmillennialism. C. C. Goen, for example, names Edwards as "America's first major postmillennial thinker" in his article.[4] Yet several scholars challenge Goen's assessment, for the term postmillennialism only appeared in the context of contemporary debates regarding the millennium, and therefore it is not an appropriate categorization for Edwards' doctrine of the millennial kingdom.[5] For instance, John Wilson contends that Goen's interpretation of Edwards' eschatology is "filtered through the mindset of the Enlightenment," and it is highly likely to reduce his rich eschatological speculations to a rigid propositional statement for defending postmillennialism in the modern millennial debate.[6] Nonetheless, their concern to prioritise the historical and geographical context of Edwards' eschatology does not undermine the fact that "the religious and theological issues embraced by the term today preoccupied Edwards from his earliest recorded years until the close of his life."[7] Hence, using the term to describe Edwards' eschatology is relevant.

Postmillennialism in the late seventeenth to the nineteenth centuries was "the default setting" in developing and promulgating "the concept of a Christian America," a peculiar form of culturally co-opted

Christianity.[8] Along with many of his Puritan forebears, such as John Winthrop (1587–1649) and Cotton Mather (1663–1728), Edwards contributed to the project of making America a redemptive nation which would save others. That project was built on the narrative which was framed by the two Puritan experimental ideas—that is, providence and progress.[9]

The Puritan settlers in New England typologically understood their existence and significance in the process of transition from one place to another and settlement in the new territory.[10] Since the late seventeenth century, Puritans gradually began to speak of their identity as a newly chosen Israel and their agenda as a missional nation by connecting between scriptural prophecy and historical events in their day. In their mind, their nation was providentially chosen and directed by God to advance "the great work of redemption by Jesus Christ" across the globe.[11] Steven Studebaker comments as follows:

> The Puritans believed they were God's chosen people, God's new Israel. America was the new Canaan, the land of promise ... New England, and more broadly the "English Nation" had received the true Protestant religion from God and, consequently, bore special status relative to the other nations of the earth.[12]

Not only did eighteenth-century New England Puritans imagine their present circumstances typologically in connection with scriptural prophecy, they also began to predict their visionary constructions through similar methods.[13] Edwards was likewise one of the visionary ministers who believed that the millennium would probably take place in America.[14] The revivals during the Great Awakening were an especially visible sign of the anticipation of the coming millennium which might be initiated in the near future.

Along with their belief in providence, the idea of progress significantly impacted the formation of the narrative of America as a Christian nation. For Puritans, these ideas were indeed two sides of the same coin in which faith in the possibility of progress was deeply rooted in a confidence in the outcome of God's redemptive plans for the ages. Furthermore, the biblical-apocalyptic warfare motif between the kingdom of God and that of Satan in post-Reformation thought was a prevalent worldview for interpreting historical circumstances, both retrospectively and prospectively. The earlier idea of progress among Puritans was apparently theological in that they, as heirs to the Protestant Reformed tradition, had strong faith in the victory of God over Satan through the suffering and death of Christ and the outpouring of the Spirit. Edwards believed that these works already inaugurated the kingdom of God on earth spiritually, and now the church is waiting for her latter-day glory on earth and the final return of Christ.[15] Edwards became assured that the advances in the history of redemption in the world were direct and mighty works of God in Christ, and the idea was surely challenging to the deistic and mechanical philosophy of history which was popular among the American intellectuals of his day.[16]

In *History of the Work of Redemption,* Edwards defined the history of redemption as a synthetic series of three major ages, which first began with the fall, second the incarnation, and last the resurrection.[17] He then divided the post-resurrection history, namely, the third age, into four Christ-centered dispensations once more: (1) the Apostles' period, (2) the Constantinian period, (3) the millennial period, and (4) the final consummation.[18] In these various ages, "the kingdom of Christ is gradually prevailing and increasing by these several great stages of its fulfillment from the time of Christ's resurrection to the end of the world," as he argued.[19] Accordingly, the kingdom of Satan and its dominion over the world has gradually been defeated and demolished since the third age ushered in through the resurrection of Christ. The rebellious will finally face the judgment of God and eternally suffer in the lake of fire (Rev 20:10).[20]

The linear-progressive understanding of history laid the foundation for a "conversionist millennium" which expected "the gradual conversion of the world to Christianity" in the eighteenth century.[21] Not long after the death of Edwards, this sacred progressive view of history was transformed into an institutional cornerstone to understand how America's salvific manifest destiny and its secular values (e.g., eudaimonia, techno-scientific, and socio-political advances) could promote the end of God's earthly plan together. Michael Ashcraft describes the later development of progressive millennialism after the American Revolution as follows:

> After Americans won their independence, millennialism became rationalist and nationalistic. The millennial future was seen as a gradual improvement in worldly conditions ... Yet this was not a completely secular perspective. God was still quite real for these preachers, writers, and leaders, who assumed that the Bible was God's Word and that Providence guided human affairs.[22]

As a result, the postmillennial viewpoint became the functional model, in which the idea of progress in Puritan tradition was gradually assimilated or at least mixed into American civil millennialism in its eighteenth and nineteenth-century cultural soil.[23]

Although Edwards' eschatology in some way could help the emergence of American civil millennialism, significant discontinuities exist between the two streams of thought. Briefly, Edwards' prioritisation of spirituality over materiality in his metaphysics was irreversible; the former was greater and truer than the latter. Don Schweitzer explains, "For Edwards, physical realities were always representative of greater and more encompassing realities ... [he] believed that the political success or well-being of a community was related to its moral condition."[24] Second, the Holy Spirit remained the primary agent for the progress of American history in his eschatology.[25] Whereas socio-political and techno-scientific successes could be adopted as a means by which God advanced his kingdom, "they were not as powerful or important as the outpourings of the Holy Spirit that occurred in revivals and awakenings."[26] Last but not least, Edwards preserved various competing ideas, for instance, divine sovereignty and human responsibility, or this-worldliness and other-worldliness, without fusing the two in his eschatology.[27] Rather he attempted to counterpoise one with the other in tension. Kyung-Chul Jang contends that his eschatology "provides valuable building blocks to our theological search for a balanced eschatology."[28]

What then did Edwards think the coming millennium would specifically look like? In "Miscellanies" no. 262, he spoke of the world in the millennium as "more like heaven."[29] For Edwards, though heaven and earth were distinct realities or different parts of the universe, the two worlds were not entirely discrete but intersecting in the way the earthly society was seen as a proleptic manifestation of the heavenly one.[30] For example, Edwards correlated the millennial and the heavenly societies with regard to advanced human thought and spirituality in both knowing and loving God. As Jesus says, "If you know me, you will know my Father also" (John 14:7); genuine knowledge of God is thus articulated and determined by the character of the God who raised Christ from the dead. For the heavenly saints, hence, their beatific vision would increase as they participate in "the immediate presence of Christ" and "the most perfect intercourse with him."[31] Moreover, the saints will also grow in knowledge about the history of God's redemption as they witness what God is doing to redeem all elect souls in the earthly world. For Edwards, in fact, the history of redemption was the primordial idea within the Trinity before creation, and God created the tri-worlds—that is, heaven, earth, and even hell—as theatrical stages for the drama of redemption.[32] In other words, not only does history precede the worlds, it also intersects them. The knowledge of the heavenly saints thus covers such a vastly larger context of history.[33]

Edwards also described heaven as a place where the Trinity resides: "[T]here dwells God the Father, and so the Son, are united in infinitely dear and incomprehensible mutual love."[34] For Edwards, the love flows from the trinitarian society *ad intra* to the world *ad extra,* for instance, "so the Father of love, who loved the world that he gave his only begotten Son."[35] Hence, heaven is also a place for the redeemed filled by the salvific work of the Trinity in relation to the world.

The saints and the angels in heaven shall receive "an infinite and unchangeable act of love" of God and love him back (vertical).[36] They shall also be united in a mutual sharing of love with one another (horizontal); in this way, they become "one family in their heavenly Father's house."[37]

As McClymond and McDermott point out, there is "a surprising continuity" between the heavenly and the earthly societies.[38] The difference between the two is rather in the degree of perfection of truth and love than kind.[39] For instance, the millennial society will also be a mutual learning community across the globe.[40] Edwards wrote that "they shall join the forces of their minds in exploring the glories of the Creator."[41] Yet, according to Edwards, such an exploration for the knowledge of God will be facilitated through globalization in that valuable philosophical and religious resources will be transported and shared from "one end of the earth and another"—for instance, "Terra Australis Incognita" (a hypothetical southern continent), "Wild Tartary" (north-central Asia), and "Hottentots" (south-western Africa).[42] Moreover, Edwards further fleshed out that such an activity among the millennial saints will be their "ordinary business."[43] This globally "ordinary business" will be a direct outcome of "a more expedite and easy and safe communication" through the latest advances in transport networks. Edwards wrote that they would be far advanced over the eighteenth century's venerated technology for voyages across the ocean with "[t]he invention of the mariner's compass" in the Age of Discovery.[44]

Not only will the millennial saints be joined together in learning knowledge of God from and sharing it with one another, they will also be united in loving and serving God. "They shall all join the forces of their minds . . . their hearts in loving and adoring him, their hands in serving him, and their voices in making the world to ring with his praise."[45] In his famous sermon "Heaven is a World of Love," Edwards contended that the saints' life in the earthly world could mirror that of "the inhabitants of heaven" and enjoy "the foretastes of heavenly pleasures and delights" by continual and lively exercises

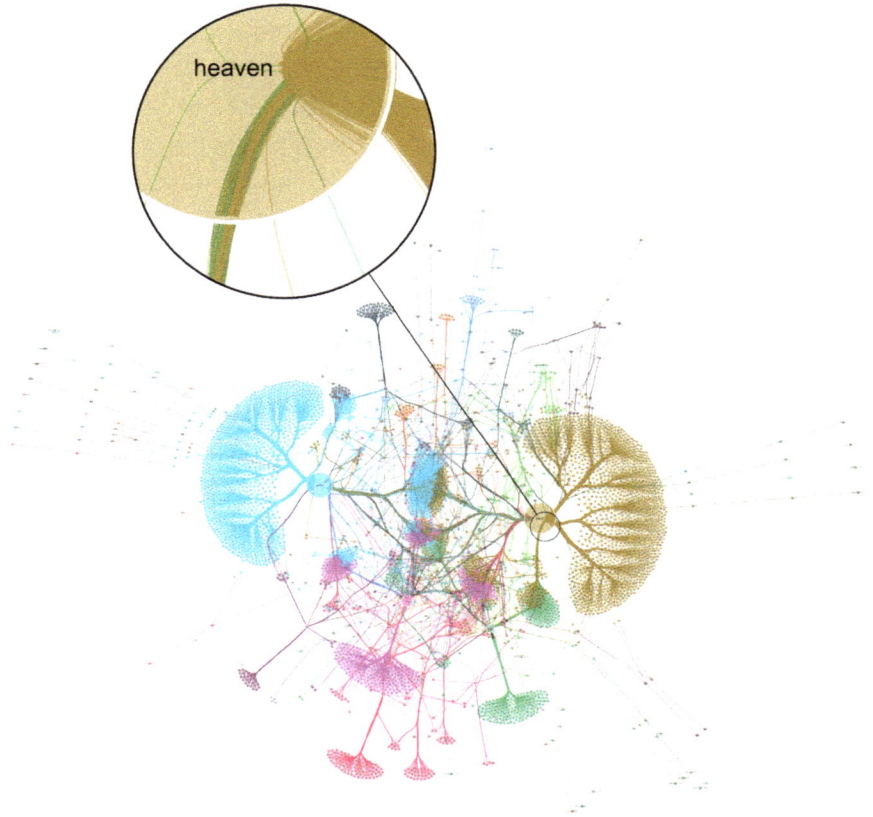

CONTEMPLATION, EMPLOYMENT, HEAVEN, MILLENNIUM, *and* SPIRITUAL—*a map of contemplate, contemplating, contemplation, contemplations, contemplative, contemplatively, employ, employed, employing, employment, employments, employs, heaven, heavenliness, heavenly, heavens, heavenward, heavenwards, millennial, millennium, millenniums, spiritual, spirituality, spiritualized, spiritually, spirituals with interconnections and page locations in WJE 1–26.*

of their love toward God and others.[46] "By living a life of love, you will be in the way to heaven. As heaven is a world of love, so that way to heaven is the way of love. This will best prepare you for heaven," as he closed the sermon.[47] Therefore, the millennial saints will be restless participants on their greatest voyage near to heaven, which is the new continent of love. This final sailing will involve exercising their holistic activities such as knowing (minds), loving (hearts), serving (hands), and praising (voices). As the saints and the angels will become "one family in their heavenly Father's house," for Edwards, the millennial saints on board ship will also be as "one community" heading for an increasing degree of perfection in their knowledge and love of God in the new creation.[48]

Notes

[1] See Michael J. McClymond and Gerald R. McDermott, *The Theology of Jonathan Edwards* (New York: Oxford University Press, 2012), 579. They write as follows: "For many thinkers in the Reformed tradition, eschatology was a theological appendage. But for Edwards eschatology was both central and integral to this thought. His philosophy of history presumed that God directed every atom in the universe toward a cosmic conclusion. His biblical typology suggested that all of nature and history teem with types of future, end-time realities." An example of this is that he extensively commented on the Book of Revelation and made this commentary a single volume.

[2] In his *Personal Narrative,* readers can identify a few of Edwards' earliest observations and expectations on the millennium. See *WJE* 16:797–800. "And my mind has been much entertained and delighted, with the Scripture promises and prophecies, of the future glorious advancement of Christ's kingdom on earth," as he wrote.

[3] *WJE* 5:178–79.

[4] C. C. Goen, "Jonathan Edwards: A New Departure in Eschatology." *Church History,* vol. 28, no. 1 (1959), 35–37, 38. See also Reiner Smolinski, "Apocalypticism in Colonial North America," in Stephen J. Stein, ed. *The Encyclopedia of Apocalypticism,* vol. 3 (New York: Continuum, 2000), 40.

[5] See Stephen J. Stein, "Editor's Introduction," in *WJE* 5:7 and "Eschatology," in Sang Hyun Lee, ed., *The Princeton Companion to Jonathan Edwards* (Princeton, NJ: Princeton University, 2005), 226; John F. Wilson, "History, Redemption, and the Millennium," in Nathan O. Hatch and Harry S. Stout, eds., *Jonathan Edwards and the American Experience* (New York: Oxford University, 1988), 136; and James West Davidson, *The Logic of Millennial Thought: Eighteenth-Century New England* (New Haven: Yale University, 1988), 121; 131–32; 138.

[6] Wilson, "History, Redemption, and the Millennium," 135. For more information on the millennial debate, see Jürgen Moltmann, *The Coming of God: Christian Eschatology,* trans. Margaret Kohl (Minneapolis, MN: Fortress, 1996), 147. He points out that it is America in where the millennial distinction/debate between premillennialism and postmillennialism largely started.

[7] Stein, "Eschatology," 226.

[8] Michael Horton, "Eschatology," in Kelly M. Kapic and Bruce L. McCormack, eds., *Mapping Modern Theology: A Thematic and Historical Introduction* (Grand Rapids: Baker Academic, 2012), 382–83. Cheryl M. Peterson, *Who is the Church?: An Ecclesiology for the Twenty-First Century* (Minneapolis, MN: Fortress, 2013), 13.

[9] See Harry S. Stout, "The Puritans and Edwards," in Nathan O. Hatch and Harry S. Stout, eds., *Jonathan Edwards and the American Experience* (New York: Oxford University, 1988), 143; 157. Stout disagrees with the revisionist interpretation that attempts to distance Edwards from his Puritan predecessors by arguing that he was indeed "even more a Puritan than Miller or his revisionists concede." For Stout, for instance, Edwards' endeavour to follow the Puritan idea of federal/national covenant was evidently shown.

[10] According to Tibor Fabiny, the term "New England" standing in contrast to "Old" is typological *per se.* See his "Edwards and Biblical Typology," in Gerald R. McDermott, ed., *Understanding Jonathan Edwards: An Introduction to America's Theologian* (New York: Oxford University, 2009), 97. For more discussion on the typological tradition of early America, see also Ursula Brumm, *American Thought and Religious Typology* (New Brunswick: Rutgers University, 1970), 27.

[11] *WJE* 16:728.

[12] Steven M. Studebaker, *A Pentecostal Political Theology for American Renewal: Spirit of the Kingdoms, Citizens of the Cities* (New York: Palgrave Macmillan, 2016), 18.

[13] Mason I. Lowance, Jr., "Typology and Millennial Eschatology in Early New England," in Earl Miner, ed., *Literary Uses of Typology from the Late Middle Ages to the Present* (Princeton, NJ: Princeton University, 1977), 228. See Gerald R. McDermott, *One Holy and Happy Society: The Public Theology of Jonathan Edwards* (University Park, PA: The Pennsylvania State University, 1992), 42

[14] *WJE* 4:353. See Studebaker, *A Pentecostal Political Theology,* 20; Smolinski, "Apocalypticism in Colonial North America," 56; Lowance, "Typology and Millennial Eschatology," 262; and Jeffrey Rosario, "The Edwardsean Roots of Manifest Destiny." *Jonathan Edwards Studies* vol. 7, no. 2 (2017): 103.

[15] *WJE* 9:435.

[16] Stein, "Eschatology," 239

[17] *WJE* 9:352–53.

[18] *WJE* 9:351. See also McClymond and McDermott, *The Theology of Jonathan Edwards,* 574–75.

[19] *WJE* 9:354.

[20]Cf. Col 2:15. For Edwards, both heaven and hell are progressive places, and they will continue to exist to reveal the glory of God for eternity.

[21]W. Michael Ashcraft, "Progressive Millennialism," in Catherine Wessinger, ed., *The Oxford Handbook of Millennialism* (New York: Oxford University, 2011), 49.

[22]Ashcraft, "Progressive Millennialism," 50.

[23]See Ashcraft, "Progressive Millennialism," 50–55. Stein, "American Millennial Visions: Towards Construction of a New Architectonic of American Apocalypticism," in Abbas Amanat and Magus Bernhardsson, eds., *Imagining the End: Visions of Apocalypse from the Ancient Middle East to Modern America* (New York: I. B. Tauris, 2002), 199.

[24]Don Schweitzer, "Jonathan Edwards," in Kwok Pui-lan, Don H. Compier, and Jo-erg Rieger, eds. *Empire and Christian Tradition: New Readings of Classical Theologians* (Minneapolis, MN: Fortress, 2007), 244; 246.

[25]See *WJE* 4:280 and *WJE* 9:460.

[26]Schweitzer, "Jonathan Edwards," 247. See also Stein, "Eschatology," 239. Analogically, when God emits energy, the Spirit is the divine enabling to bear fruits in season (e.g., the periods of Constantine, the Reformation, and the Great Awakening) and transforms the wilderness into a garden (e.g., the millennium), as if energy emanating from the sun hits the earth and starts life.

[27]Jang Kyoung-Chul, "The Logic of Glorification: The Destiny of the Saints in the Eschatology of Jonathan Edwards." PhD diss., Princeton Theological Seminary, 1994, 4.

[28]Jang, "The Logic of Glorification," 4. For much debate on the thesis among scholars, see Stein, "American Millennial Visions," 196–99 and McDermott, One Holy and Happy Society, 37–43.

[29]"Miscellanies," no. 262, in *WJE* 13:369.

[30]See Owen Strachan, "Heaven," in Harry S. Stout, ed., *The Jonathan Edwards Encyclopedia* (Grand Rapids: Eerdmans, 2017), 280. He explains that "heaven was a living reality for Edwards. The Christian did not merely *go there* at the end of life; the Christian lived with heaven constantly on the mind, the doctrine of eternal glory filling each earthly moment with purpose, shaping faith and practice." See also Gerald R. McDermott and Ronald Story, *The Other Jonathan Edwards: Selected Writings on Society, Love, and Justice* (Amherst: University of Massachusetts, 2015), 90. They also describe Edwards' prospect of a great millennial era as "a time of heavenly peace and joy for roughly one thousand years." See also Hans Boersma, "The "Grand Medium": An Edwardsean Modification of Thomas Aquinas on the Beatific Vision." *Modern Theology* vol. 33, no. 2 (2017): 188. To borrow from Hans Boersma's idea, Edwards' theology of heaven is sacramental in terms of its continuity with the present life, and he explains that it can be understood as "the sacramental presence of our supernatural end within the created realities around us."

[31]*WJE* 25:237. For further information on Edwards' vision of heaven, see Steven M. Studebaker and Robert W. Caldwell, *The Trinitarian Theology of Jonathan Edwards:*

Text, Context, and Application (Farnham, UK: Ashgate, 2012), 213–28. Therefore, the knowledge of the heavenly saints far exceeds that of the earthly believers in quality.

[32] *WJE* 16:727–28; *WJE* 9:513–14; "Miscellanies," no. 777, in *WJE* 18:430. He wrote that the history of redemption is the "eternal covenant of redemption that was between the Father and the Son before the foundation of the world."

[33] See Caldwell, "A Brief History of Heaven in the Writings of Jonathan Edwards." *Calvin Theological Journal* vol. 46 (2011): 63. The differences between the knowledge of the heavenly and earthly saints are also quantitative, not just qualitative.

[34] *WJE* 8:369.

[35] *WJE* 8:369.

[36] *WJE* 8:373; 374.

[37] *WJE* 8:374; 380.

[38] McClymond and McDermott, *The Theology of Jonathan Edwards*, 296.

[39] See "Miscellanies," no. 1131, in *WJE* 20:510.

[40] See "Miscellanies," no. 26, in *WJE* 13:212.

[41] See "Miscellanies," no. 26, in *WJE* 13:213.

[42] See "Miscellanies," no. 26, in *WJE* 13:212. See also McDermott and Story, *The Other Jonathan Edwards*, 30–32.

[43] "Miscellanies," no. 262, in *WJE* 13:369.

[44] "Miscellanies," no. 262, in *WJE* 13:369. See Nancy Koester, "The Future in Our Past: Post-millennialism in American Protestantism." *Word and World* vol. 15, no. 2 (1995): 138.

[45] "Miscellanies," no. 26, in *WJE* 13:213.

[46] *WJE* 8:396

[47] *WJE* 8:396.

[48] "Miscellanies," no. 262, in *WJE* 13:369. See "Miscellanies," no. 421, in *WJE* 13:478. From Edwards' eschatological perspective, the saints in heaven and on earth are one and the same family of God. In "Miscellanies" no. 421, Edwards wrote that, "The church in heaven and the church on earth are more one people, one city, and one family than generally is imagined." See also *WJE* 9:483–84. It is written as follows: "And then shall all the world be united in peace and love in one amiable society; all nations, in all parts, on every side of the globe, shall then be knit together in sweet harmony, all parts of God's church assisting and promoting the knowledge and spiritual good one of another ... all the world [shall then be] as one church, one orderly, regular, beautiful society, one body, all the members in beautiful proportion."

EDWARDS IN DEFENSE OF A LITERAL MILLENNIUM

Bonghyun Yoo

'Tis manifest that the saints in heaven, holy martyrs and others, do behold and rejoice in the prosperity of Christ's church on earth, and do rejoice in the nations of the world, and the heathen, being brought under Christ, and have a great share in this prosperity by that kind of union and communion that the Scripture reveals that they have with Christ.

— Jonathan Edwards, *Miscellany no. 836*

S TEPHEN STEIN DIVIDES THE DEVELOPMENT of Edwards' eschatological thought into three stages.[1] He then concludes that, although Edwards' eschatology maintained contextual flexibility in response to fluid situations, it did not undergo significant changes, and the Millennium steadily remained central to his eschatology throughout every stage of his life.[2] His "Miscellanies" entries pertaining to the theological locus prove the point. For instance, the Millennium functioned as an integral part of his eschatological thinking, from his early to his late period.[3] In addition, Edwards' millennial logic was consistent in that he affirmed that the Millennium would be fulfilled in history and last for a thousand years or a similar length on earth. Unlike Luther and Calvin, he was a millenarian or chiliast who affirmed that

Revelation 20 literally refers to Christ's millennial kingdom on earth, in which he would spiritually reign with the saints for a period of one thousand years.[4]

Edwards' eschatology could be understood as a prototype of contemporary postmillennialism in that the overall outlines of the nature of the Millennium and the order of Christ's final coming can cohere with one another.[5] To be specific, Edwards and modern postmillennialists would broadly agree that the Millennium will occur through the global advance of the gospel and its gradual dominance over the power of Satan.[6] They would all strongly urge the involvement of the church in God's redemption through her spiritual exercise for a speedy and swift advance of the gospel across the globe, though God remains the sole agent who brings about the ultimate outcome.[7] Also, they would concur that Christ will gloriously return at the end of the millennial kingdom and bring the last judgment in the final epoch of the redemptive history.[8]

For examples, Kenneth Gentry, one of the current advocates of postmillennialism, defines it as such:

> Postmillennialism expects the proclaiming of the Spirit-blessed gospel of Jesus Christ to win the vast majority of human beings to salvation in the present age. Increasing gospel success will gradually produce a time in history prior to Christ's return in which faith, righteousness, peace, and prosperity will prevail in the affairs of people and of nations. After an extensive era of such conditions the Lord will return visibly, bodily, and in great glory, ending history with the general resurrection and the great judgment of all humankind.[9]

As can be seen from above, Christology occupies a central place in the definition of postmillennialism. This view is also observed in Edwards' theological notebooks. In "Miscellanies," no. 804, for instance, he wrote that the Millennium is the reward that God gave to Christ for his righteous suffering and death: "'Tis the joy that was set before him, for which he endured the cross. 'Tis given him as the reward of what he did and suffered in the work of redemption."[10] Not only did God give the inheritance of the Millennium to him, Christ also purchased it in order to partake of its joy, glory, and victory with the body of Christ for a thousand years.[11] In the same entry, moreover, Edwards interpreted the millennial kingdom in the broader context of God's providence, which is Christologically unfolded and finalized. According to him, "Christ's mediatorial glory" and the "reward that he has for his own sufferings and righteousness" continue to be multiplied by degrees in successive times, being gradually firmer and fuller since the first dispensation.[12] Hence, it becomes like snowballing in that God's future plan and glory in Christ would continue to become more evident in a gradual advance of the salvation history. So finally, it would become "vastly higher" enough to capture his enemies in hell for eternity.[13] At the judgment day, the souls of the wicked shall be miserable, whereas those elected shall be joyful before Christ the Judge, whose throne will "be fixed in the air in the region of the clouds, whence he may be seen by all that vast multitude that shall be gathered before him."[14] As a result, Edwards' eschatology cannot be torn apart from his Christology, for it is a Christologically informed anticipation.[15] Furthermore, as the eschaton itself is an act of God's redemption, Edwards' eschatology should be understood as a function of soteriology.

Despite such similarity, Edwards and recent postmillennialists differ in opinion as to several details related to the Millennium, including its nature, time, and duration. For instance, should the millennial kingdom be understood historically or figuratively? If it is historical, would it be understood as extended out of the present age ("already") or transmuted into a new era ("not yet")? When will the Millennium begin and end? How long will a golden era last before the end of it? Gentry explains these issues in detail in a chapter of *Three Views on the Millennium and Beyond*. He is convinced that God's will for the advancement of the kingdom "shall be done on earth as it is heaven."[16] Though the rise of the millennial kingdom seems slow and deliberate, he believes, its progress with spiritual awakenings on earth is appointed and assured under divine providence.[17] Pertaining to the interpretation of the thousand years in Revelation 20, however, he conceives it in a symbolic sense, writing that it seems to "function as a symbolic value, not strictly limited to a literal thousand year period" or refers to "the long-lasting glory of the kingdom Christ established at his first coming."[18] John Davis is another postmillennialist today who also believes that Christ will return after the Millennium.[19] His belief in the emergence of the millennial kingdom is fundamentally grounded in Christ the Victor, who was raised from the dead and ascended to the Father, and whose reign is now expanding to the entire cosmos.[20] Similar to Gentry, Davis argues that the thousand years in Revelation 20:4–6 are not likely literal. For him, it is more compelling to interpret the number "thousand" in Revelation 20 as "a long period of spiritual prosperity for the church" from the immediate context of the passages than as a literal thousand years.[21]

Edwards also sustained an optimistic expectation for the future, urging that the millennial society will be ushered in with the global expansion of Christianity through the gospel movement.[22] Yet he held that the Millennium belongs to the latter days in which there are more glorious times and things to come, not the present church age until the second coming of Christ.[23] For him, the church could not imagine anything worse than losing the hope for the advent of the millennial kingdom. "It would be a great discouragement to the labors of nations or pious magistrates and divines, to endeavor toward the advancing of Christ's kingdom, if they understood that it was not to be advanced," he wrote.[24] For him, Christ will surely return to a civilized and prosperous world in which the gospel of Christ affects every realm of human life in the world.[25] Therefore, the millennial kingdom would not be seasonal blessings in a certain place but a global society of peace and prosperity with serious long-term triumphs.[26]

Unlike Gentry and Davis, nevertheless, Edwards preferred to hold a literal interpretation of the millennium in Revelation 20:4–6, the length of which shall be literally one thousand years. In "Miscellanies," no. 836, Edwards supported his thought by urging the following: "When the duration of the glorious times of the church on earth after the fall of Antichrist is spoken of in the 20th chapter of Revelation as being a thousand years, the words are to be literally understood that it will be about that space of time."[27] To be more concrete, the gist of his argument here in the "Miscellanies" is that the Millennium would not be "vastly longer than a thousand years" on earth.[28] He admitted that the length of time would be an approximation, for it is difficult to set the precise time of its beginning and end.[29] Also, Edwards was clearly aware that certain biblical numbers in prophetic messages do not always demand literal interpretations. He knew that they are often interpreted in a way that deviates from their literal meaning or denotation—for instance, "a prophetical day is a year, a prophetical week seven years, a prophetical month thirty years, a prophetical year 360 years."[30] Another typical example of Edwards' figurative interpretation of biblical numbers is that he transposed the six days of creation into the entire of human history, believing that it is reckoned at about six thousand years old, and the millennial age is parallel to the seventh day of creation which represents the Sabbath.[31] He then claimed that the church will enjoy a sabbatical age of rest and peace for the last one thousand years on earth before the new creation.[32] Thus, a prophetical day was equivalent to a thousand years in his millennial logic, and he described it as follows: "For the manner of Scripture prophecy is to represent the true time by other times are vastly less."[33]

Nevertheless, he provided several reasons why it is likely that the Millennium would not last longer than one thousand years.[34] If it were not so, Edwards speculated, the earth would be overpopulated "under such great universal and uninterrupted prosperity, health and long life ... without being diminished with wars, pestilences and other desolating calamities."[35] It was his rationale that if the rate of population growth steadily rose at the beginning of the Millennium by the standard of his day and place, its population would increase

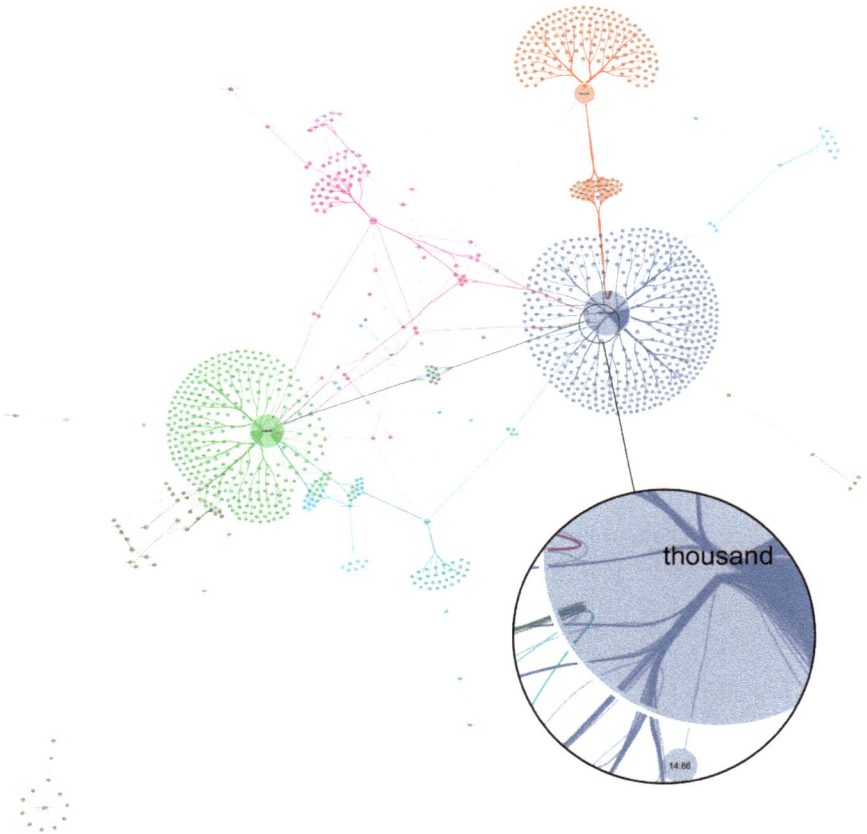

MILLENNIUM, SABBATH, and THOUSAND—*a map of millennial, millennium, millenniums, sabbatarians, sabbath, sabbaths, sabbatical, sabbatism, sabbatiz-ing, thousand, thousandfold, thousands, thousandth with interconnections and page locations in WJE 1–26.*

in a thousandfold at the end of the period.[36] Furthermore, most of population during the millennial age would be regenerate due to the universal advance of the gospel across the globe. Hence, if its actual duration continued on for several thousand years, then "such multitudes shall be saved," but for Edwards, that is hardly consistent with the biblical truth that only a few elected will be saved.[37]

Not only with the soteriological concern, if the day of the Parousia were delayed far too long, it would raise an ecclesiological dilemma, as well. In other words, if the "glorious state of the church" continued to exist for a vastly long time, then the church would lose her diasporic identity by distancing from her "true rest and glory" in the new heavens and new earth.[38] Although the ultimate future of the church could be tasted in the penultimate millennial world, he warned, the church shall long for Canaan, the promised land, not the wilderness that shall be a figurative interval of one thousand years' peace and rest.[39] Moreover, Edwards claimed that the whole visible universe, including the (old) heavens and earth, will gradually decay and pass away.[40] At the day of judgement, the earthly world, which the millennial society will inhabit, will become "an accursed world ... burnt, as having been for the most part a stage of wickedness and the kingdom of the devil."[41] Once the sun was created to reveal God's grace, it, too, shall be under curse and blazing with fury to consume the whole world, "so it will hereafter be the grand instrument of God's wrath and all outward torment," as he wrote in "Miscellanies," no. 931.[42]

In Edwards' day, as today, there was considerable literature which approached the Millennium from different theological perspectives.[43] According to Stein, post-Reformation millennial theology in sixteenth- and seventeenth-century England gradually began to fade from the line of the Augustinian anti-millenarian tradition and diverged from that of the earlier Protestant Reformers.[44] For instance, John Cotton (1584–1652), an English and New England Puritan clergyman, argued that the coming of the millennial kingdom was near.[45] In the seventeenth and eighteenth centuries, especially, the millennial discourse continued to develop in various ways—for instance, Joseph Mede (1586–1638) for anti-Roman Catholicism, Isaac Newton (1614–1727) for an interdisciplinary studies of biblical prophecy and scientific method, William Twisse (1578–1646) and Thomas Goodwin (1600–80) for the Fifth Monarchy political movement, and Hugo Grotius (1583–1645) and Henry Hammond (1605–60) for Arminian theology.[46] Furthermore, Daniel Whitby (1638–1726), an eighteenth-century liberal theologian, took an unusual position pertaining to the doctrine of the millennium in those days. That is, his work was "the first example of a postmillennial formulation" in eighteenth-century England.[47] In his postmillennial thought, the Jews played a major role in the millennium, and he believed that it would be a figurative, not literal, thousand year promised to the Jewish Christians primarily and the Gentile believers next.[48] So when viewing Edwards' millennial thought in light of these theological formulations, as John Wilson once reminded his readers, his position was neither as outstanding nor innovative as one could imagine in the context.[49] Consequently, it can be said that Edwards developed his *sui generis* system of thought about eschatology by interacting with those newly emerging theological ideas.

Notes

[1] Stephen J. Stein, "Eschatology," in Sang Hyun Lee, ed., *The Princeton Companion to Jonathan Edwards* (Princeton, NJ: Princeton University, 2005), 227. According to Stein, (1) the early stage of his eschatological thought grew from his youth to 1733, (2) the prime of his life as a public figure who involved in a series of Christian revivals was from 1734 to 1748, and (3) the most productive stage of his life as a prolific writer was in the last decade before his death.

[2] Stein, "Eschatology," 236, 238–40. The five common denominators in Edwards' eschatology throughout the whole stages are as follows: (1) glory, (2) providence, (3) the Spirit, (4) cosmic warfare, and (5) progression.

[3] See Michael J. McClymond and Gerald R. McDermott, *The Theology of Jonathan Edwards* (New York: Oxford University Press, 2012), 579. For Edwards, eschatology is neither "a theological appendage" nor a closing chapter. They wrote that the locus was "both central and integral to his thought."

[4]"Miscellanies," no. 804, in *WJE* 18:506. For discussion on the Reformers' views about the Millennium, see Stein, "Editor's Introduction," in *WJE* 5:3. The belief in a future thousand year reign of Christ on earth in Revelation 20 can be called millenarianism/millennialism (from the Latin word *mille* "thousand" plus *annus* "year") or chiliasm (from the Greek equivalent *chília étē* "one thousand years").

[5]In Edwards' day there existed no such theological terms as "postmillennialism" or "eschatology" that people use today.

[6]See "Miscellanies," no. 158, in *WJE* 13:307 and "Miscellanies," no. 613, in *WJE* 18:146. Edwards wrote as follows: "It seems probable there will be a time wherein the gospel will prevail so far, as to be a very great defeat and glorious disappointment of Satan in his design of making man miserable." See also Nancy Koester, "The Future in Our Past: Post-millennialism in American Protestantism." *Word and World* vol. 15, no. 2 (1995): 139. In Edwards' millennial theology, it was always "a two-fold strategy" to advance the millennial kingdom by means of (1) the outpouring of God's grace upon the church and (2) that of God's wrath upon her enemies.

[7]Don Schweitzer, "Jonathan Edwards," in Kwok Pui-lan, Don H. Compier, and Jo-erg Rieger, eds. *Empire and Christian Tradition: New Readings of Classical Theologians* (Minneapolis, MN: Fortress, 2007), 247.

[8]"Miscellanies," no. 804, in *WJE* 18:506–7.

[9]Kenneth L. Gentry Jr., "Postmillennialism," in Stanley N. Gundry and Darrell L. Bock, eds., *Three Views on the Millennium and Beyond* (Grand Rapids: Zondervan, 1999), 13–14; orig emph. For more definition on postmillennialism, see John Jefferson Davis, *Christ's Victorious Kingdom: Postmillennialism Reconsidered* (Grand Rapids: Baker, 1986), 10–11.

[10]"Miscellanies," no. 804, in *WJE* 18:506.

[11]"Miscellanies," no. 804, in *WJE* 18:506.

[12]"Miscellanies," no. 804, in *WJE* 18:506–7. According to Edwards, the first dispensation started with Christ's resurrection and ascension in the first century and signified "the days of the apostles." The second dispensation was during the reign of the Roman Emperor Constantine the Great (AD 306–337). The third dispensation would start with the emergence of the Millennium, which would bring about the spiritual reign of Christ for a literal thousand years, as well as "the destruction of Antichrist." And the last dispensation would be initiated by "the day of judgment" after the millennial kingdom. Edwards characterized the dispensations as the four different comings of Christ (e.g., bodily–spiritual–spiritual–bodily), and they succeed one after another in history. For further information about the fourfold comings of Christ, see Christopher B. Holdsworth, "The Eschatology of Jonathan Edwards." *A Quarterly Journal for Church Leadership* vol. 5, no. 3 (1996): 135.

[13]"Miscellanies," no. 804, in *WJE* 18:507.

[14]*WJE* 14:525–26; *WJE* 9:498.

[15]See "Miscellanies," no. 1131, in *WJE* 20:510–12.

[16]Kenneth L. Gentry Jr., "Postmillennialism," in Stanley N. Gundry and Darrell L. Bock, eds., *Three Views on the Millennium and Beyond* (Grand Rapids: Zondervan, 1999), 56.

[17]Kenneth L. Gentry Jr., "Postmillennialism," in Stanley N. Gundry and Darrell L. Bock, eds., *Three Views on the Millennium and Beyond* (Grand Rapids: Zondervan, 1999), 56.

[18]Kenneth L. Gentry Jr., "Postmillennialism," in Stanley N. Gundry and Darrell L. Bock, eds., *Three Views on the Millennium and Beyond* (Grand Rapids: Zondervan, 1999), 51.

[19]See John Jefferson Davis, *Christ's Victorious Kingdom: Postmillennialism Reconsidered* (Grand Rapids: Baker, 1986), 93.

[20]See John Jefferson Davis, *Christ's Victorious Kingdom: Postmillennialism Reconsidered* (Grand Rapids: Baker, 1986), 129–30.

[21]John Jefferson Davis, *Christ's Victorious Kingdom: Postmillennialism Reconsidered* (Grand Rapids: Baker, 1986), 94.

[22]For more discussion on Edwards' optimistic eschatology, see James West Davidson, *The Logic of Millennial Thought: Eighteenth-Century New England* (New Haven: Yale University, 1988), 29–36.

[23]"Miscellanies," no. 1131, in *WJE* 20:510.

[24]"Miscellanies," no. 351, in *WJE* 13:427.

[25]"Miscellanies," no. 262, in See *WJE* 13:369.

[26]Gerald R. McDermott, *One Holy and Happy Society: The Public Theology of Jonathan Edwards* (University Park, PA: The Pennsylvania State University, 1992), 41. See also Davis, *Christ's Victorious Kingdom,* 15.

[27]"Miscellanies," no. 836, in *WJE* 20:50.

[28]"Miscellanies," no. 836, in *WJE* 20:50 and "Miscellanies," no. 1224, in *WJE* 23:156.

[29]"Miscellanies," no. 836, in *WJE* 20:50.

[30]"Miscellanies," no. 836, in *WJE* 20:50.

[31]*WJE* 5:129–30. Edwards wrote in "Notes on the Apocalypse," "The first 6000 years are 6 days of labor, and the seventh is a sabbath of rest. As the world was six days in making, so I believe that the kingdom of God, that it will be six days in making before 'tis finished. That is, things will be overturning six days in order to it; and the seventh day there shall be rest, putting a thousand years for a day." Like many of his contemporaries, he thought that the millennium would come by the year two thousand or earlier: "The sabbath of the world will begin near about the beginning of the seventh thousand year of the world . . . it cannot be far."

[32]*WJE* 5:178–79.

[33]"Miscellanies," no. 836, in *WJE* 20:50.

[34]See "Miscellanies," no. 1224, in *WJE* 23:156 which provides a condensed version of "Miscellanies," no. 836.

[35]"Miscellanies," no. 836, in *WJE* 20:51.

[36] "Miscellanies," no. 836, in *WJE* 20:51.

[37] "Miscellanies," no. 836, in *WJE* 20:51–2. See "Miscellanies," no. 520 in *WJE* 18:64–66.

[38] "Miscellanies," no. 836, in *WJE* 20:52.

[39] "Miscellanies," no. 836, in *WJE* 20:52.

[40] "Miscellanies," no. 931, in *WJE* 20:176.

[41] "Miscellanies," no. 836, in *WJE* 20:51. See *WJE* 14:530 and "Miscellanies," no. 863, in *WJE* 20:93; "Miscellanies," no. 931, in *WJE* 181–82.

[42] "Miscellanies," no. 931, in *WJE* 20:181.

[43] See Stein, "Editor's Introduction" in *WJE* 5:1–8.

[44] *WJE* 5:4.

[45] *WJE* 5:5.

[46] *WJE* 5:5–7. For more discussion on how Edwards' contemporaries impacted upon the formulation of his eschatology, see Michael J. McClymond and Gerald R. McDermott, *The Theology of Jonathan Edwards* (New York: Oxford University Press, 2012), 572–74.

[47] James West Davidson, *The Logic of Millennial Thought: Eighteenth-Century New England* (New Haven: Yale University, 1988), 141.

[48] James West Davidson, *The Logic of Millennial Thought: Eighteenth-Century New England* (New Haven: Yale University, 1988), 141. See also *WJE* 5:7.

[49] John F. Wilson, "History, Redemption, and the Millennium," in Nathan O. Hatch and Harry S. Stout, eds., *Jonathan Edwards and the American Experience* (New York: Oxford University, 1988), 140.

EDWARDS ON HAPPINESS

Matthew Everhard

*When I think how great this happiness is, sometimes it is
ready to seem almost incredible. But the death and sufferings of Christ make everything credible that belongs to this
blessedness; for if God would so contrive to show his love in
the manner and means of procuring our happiness, nothing
can be incredible in the degree of the happiness itself.*

— Jonathan Edwards, *Miscellany no. 576*

Introduction

HAPPINESS IS ONE OF THE PRIMARY motifs and theological preoc-
cupations of Jonathan Edwards as both a philosopher and a
theologian. If the Genevan Reformer John Calvin is often referred
to as the "Theologian of the Holy Spirit," it would be fitting to call
Jonathan Edwards the "Theologian of Joy."[1] The pursuit of happiness
in and through Jesus Christ consumed his heart, both as a public theologian and as an individual and private Christian. Edwards himself
experienced great rushes of joy at his own conversion[2] and vowed
early in his career in his "Resolutions" to pursue this happiness in-
tensely.[3] Just as it was young Sarah Pierpont's youthful joy that
initially drew Jonathan to her,[4] so also Edwards saw happiness as
being the loving bond between the Savior and His own bride, the
elect church.[5] Joy permeates the preaching of Jonathan Edwards,

even if he is better known anecdotally for his hellfire and brimstone orations.[6] Readers who are only superficially familiar with his most famous sermon, "Sinners in the Hands of an Angry God"—which reeks of fire and fresh smoke—would do well to pair it with his "Heaven is a World of Love," which charms with a gladdening perfume. In the *Religious Affections,* he places joy as the penultimate affection, second only to love, treating its apprehension and experience as essential to true conversion.[7] In *The End for Which God Created the World,* happiness is seen as the chief end and purpose of creation, especially as manifested in the Beatific Vision, where the creatures yield back holy joy to the Creator who made them through the Savior that redeemed them.[8] In his mature theological writings, Edwards even saw happiness as an integral part of his Trinitarian theology, likening the Spirit of God Himself to the bond of joy between the Father and the Son.[9] Happiness, as a primary loci, is ubiquitous throughout Edwards' entire corpus for those who have eyes to see it. Found plentifully in almost all of his primary writings, including the "Miscellanies," the theme of joy or happiness runs through all of his manuscripts and published papers like a golden thread. Joy sweetens and enlightens his personal journals and public orations like sprinkled sugar over almost every composition. In the material that follows, we will look at joy as a theme in the "Miscellanies," particularly numbers 501–832, which comprise Volume 18 of *The Works of Jonathan Edwards.*

Although joy or happiness can be found throughout the "Miscellanies," (there are dozens of entries which treat of this topic particularly),[10] we must necessarily limit our scope here. I have selected six entries as follows: nos. 576, 585, 701, 721, 741 and 777. These are all important entries—though of various lengths—and aptly summarize Edwards' conceptions of joy as a whole. Taken together, these entries give the reader a brief, general overview as to what Edwards believed about joy; a quick crash-course of Edwards' overall conceptions representative of his entire literary corpus. Volume 18 in the "Miscellanies" is also rather important because these entries were written primarily during the 1730s while Edwards was maturing as a minister and emerging as a public voice for orthodox Calvinism, buoyed by his highly successful work *A Faithful Narrative,* which brought him into international acclaim. Moreover, this set of entries (Nos. 501–832) were written during the dawning prime of his own life: while his church was experiencing astounding local revival (1734–1735), his ministry was growing in international reputation (1737), and his home life was blossoming through a blissful marriage and abundant childbearing.

For the sake of convenience, let me attempt to define happiness as I believe Jonathan Edwards would have. This will help our more detailed study to unfold more smoothly below when we get into the particulars of our selected "Miscellanies:"

> **Happiness:** A holy affection of mutual pleasure, intrinsic to the very nature of the Three Persons of the Holy Trinity; wrought in the heart of the sinner by God at conversion as a fruit of the Spirit; in which converted persons truly delight not only in the temporal blessings of the created order, but even more so in the person and work of Jesus Christ through redemption; culminating and progressing for eternity in Heaven, especially as the saints gaze upon the infinite goodness of God in the Beatific Vision.

Analysis of Several Important "Miscellanies" on Happiness

With that working definition, let's go ahead and survey the six selected entries we have chosen.

No. 576 is entitled "Heaven's Happiness" and consists of only one paragraph. Its first line hints that happiness is a topic to which Edwards has given significant thought from time to time. His biography and journals, of course, bear this fact out. In contemplating these matters, Edwards has attempted to probe the heights and depths of the joys that will be available to the redeemed in Heaven. He finds their extents nearly incredible, and most certainly entirely undeserved! And yet, Edwards sees the proof of these joys to come in the extraordinary death of Jesus Christ. He summons Romans 8:32 to prove the point scripturally, and remarks that joy must be a correspondingly radical experience, since God did something extraordinarily radical in the giving of His own Son unto death. In line with Edwards' love for balance, symmetry, and harmony in all things, he concludes that certainly the joys of Heaven must correspond in degree to the "manner and means of God's procuring our happiness"[11] through the events of Calvary.

No. 585, although given the already familiar title of "Heaven's Happiness," regards time, providence, and eternity. Here, Edwards is perplexed by the fact that joy sometimes seems elusive in this world. He finds that providence directs this frustrating inevitability and "won't suffer any great degree" of happiness now. That is to say, fortune will not permit sustained levels of joy in the mortal realm. Just as it appears that some joys are just barely attainable in this life, so also are they all the more fleeting once obtained! "Providence," he says, "seems watchfully to take care that [men] should have no exceeding joy and satisfaction here in this world."[12] This is because it is not the right time for joy to be culminated in God's economy. No effort or invention of man will be able to grab now what God decrees to mete out so abundantly *later*. Of course, he is right. Even the best wine and feasts can only be enjoyed for a few moments. Sex is pleasurable for a limited duration of time and then fades quickly. Physical health, as well as youth, are here now, but gone tomorrow.

Edwards chooses to illustrate this fact with an extended metaphor of kings and kingdoms in the second paragraph. He remarks that throughout history, it seems that certain monarchs are invincible one day, and yet their fall is determined and decreed for the next. Despite their best strategy and efforts, mortal men cannot maintain what they worked so hard to acquire. Thus their temporal realms collapse inevitably. All things, he concludes, must find their fulfillment in God's design and in His providential order. Since God has decreed to

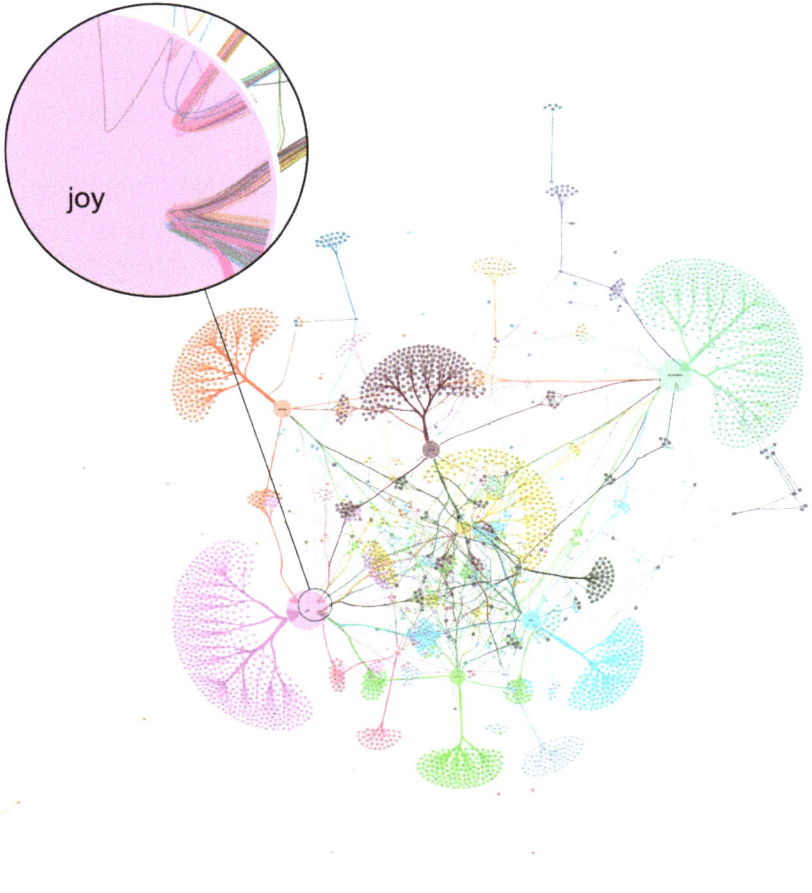

JOY, PROVIDENCE, and SATISFACTION—*a map of dissatisfaction, enjoy, enjoyed, enjoyer, enjoying, enjoyment, enjoyments, enjoys, joy, joyful, joyfulest, joyfully, joyfulness, joying, joyous, joys, providence, providences, providential, providentially, satisfaction, satisfactions, satisfactorily, satisfactory, unsatisfactoriness, unsatisfactory with interconnections and page locations in WJE 1–26.*

fulfill all longings for joy in the eternal state—and not in this life—no effort of man to usurp them before their time or to snatch them from their place in redemption history will be successful.

No. 701: This entry is entitled "Happiness of Heaven Increasing" and consists of two short sentences and a cross reference to Ridgley's *Body of Divinity,* vol.1, pp. 61–62. Here, Edwards remarks briefly that the saints' knowledge will increase in Heaven, just as the angels' curiosity and knowledge increases in redemption history (see 1 Peter 1:12). Knowledge and joy are related, as greater knowledge of Christ brings about greater joy in His presence. Alert readers will note that this is a conjunction where Dr. Boss's visualizations of the "Miscellanies" through computerization could further our current understandings of Edwards' conceptual overlap on the themes of knowledge and happiness. This would be an example of a fruitful study for scholars of the "Miscellanies" using these cutting edge advances in digital technology.

No. 721, entitled, "Happiness of Heaven after the Resurrection" is very interesting and takes our study in an invigorating, if somewhat speculative, direction. Here, Edwards explores the potentiality of embodied experiences of happiness after the resurrection of the dead when believers are given their new physicalities (cf. 1 Corinthians 15:35–49). He notes references to Nos. 95, 182, and 263, which students likewise should consult for overlapping themes. He suggests provocatively that "every perceptive faculty shall be an inlet of delight."[13] He then selects the eyes for further consideration, suggesting that we will, perhaps, be able to see colors and variations which are heretofore unknown to us. To describe these colors, Edwards suggests that this is somewhat akin to trying to explain to a blind man how colors appear in this world—so bright and clear to seeing people, and yet so mysterious and otherworldly to the physically impaired. Common themes of "sun," "light," and "delight" emerge in this entry, so profuse in his writings on happiness and joy in other major works. Edwards is sure, however, to direct the most focused attention on God

Himself. He is the great joy. He is the fullest source of all true and lasting happiness for the redeemed. He writes:

> But yet this pleasure from external perception will in a sense have God for its object. It will be in a sight of Christ's external glory. And it will be so ordered in its degree and circumstances, as to be wholly and absolutely subservient to a spiritual sight of that divine spiritual glory, of which this will be a semblance and external representation; and subservient to the superior spiritual delights of the saints, as the body will in all respects be a spiritual body, and subservient to the happiness of the spirit.[14]

References in this entry to the transfiguration of Christ, Moses' vision of God (Ex. 33:18), and to the New Jerusalem of God (Rev. 21:11) give the reader some glimpse—even if veiled by the mystery of these biblical passages—into the directions that Edwards' sanctified imagination was leading him.

No. 741 is entitled once again "Happiness of Heaven" and extends the thoughts and themes already given. In fact, with No. 777, it is among the longer entries considered here, being about seven pages of print text. It is notable for its darker themes however, since this Miscellany focuses on the death of Christ as being the means by which the joy of the saints is secured. Among those studied so far, it is clearly the most Christocentric. It follows a condescending, humiliating trail towards the cross. Language on blood, suffering, and death abound. All of this is necessary, though, as Edwards shows us how the incarnation was instrumental in winning and securing our eternal joy. Christ had to suffer in the body, mind, and soul (key thought) so that the saints could experience the joys of body, mind, and soul in Heaven. The wrath of God upon guilty creatures had to be poured out upon Christ in our stead, so that we the guilty could experience the fullness of redemption through His blood. Without suffering and death, joy is impossible and inaccessible to us. Our own guilt and sin would have plunged us into Hell had not Christ atoned for our guilt and sin through His cross. Thus, this Miscellany becomes an extraordinary explanation of the very heart of the Gospel; Christ's death and resurrection for sinners is granted for our joy. Suffering and happiness are brought into such close quarters here that the reader is stunned by the necessity of such violence upon Christ for the gladdening redemption of the elect. Rarely are the themes of suffering and joy drawn so close to one another in such a tight space. Readers of this Miscellany are compelled to feel their own guilt and invited to rejoice in its having been remitted through Christ's death. Thus the portal of joy and true happiness is opened wide for those who would receive it:

> Though an admission to such a kind of fellowship with God perhaps could not be without God's own suffering, yet when a divine person has been slain, way is made for it, seeing that he has been dead. The veil is rent from the top to the bottom by the death of Christ. The debt is all paid to the awful attributes of God; there is no need of any more. Nothing of awful distance towards the believer can be of any use after this. Now the veil is removed, the way is all open to the boldest and nearest access; and he that was dead and alive again is ours fully and freely to enjoy.[15]

Finally, we consider No. 777, entitled "Happiness of Heaven is Progressive." Just like the previous, it contains about seven full pages of print in the Yale edition. In addition to the main idea, it contains three minor corollaries appended to the primary thought. I have a hunch that readers will find this the most difficult entry, and no doubt one that needs some clarification. Here, Edwards is wearing his philosopher's hat and speaks in a tone that is somewhat different from his pastoral and theological voice. His primary idea here has to do with "minds" and their ability to fully access the existential mentality of another. No mind, he says, can fully access what is in the mind of God the Father, except Jesus Christ, who is in His bosom. For two minds to be coextensive in this way would require their unity of personhood. For this reason, all knowledge of God's mind must be *mediate* rather than *immediate*.[16] Edwards then tells us that mediate knowledge of God can come through signs, images, words, and divine actions; especially divine actions in redemption history. In this way, Edwards points to Christ who is the image of God, revealing the Father to His fullest extent to redeemed creatures.

Now for the corollaries. As mentioned above, there are three. The first pertains to Christ as the image of God, the revealer of the Father. In heaven, the saints will look upon Christ as the primary subject of the joy-imparting Beatific Vision. Edwards writes, "And so we may infer that [the] business and employment of the saints, so far as it consists in contemplation, praise, and conversation, is mainly in contemplating the wonders of this work, in praising God for the displays of his glory and love therein, and in conversing about things appertaining to it."[17] The second corollary pertains to the fact that the church in heaven (read: departed saints, now glorified with Christ in His presence) can see the church on earth. Because mediate knowledge can be imparted through actions in redemption history (recall: above), the church in heaven has an ability to see what is transpiring down here on earth. The third corollary is the payoff in terms of joy and happiness. Since the church in heaven can see and rejoice in what transpires on earth, their joy progressively increases as they see the progress of human history unfold according to God's redemptive plan. As God called the church out of slavery in Egypt, those already glorified rejoice. As God established the Davidic Kingdom, joy increases even more. When God delivers Israel from the Exile of Babylon, more happiness ensues. As the saints accumulate in number, filling heaven's gargantuan ethereal space, as time progresses towards the culminating acts of redemption history (incarnation, cross, resurrection, ascension), so also the joy and happiness of Heaven increase, accumulating joyous reasons to praise God for His wonders, acts, and works. This joy, Edwards holds, will continue unto and throughout the millennial state as the Kingdom is established in the world and the Lord's Prayer is fulfilled: "Thy

Kingdom come; Thy will be done on earth as it is in Heaven." Thus Edwards sees heaven's joys increasing exponentially as the history of redemption unfolds in real time and space.

But what about *after* the millennial age? What about *after* the return of Christ and the judgment of the living and dead? What about after the eternal state has begun, and all of human history has unfolded according to God's triumphant plan; does joy still progress there, too? It does, in fact, Edwards believes. But readers will have to turn to other places such as his sermon "Heaven is a World of Love" to find this glorious thought elaborated. For now, our space has almost run out on this handful of his important "Miscellanies." Before we end this section, however, we should add some summary thoughts.

Concluding Observations

After looking at each of these entries in turn, it would do us a service to note several hallmark terms that "connect the dots" between these entries. Each of these search terms will bear fruit should the reader follow them across the visual spectrum of Dr. Boss's three dimensional computer analysis of the "Miscellanies." Edwards frequently speaks of "light," "the sun," "blessedness," and "glory" while speaking of joy. Likewise, researching the Beatific Vision will bear much fruit in this regard, as well. But without a doubt, the term "Heaven" must be seen as the matrix of joy itself. Here is where Edwards places the weight of all holy joys as an experience. Though earthly joys abound, they all point forward in some significant ways to the eternal state. Because Edwards constantly places joy in the eternal location of Heaven, we cannot quite understand what Edwards means by happiness without doing further study there. As for the joys and happiness of this life, Edwards find them to be real, if somewhat elusive and temporary. Students of Edwards' theology of joy would do well to use the three-dimensional digital analysis of Dr. Boss to consult and follow trails regarding "knowledge," "intimacy," and "communion," as well as those just mentioned.

May all readers—whatever lines their course of study should follow—be given the abundant joy that Edwards discovered in and through Jesus Christ.

Notes

[1] See my fuller treatment on Jonathan Edwards' comprehensive understanding of happiness in my book *A Theology of Joy: Jonathan Edwards and Eternal Happiness in the Holy Trinity* (Fort Worth, TX: JESociety Press), 2018.

[2] Early in his life, he wrote, "I think I find in my heart to be glad from the hopes I have that my eternity is to be spent in spiritual and holy joys, arising from the manifestation of God's love, and the exercise of holiness and burning love to him." Iain H. Murray, *Jonathan Edwards: A New Biography* (Carlisle, PA: Banner of Truth, 2008), 44. See also *WJE* 16:803.

[3] He vows, for instance, "Resolved, to endeavor to obtain for myself (as much happiness, in the other world,) as I possibly can, with all the power, might, vigor, and vehemence, yea violence, I am capable of, or can bring myself to exert, in any way that can be thought of." See especially "Resolutions" nos. 22, 45, and 55. *WJE* 16:753–759.

[4] See his "Apostrophe to Sarah Pierpont" in *WJE* 16:789-790.

[5] Jonathan Edwards, *Sermons of Jonathan Edwards on the Matthean Parables: True and False Christians (On the Parable of the Wise and Foolish Virgins), vol. 1,* eds. Kenneth P. Minkema, Adriaan C. Neele, and Bryan K. Kimnach (Eugene, OR: Cascade Books, 2012), 41–53.

[6] He declares to his congregation for instance in one place, "Man is of such a nature, that he is capable of an exceedingly great degree of happiness; he is made of a vastly higher nature than the brutes, and therefore he must have vastly higher happiness to satisfy…It must be an incomprehensible object that must satisfy the soul; it will never be contented with that, and that only, to which it can see an end, it will never be satisfied with that happiness to which it can find a bottom." In "Safety, Fullness, and Refreshment in Christ" in *Sermons of Jonathan Edwards* (Peabody, MA: Hendrickson, 2005), 29–30.

[7] *WJE* 2:236, 277–278, 241.

[8] *WJE* 8:442.

[9] Jonathan Edwards, *Treatise on Grace and Other Posthumous Writings Including Observations on the Trinity,* ed. Paul Helm, (Cambridge: James & Co., 1971), 99–108.

[10] Besides the "Miscellanies" considered in this essay, readers would do well to consider nos. f, 3, 87, 95, 97, 106, 198, 233, 272, 477, 930, 934, 1059, 1061, 1072, 1081, 1137, 1274, and 1275.

[11] "Miscellanies," no. 576, in *WJE* 18:114.

[12] "Miscellanies," no. 585, in *WJE* 18:120.

[13]"Miscellanies," no. 721, in *WJE* 18:350.

[14]"Miscellanies," no. 721, in *WJE* 18:351.

[15]"Miscellanies," no. 741, in *WJE* 18:371.

[16]That is, conveyed through some sort of medium of communication and not apprehended directly.

[17]"Miscellanies," no. 777, in *WJE* 18:431.

EDWARDS' VISION OF HAPPINESS AS THE DIVINE AND HUMAN GOALS OF GOD'S CREATION

David Luke

> *An understanding of the perfections of God, merely, cannot be the end of the creation; for he had as good not understand it, as see it and not be at all moved with joy at the sight. Neither can the highest end of the creation be the declaring God's glory to others; for the declaring God's glory is good for nothing otherwise than to raise joy in ourselves and others at what is declared.*
>
> — Jonathan Edwards, *Miscellany no. 3*

IN NOTES FOR A SERMON ON PSALM 115 Jonathan Edwards wrote that the Christian "loves to attribute to God the Glory of what he is what he has and what he does. The believer delights in Giving the Praise of all that he has all that he is and all that he enjoys to God."[1] The theme of God's glory and the believer's delight in that glory was a theme that was central to Edwards' thought. It was not, however, merely a shibboleth but the fruit of Edwards' careful reflection upon this theme, the development of which can be traced through the "Miscellanies."

"Miscellanies" no. 3. HAPPINESS IS THE END OF THE CREATION was one of Edwards' early "Miscellanies," but already it touched upon many of the themes to which he would return both in subsequent entries and in his wider writings. This entry, from 1723, arose from his contemplation of one of the great questions that confronts humanity: Why did God create the world?

He began by noting that it is "the goodness of the Creator that moved him to create."[2] Edwards does not fully develop this idea at this point, but he works it out in subsequent entries. Here he is concerned mostly with the "end proposed by goodness."

While it is not unexpected that God as the Creator was an important locus of Edwards' theology, it is striking to see how frequently he turned to the theme of the "end" of God's creation, to consider why God created the world. The importance of this for Edwards is evident here as he reflected that it was God's goodness that moved him to create and that goodness, as he sought to demonstrate, is closely connected to the display of his glory. As he later wrote in "Miscellanies" no. 679. GOODNESS OF GOD. LOVE OF GOD. HAPPINESS OF HEAVEN, "as he delights in his own goodness, so he delights in the exercise of his goodness."[3]

Such a display of God's goodness or glory is futile, however, if God himself cannot "delight in seeing the creatures he made rejoice in that being that he has given them."[4] Edwards argued that God's goodness or glory is not a sufficient end in itself without his creatures rejoicing in it because they are deeply moved by that glory. This is not because God's happiness is dependent upon the happiness of the creature; rather it is because, as "Miscellanies," no. 679 noted, "It is a fit and condecent [appropriate] thing that God's glory should shine forth."[5]

In the same manner, it is not enough that his creatures declare his glory to others unless they themselves delight in what they are declaring. Without creatures to rejoice in God's glory, Edwards concluded that the creation might as well not have come into existence.

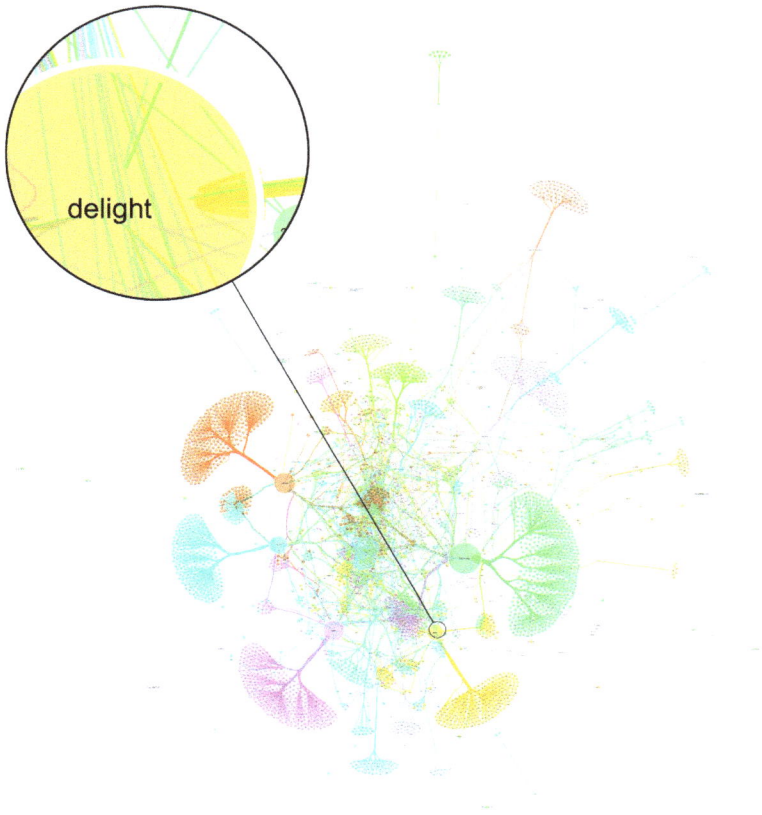

COMMUNICATE, CREATURE, DELIGHT, and HAPPINESS—*a map of communicability, communicable, communicant, communicants, communicate, communicated, communicates, communicating, communication, communications, communicative, communicativeness, communing, communion, communions, creature, creatures, delight, delighted, delightest, delighteth, delightful, delightfully, delightfulness, delighting, delights, delightsome, delightsomeness, excommunicable, excommunicate, excommunicated, excommunicating, excommunication, excommunications, happier, happiest, happifying, happily, happiness, happinesses, happy, incommunicable, unhappily, unhappiness, unhappy with interconnections and page locations in WJE 1–26.*

Such creatures must be intelligent. In a phrase he would use again he declared, "Intelligent beings are that consciousness of the creation."[6]

This rejoicing in the display of God's glory not only revealed something about God; it also revealed something about humanity's place in God's plan. In the first instance, as noted above, it is only intelligent beings who can rejoice in the goodness of God's creation. Then, as they rejoice in God's goodness, they discover the true happiness for which God created them. This is a happiness, Edwards noted, that is the all surpassing happiness of those who "are made eternally happy." The idea of eternal happiness was again an important theme for Edwards and one that he returned to in subsequent entries. Thirteen of the "Miscellanies" have the phrase "Happiness of Heaven" included in their title.

This focus on happiness may come as a surprise to those who only know Edwards as the preacher of "Sinners in the Hands of an Angry God." For Edwards, however, happiness was a subject to be taken seriously, not least as the goal of human happiness became an important theme amongst men of letters in the eighteenth century. Edwards did not deny the importance of human happiness as a natural and worthy goal, as he made clear in in "Charity and Its Fruits." Here he noted, "That a man should love his own happiness is necessary to his nature, as a faculty of will is."[7] If this was not the case, then "their happiness, which God has given them, would be no happiness to them; for that which anyone does not love he can enjoy no happiness in."[8] The problem, as he went on to point out, was that mankind sought its happiness apart from God, which was increasingly the direction in which Enlightenment thought travelled. Indeed, there was a growing sense that God's role was to serve human happiness.

With this focus on the importance of happiness, it then follows that for Edwards happiness is the business of true religion. This is evident in "Miscellanies," no. gg. RELIGION, which is another entry from 1723. Once more Edwards traced the familiar ground covered in "Miscellanies," no. 3, as he stated, "Tis most certain that God did not create the world for nothing."[9] Again he pointed out the importance of intelligent beings in God's scheme if creation is to serve some end. The creation would in fact "be useless if there were no intelligent beings at all." If this was the case, God could neither communicate nor receive good. There would be no purpose in the excellence of the created order. In this sense he again noted that "it necessarily follows that intelligent beings are the end of the creation." This is why God has created intelligent beings "to behold and admire the doings of God, and magnify him for them, and to contemplate his glories in them." He continued that it is "for this end God has placed us on this earth."

Religion, then, must also be the end of creation, "the great end, the very end."[10] This is because religion is the vehicle by which the end of God's creation is pursued, i.e., through religion the creature glorifies the Creator. Again he reiterated that if this was not the case, then all of the excellence of creation evident in the skill of the creator, the proportion of the creation and the laws which govern it, would be in vain. Religion was for Edwards "the very business" of intelligent beings. This is why God had created humanity, so that it might comprehend the glory of God as revealed in creation and magnify his name. In this way God spreads his happiness and his creatures enjoy God's own delight in himself.

We see in Edwards' unfolding thought a pattern developing. God had created this world with an end in view. The ultimate end was that he might express his glory. However, the expression of God's glory necessarily involved the creation of intelligent beings so that his glory might be apprehended and returned to him. This apprehension of God's glory and the return of that glory to God is the chief business of religion. It is the inter-relationship of these "ends" that meant Edwards could speak of God, intelligent beings and religion as all being the end of creation. This apparently overlapping use of the term "end," which may at first even appear contradictory, became more developed and clearly differentiated in his introduction to *Dissertation I: Concerning the End for Which God Created the World.*

He concluded, It follows from this that we must be immortal."
For, as he went on to note, if it is only for a short time that humanity
apprehended God's works and returned glory to him them then, using
similar language to that of "Miscellanies," no. 3, it might as well
never have existed. He cross-referenced this conclusion by adding,
"The same argument seems to be used, Isaiah 45:17–18."[11] His entry
on these verses in the *Blank Bible* simply refers back to this entry in
the "Miscellanies" without further comment.[12] The link for Edwards
seems have been that these verses from Isaiah speak of the eternal
nature of God's salvation and how God "created [the world] not in
vain, he formed it to be inhabited."

Edwards added a later cross-reference "See No. 1292." This refers
to "Miscellanies" no. 1292. IMMORTALITY OF THE SOUL which was
written in 1751/52. It reiterated the view that without immortality
for God's creatures the world might as well never have been created.
"Miscellanies," no. 87. HAPPINESS also belongs to the first collection
of entries written in 1723. It was one of only two "Miscellanies" that
first appeared in draft form. It was written on the back of a sermon
on Romans 12:18, along with a draft of a note on Revelation. The
opening of the entry touched upon familiar themes as Edwards wrote,
"Tis evident that the end of man's creation must needs be happiness,
from the motive of God's creating the world, which could be nothing
else but his goodness."[13] However, what seems to have led him to
return to this subject is the question "*why* God would make known
his power, wisdom, etc.," in this way. Also the question of why God
should create beings who might know his power and wisdom. His
answer was, "It could be nothing else but his goodness."

As he went on to point out, the particular stimulus for this enquiry
is to examine which of God's attributes moved him to exert his power
in this way. It is a consideration not of the "subordinate ends but
of the ultimate end, of that motive into which all others may be
resolved."[14] Here Edwards began to demonstrate the different ways
in which he employed the term "ends," which he explained more

fully in *Dissertation I*. Once more he turned to God's goodness as his motivation.

He wrote that "goodness [has] an inclination to show goodness." The display of God's power can never be a naked, purposeless display of his power; it must always be displayed in order to obtain an end. If it had no end in view, then it would be the very antithesis of wisdom, which must serve some end. So if God is moved by goodness, then "that goodness must necessarily ultimately terminate in the consciousness of the creation." Why? Because, again using the language of "Miscellanies," no. 3, only "intelligent beings are the consciousness of the world." Therefore, they alone can appreciate the goodness of God and in that appreciation of the God's goodness they discover their happiness. Edwards noted that only intelligent beings can "perceive what God is and does." It is in doing so that they perceive its "excellence."

In this entry Edwards traversed the familiar ground of previous entries. However, he also offered a different nuance. Here he pictured God's goodness as something which cannot help but overflow. This was a theme in the writings of the English Puritans, notably the group often referred to as "the Spiritual Brethren," who spoke of God's communicative and spreading goodness. It was part of the tradition in which Edwards was rooted. This theme of God's overflowing goodness was one to which he would often return in his writings. Whilst God's goodness must overflow, it does not, however, do so in way that is out of control or lacking in purpose. God wills it to overflow so that those intelligent beings whom he has created might share in that goodness. It is as humanity perceives the excellency of God's goodness that they discover true happiness. Humanity's greatest happiness is found in perceiving God's excellency and, therefore, it has God as its true object. As he would later state in a sermon on Hebrews 11:13–14, "God is the highest good of the reasonable creature. The enjoyment of him is our proper happiness, and is the only happiness with which our souls can be satisfied. To go to heaven, fully to enjoy God, is infinitely better than the most pleasant accommodations here."[15]

This is not, however, to suggest that humanity's enjoyment of God is the ultimate end of creation. In another early entry, "Miscellanies," no. 92. END OF THE CREATION, Edwards reflected further on this issue posing the question, "How then can it be said that God has made all things for himself, if it is certain that the highest end of the creation was the communication of happiness?"[16] His answer was that "God takes complacence in communicating felicity, and he made all things for this complacence." As noted above, the communication of God's happiness to the creature is not the ultimate end of creation. God's love is ultimately delightful and pleasing to himself.

"Miscellanies," no. 106. HAPPINESS, written in 1724, offers an insight into how Edwards used the "Miscellanies." For we see how he used this entry to trace his thinking on this subject to date, making reference both explicitly and implicitly to his previous writings on this subject. He also added an eschatological dimension to his thought that is not as evident in the earlier entries. Having reiterated that God has created the world for his glory, he added that "he will glorify himself exceeding transcendently."[17] Referring to "Miscellanies," no. 3, he pointed out that humanity's glorifying of God is nothing more than rejoicing in God's manifestations of himself. God is glorified not by what is given to him but by the creature's joy in him. This, in turn, has significant implications for the happiness of humanity. As he continued to note, human happiness is not only inseparable from God, as its supreme object it is actually the same happiness. This happiness is the glory of God, and it is therefore transcendent. Such an observation helped to steer Edwards away from any suggestion that human happiness in some way increased God's happiness.

He then returned to the point from "Miscellanies," no. gg. "that God has created man as the intelligence of the creation" so that he may behold God's excellency. Again he reiterated that humanity's happiness is found in perceiving God's excellency. Indeed, happiness is found in proportion to the manifestation of God's excellency. It was therefore beyond doubt for him, as he contemplated transcendent happiness, that "man shall be exceeding happy beyond conception."[18]

Having noted this, Edwards then developed this idea still further. He added that "the saints will be full of happiness, will have as much happiness as they can contain." Indeed, the only thing that can inhibit their happiness is their lack of capacity for happiness, as true happiness consists of "the perception and the possession of excellency." Since God is infinite in his excellency, our lack of happiness cannot be due to any absence of excellence on his part. Rather, looking forward to the eternal state, Edwards noted the ultimate reality is that there will be no want of perception or possession of the excellency of God.

From this entry, it is clear that Edwards was conscious of the criticism that the glory given to God by his creatures added to his glory *ad intra* or made up for some deficit in his being. He was keen to avoid this charge and repeatedly made clear in his writings that he was not suggesting this. For example, in "Miscellanies," no. 679, he stated that God "is not dependent on the creature for anything, nor does he receive any addition from the creature." Nonetheless, he added, "yet in one sense it can be truly said that God has the more delight for the loveliness and happiness of the creature." Using the qualification "in one sense," Edwards tried to navigate the perilous path of making human happiness the end of God's creation without making God contingent upon human happiness or suggesting that God's happiness was added to by his creation.

God's end in creation was a subject which occupied Edwards in many of his "Miscellanies." More than thirty entries have titles related to the "end of creation." It had its fullest expression, however, in *Dissertation I.* Written, probably, some thirty years after "Miscellanies," nos. 3, gg, 87 and 106, it reiterated many of the themes expressed in these early observations.

At the outset, Edwards plotted the labyrinth way in which he thought about "ends." Of particular importance is the way in which he distinguished between "ultimate ends" and "subordinate ends."[19] For Edwards, an "ultimate end" is that which is sought for its own sake, and a "subordinate end" is that which is followed in pursuit of an "ultimate end." For Edwards, that ultimate end is clear. He summarised it, writing,

> What has been said may be sufficient to show how those things, which are spoken of in Scripture as ultimate ends of God's works, though they may seem at first view to be distinct, all are plainly to be reduced to this one thing, viz. God's internal glory or fullness extant externally, or existing in its emanation. And though God in seeking this end, seeks the creature's good; yet therein appears his supreme regard to himself.[20]

Here Edwards wove together the themes of the earlier "Miscellanies." God's ultimate end is the display of his glory. This glory is revealed in his goodness which overflows. As he wrote in *Dissertation I*, "we may suppose that a disposition in God, as an original property of his nature, to an emanation of his own infinite fullness, was what excited him to create the world; and so that the emanation itself was aimed at by him as a last end of the creation."[21] Edwards used the term "fullness" as he noted "as signifying and comprehending all the good which is in God natural and moral, either excellence or happiness."[22]

Similarly, he returned to the relationship between God's happiness and the creature's happiness. He wrote, "Another part of God's fullness which he communicates is his happiness. This happiness consists in enjoying and rejoicing in himself, and so does also the creature's happiness ... The happiness of the creature consists in rejoicing in God."[23] Again he was careful to make clear that while "God may have a real and proper pleasure or happiness in seeing the happy state of the creature," his happiness is not increased by nor is it dependent upon the happiness of the creature. As he noted, "is delight which God has in his creature's happiness can't properly be said to be what God receives from the creature."[24] This is because ultimately God's happiness and the happiness of the creature are the same happiness. As he later wrote in *Discourse on the Trinity,* "Christ purchased for us spiritual joy and comfort, which is in a participation of God's joy and happiness."[25]

For Edwards the display of God's glory and the creation of beings with the capacity to enjoy that glory and to find their happiness in it was an important line of development in his doctrine of creation. It also had important pastoral implications as it spoke to the deepest longings of fallen humanity. Furthermore, Edwards saw the apologetic significance of this line of reasoning in an age which saw "the pursuit of temporal happiness as the *summum bonum*."[26]

Notes

[1] *WJEO* 42. The quotation is lightly edited for clarity.
[2] "Miscellanies," no. 3, in *WJE* 13:199.
[3] "Miscellanies," no. 679, in *WJE* 18:238.
[4] "Miscellanies," no. 3, in *WJE* 13:199.
[5] "Miscellanies," no. 679, in *WJE* 18:238.
[6] "Miscellanies," no. 3, in *WJE* 13:200.
[7] *WJE* 8:254.
[8] *WJE* 8:254.
[9] "Miscellanies," no. gg, in *WJE* 13:185.
[10] "Miscellanies," no. gg, in *WJE* 13:185.
[11] "Miscellanies," no. gg, in *WJE* 13:185.
[12] "Blank Bible," note on Isaiah 45:17–18, in *WJE* 24:680.
[13] "Miscellanies," no. 87, in *WJE* 13:251.
[14] "Miscellanies," no. 87, in *WJE* 13:252.
[15] *WJE* 17:437.
[16] "Miscellanies," no. 92, in *WJE* 13:256.
[17] "Miscellanies," no. 106, in *WJE* 13:276.
[18] "Miscellanies," no. 106, in *WJE* 13:277.
[19] *WJE* 8:405ff.
[20] *WJE* 8:530.
[21] *WJE* 8:435.
[22] *WJE* 8:433.
[23] *WJE* 8:442.
[24] *WJE* 8:446.
[25] *WJE* 21:136.
[26] Roy Porter, *The Creation of the Modern World: The Untold Story of the British Enlightenment* (New York: W.W. Norton & Co., 2001), 258.

Edwards and the Timeless Time of God's Decrees

Toby K. Easley

> *What divines intend by prior and posterior in the affair of God's decrees, is not that one is before another in the order of time, for all are from eternity, but that we must conceive the view or consideration of one decree to be before another, inasmuch as God decrees one thing out of respect to another decree that he has made . . .*
>
> — Jonathan Edwards, *Miscellany no. 704*

JONATHAN EDWARDS HAS BEEN DESCRIBED as America's preeminent theologian, preacher, pastor, and philosopher.[1] The topics covered in his lifetime can be summed up as voluminous and, for some, daunting to absorb. However, there was perhaps one colossal topic that captivated his mind and imagination for much of his life. The topic revolved around God's decrees in the work of creation, the fall, the history of redemption, the eschaton, and his eternal purposes in light of his decrees and providence. For Edwards, God is timeless; man lives in small gaps in time, but only God can see the whole entire span of his decrees in light of all eternity.

In describing God's decrees, Edwards used one of his favorite terms "excellent." He wrote, "What we would we completely express thus, that God decrees all things harmoniously and in excellent order;

one decree harmonizes with another, and there is such a relation between all the decrees as makes the most excellent order."[2] Edwards was not one to use the term "excellent" in a frivolous manner. One can imagine him even trying to make an onomatopoeia out of the word while it echoed from his pulpit. He also vividly saw "excellency" in the Triune Godhead and in the concept of Godly love, as well. He wrote, "Excellency therefore seems to consist in equality . . . one of the highest excellencies is love . . . The highest excellency, therefore, must be the consent of spirits one to another."[3] Furthermore, because God is love and has many other attributes that are "excellent," he saw the harmony of God's decrees, even though men often try and find inconsistencies and impose their own definition of decrees. "Thus," he went on to say, "All the decrees of God are harmonious."[4]

Man, on the other hand, does not represent "true excellency," due to the fall, and man will always have a limited comprehension about the overall vastness of history. God, however, "knows and perfectly sees all things, great and small, in heaven and earth, *continually at one view;* which cannot be without infinite understanding."[5] Understanding Edwards' concept of God seeing "all things, great and small, in heaven and earth, *continually at one view"*[6] may possibly be the key to unlocking his foundational thought process that set his theological scope regarding God's decrees, cause and effect, and his thoughts of God *"who is the first cause of all things."*[7] Nevertheless, at times when reading what Edwards wrote about God's decrees, one is left to ponder whether Edwards himself really comprehended a few of the ambiguous thoughts he jotted down. For the most part, however, he seems to stay consistent within the scope of his foundational concepts with one example in the following sentences:

> There is no new act of the will in God, but only the same acts of God's will that [were] before, because the time was not come [that] respected future time, and so were called decrees. But now the time being come, [they] respect present time, and so ben't called by us decrees, but acts executing decree. But 'tis evidently the same act in God;

and therefore, these acts in executing must certainly be conceived of in the same order, with the same dependence, as the decrees themselves.[8]

The first line of the previous quote, "There is no new act of the will in God but only the same acts of God's will that [were] before," seems to be Edwards' effort at staying within his own theological framework of God "seeing all things . . . continually, at one view."[9] With these initial concepts of Edwards in mind, the following pages will evaluate various subject matters within the parameters of his thought process on decrees. Furthermore, other concepts will be explained and critiqued not only to discern what he believed concerning decrees but also to discover whether he remained consistent.

With this purpose in mind, five particular subject matters will be discussed and questions answered. First, why did Edwards believe there was such a span between man's finite knowledge and God's infinite knowledge regarding decrees? Second, Edwards believed in cause and effect, but how did he answer any dilemmas? Third, did Edwards find the decrees a reason for optimism or pessimism? Fourth, how do the decrees of God impact individual salvation? Fifth, are the decrees of God sure enough to solidify God's triumph throughout the end of history?

Knowledge of Decrees

One of the reasons Edwards believed there was such a span between man's finite knowledge and God's infinite knowledge went back to the fall in the Garden of Eden. Edwards believed if Adam and Eve had never sinned they would have continued to grow more in their knowledge since the time of their creation, without the interruption of sin and death. As a result mankind ever since the fall has entered the world running from, not seeking to know more of God. Edwards said of Adam in his sermon "East of Eden,"

His soul was in a perfect state, the faculties of it in full strength, not broken, impaired, and weakened and ruined, as they are now. The soul of man with regard to the quickness and clearness of its faculties was then like the heavenly intelligences—as a flame of fire. The natural image of God that consists in reason and understanding was then complete.[10]

Edwards then went on to say as a result of the fall in the Garden, man's "understanding was clouded and broken, and the whole man in all its faculties was but the ruins of what it before was."[11] As a consequence, he believed there is now an ongoing battle between man ignoring God altogether, or resisting the fact that God has decreed the destiny of salvation history. For Edwards, these two battles took the form first of the lost condition of humankind in general and second of the refusal of some theologians to give God the complete credit for his work in salvation history. The dilemma regarding decrees was often conjured up in the minds of men, and that is why the decrees deserved to be viewed not in light of man's finite understanding but in light of an infinite God who sees "the end from the beginning, and from ancient times things that are not yet done, and I will do all my pleasure" (Isaiah 46:9–10). Consequently, in Edwards' sermon "East of Eden," he concluded, "If men deny God's authority, God will cause it to take place one way or other. God will appear as man's supreme Lord either in having his law obeyed or in having it executed; the law of God must some way or other take place with respect to him who is the subject of it."[12] At the end of the day, Edwards still believed there was a vast span between man's finite knowledge and God's infinite knowledge regarding decrees, and he certainly let it be known who he believed would be triumphant on the final day.

Cause and Effect

The second aspect of Edwards' view of decrees dealt with cause and effect and any apparent dilemmas surrounding God's decrees. In his effort to explain himself he said, "The decrees of God must be conceived of in the same order, and as antecedent to and consequent on one another, in the same manner as God's acts in execution of those decrees."[13] In this statement, Edwards was setting some parameters for individuals analyzing decrees. Due to the fact that men are isolated in a time slot in history, we often think of events as they occur sequentially. We have a tendency to analyze "antecedent" actions and events and then fast forward to the consequences in the present. Even with events that occur and provide much data to the observers, there is a limited knowledge of every detail. However, not so with God, as he looks at the "antecedent" and the "consequent." Edwards admitted there were "effects" of the "acts" themselves that are often looked at as peripheral, and some may categorize them as inconsistent with God and his purpose. He would argue that man sees things this way because of the inability to know how things in the past affect the present and the future. On the other hand, God sees past, present, and future, and man often quibbles over items with insufficient knowledge.

One of the key sentences Edwards used for explaining his argument was, "For, on the one hand, the decrees of God are no other than his eternal doing what is done, acted or executed by him in time."[14] The question that naturally arises regards man's evil acts and understanding why God allows them. There is quite a paradox in many of the events of history that are difficult to explain regarding the question of God's decrees and evil. However, the late theologian R.C. Sproul gave perhaps as good an explanation as any regarding the concepts of antinomy, paradox, and contradiction in relation to the accusation of God's "contradicting" ways:[15]

> I once read a statement by a Christian who said, "God's sovereignty can never restrict human freedom." Imagine a Christian thinker making such a statement. This is sheer humanism. Does the law of God place restrictions on human freedom? Is God not permitted to impose limits on what I may choose? ... Contradictions can never co-

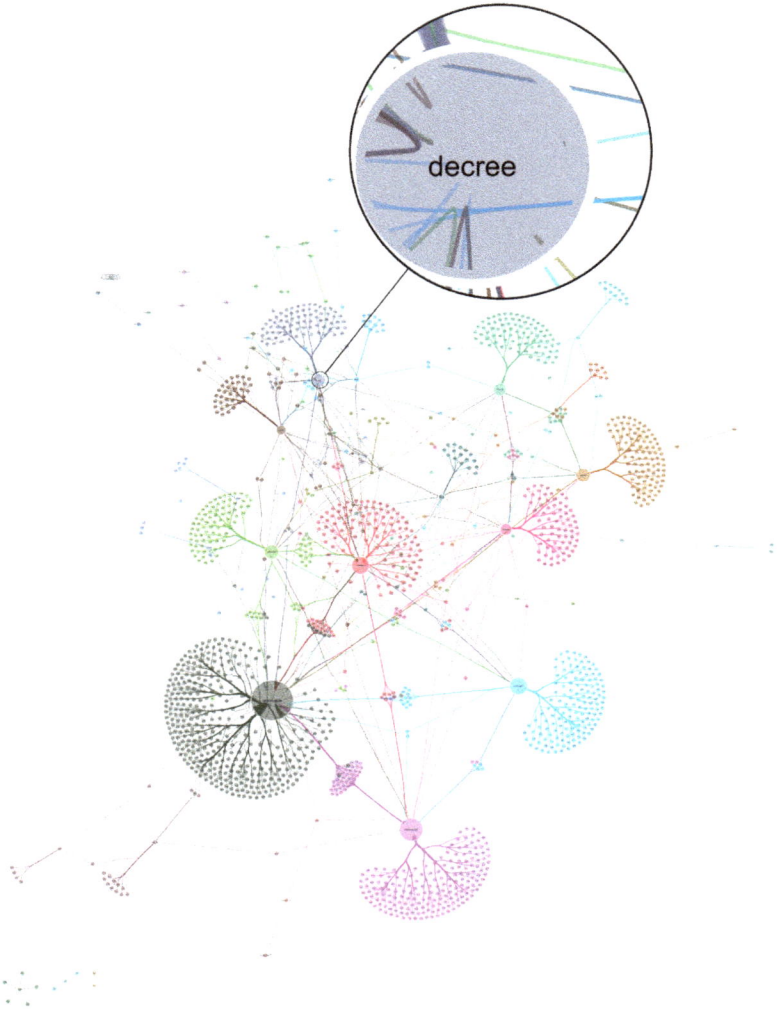

ANTECEDENT, CONSEQUENT, DECREE, *and* EXECUTION—*a map of antecedence, antecedent, antecedently, antecedents, consequence, consequences, consequent, consequential, consequentially, consequently, consequents, decree, decreed, decreeing, decrees, execute, executed, executes, executeth, executing, execution, executioner, executioners, executions, executive, executor, executors, undecreed with interconnections and page locations in WJE 1–26.*

exist, not even in the mind of God . . . A paradox is an apparent contradiction that upon closer scrutiny can be resolved . . . The Trinity is a paradox, but not a contradiction . . . Antinomy, its primary meaning is a synonym for contradiction but its secondary meaning is a synonym for paradox . . . Confusion creeps in when people use the term antinomy not to refer to a genuine contradiction but to a paradox or apparent contradiction . . . I am convinced that Dr. Packer uses antinomy to mean paradox and not contradiction . . . Mystery refers to that which is true but which we do not understand. The Trinity for example, is a mystery . . . Mysteries are capable of being misunderstood . . . All contradictions are mysterious. Not all mysteries are contradictions. Christianity has plenty of room for mysteries. It has no room for contradictions. Mysteries may be true. Contradictions can never be true, neither here in our minds, nor there in God's mind.[16]

These twentieth century words by Sproul in many ways reflect the mindset of Edwards in the eighteenth century. It seems apparent that Edwards believed the key to approaching God's decrees in light of world events and any perceived contradictions was not man's lack of an ability to see the minute details, but ultimately the biblical perception of God's overall purpose in relation to redemption history. He even saw Ezekiel's chariot and the wheels as representing God's turning and rotation of the ages. "The wheels of providence are not turned round by blind chance, but they are full of eyes round about as Ezekiel represents."[17] Edwards viewed the entire universe as a machine or chariot for God's own use and viewed God as having his seat in heaven where he governs. The inferior part of creation, this visible universe that is subject to changes and revolutions, are the wheels of the chariot, and the constant revolutions represent God's decrees in the alterations and successive events.[18] Not only is God in control of his creation, according to Edwards, but God also sees all things that transpire in the universe as many parts to the whole,

THE MISCELLANIES COMPANION

like a chain with many links: "the first link is from God and the last is to him."[19] Any seeming dilemmas or contradictions on man's part is due to the fact that man looks at the chronological sequences since creation in his finite mind, but God sees all in infinity. Man thinks about and observes pieces of the works of God, but God sees and conglomerates all of his works into his perfect "work of providence."[20] God's conglomeration of the whole is not therefore contradictory; neither is God the author of sin because he permitted sin. Man is held accountable for his sin in time, even though God permitted man's sin to occur in time in sequence of God's decrees. Edwards reiterated this theme as he sketched his thoughts in "Miscellanies" no. 704:

> So who will deny but that God's act in punishing sin is grounded on what God antecedently hath done in permitting sin or suffering it to be, because the former necessarily supposes the latter; and therefore that the actual permission of sin is prior in the order of nature to the punishment of it?[21]

Therefore, God, according to Edwards, did permit sin without being the author of sin and knew there would be redemption from sin and a future punishment for sin. In other words, Edwards never ignored the negative consequences that sin had caused and did not blame God for how he handled man's sin, nor did he react by creating his own man-centered thought process of dilemmas. Edwards explained,

> We do not mean by decreeing an action as sinful, the same as decreeing an action so that it shall be sinful; but by decreeing an action as sinful, I mean decreeing [it] for the sake of the sinfulness of the action. God decrees that it shall be sinful for the sake of the good that he causes to arise from the sinfulness thereof, whereas man decrees it for the sake of the evil that is in it.[22]

The fall of man for Edwards was something he could not change, so he instead reflected on what God had done through reconciliation and redemption to right the wrong of man's sin. He writes,

> The wrath of God drove us out of paradise, but the grace of God invites us to return. The Son of God in the name of his father comes and calls to us to return from our banishment; he ceases not to call us. He beseeches us to return again. He is come forth on purpose to make known those joyful tidings to us, Christ calls us away from this cursed ground, that brings forth briars and thorns, to a better country. Our first parents were driven away very loath and unwilling to go, but we are invited back again.[23]

Optimism or Pessimism

The previous quote may also serve as an appropriate introduction to our third issue regarding Edwards and God's decrees: Did Jonathan Edwards find the decrees of God a reason for optimism or pessimism? Perhaps some may answer both, but the accusation cannot be substantiated that he was imbalanced. Certainly, there are numerous instances where he found optimism in light of creation, the chaos of the fall, and God's ultimate decree to reverse the effects of Eden. Due to the fact that God has the ability to know and declare all things "before the world was created, yea from all eternity," he preached that the Trinity made agreements "before man fell."[24] Even though he acknowledged the pessimism of the fall of Adam and Even, he believed that if the New Testament Church would view the scope of biblical history in light of God's decrees, "consistence, order, and beauty"[25] would result rather than "confusion"[26] and pessimism. He found his optimism in the truth of God's ceaseless involvement and offered encouragement to his congregation that God's dealings with mankind were not only reasonable; He also had their best interest in mind.

Let us therefore be exhorted to yield and resign ourselves to God's providence, patiently submit to whatever he is pleased to bring upon us in the world, and be willing that he should dispose of us as he pleases, seeing we know that all his providential dealings are most reasonable and we can be assured that God can do us no wrong.[27]

In his effort to optimistically describe God working out his decrees in time, he used three categories to communicate how the least important events of God's end of creation are still important in the overall scheme of things. His trio was made up of "subordinate" and "ultimate ends," and a "chief end." He used the example of a man selling a garment in order to buy tools. Selling the garment was a subordinate end in order to reach the ultimate end of buying the tools.[28] However, the chief end remains different from the subordinate and ultimate end because "it is most valued, and therefore most sought after by the agent in what he does."[29] Edwards used these metaphorical angles to reflect on God's decrees on levels of importance as he searched for the biblical answer to God's chief end in creating the universe. His point of the "tools" example was to point out that what man often sees as perhaps insignificant actions and events in time are all a part of the overall process leading to God's "chief end." Only God can see and know the significance of every minute detail that occurs throughout the universe at one time. This to Edwards is the magnitude of our God, and his omniscience is only one of his attributes that set him apart from our feeble finite makeup and his infinite majesty.

Consequently, Edwards believed when people stubbornly reject God's ways and look upon his decrees in a pessimistic manner, they miss out on tremendous blessings. He believed the Scriptures were a tremendous treasure to the ones who read and appreciated God's word. To Edwards these "doctrines, promises, types, songs, histories, and prophecies" of the Bible were treasures, and he let it be known that a man who has a Bible and does not observe the contents "is like a man that has a box full of silver and gold, and don't know it. Don't observe that it is anything more than a vessel filled with common stones. As long as it is thus with him, he'll be never the better for his treasure."[30] On a similar note regarding prayer, he knew people when observing his view of decrees could be perplexed and question why he prayed if God determined all before. He believed this was a "wrong" and pessimistic viewpoint. "But to say that all was determined before these prayers and striving is very wrong way of speaking, and begets those ideas in the mind which correspond with no realities with respect to God."[31]

Furthermore, Edwards would optimistically continue to write in his "Miscellanies" and his sermons that it was God's desire to make himself known through all eternity to his redeemed people.[32] Furthermore, God's desire to be one with his people is why he will bring them home and unite them to himself. He believed this was a direct fulfillment of Jesus' words "that they all may be one, as thou Father art in me, and I in thee, that they also may be one in us; I in them and thou in me, that they may be made perfect in one" (John 17:21, 23).[33] God's purpose, then, in communicating his fullness is for himself because their good he desires "is so much in union and communion with himself."[34] This optimism also reflects a future "happiness," about which he wrote, "Tis evident that the end of man's creation must needs be happiness, from the motive of God's creating the world, which could be nothing else but his goodness . . . Yea, he is nothing but excellency; and all that he does, nothing but excellent."[35]

Individual Salvation

The fourth issue in relation to decrees has perhaps been the most controversial historically. The question to be answered is: In the "Miscellanies" how do the decrees of God impact individual salvation? Four of the catchwords are foreknowledge, reprobation, election, and predestination. It has not been a secret in the past or the present where Edwards stood regarding his soteriological position. However, for the "Miscellanies" in particular, it is important to discover whether

Edwards remained consistent with his sermons, treatises, and books. Thomas A. Schafer seemed to have no doubt about the consistency of Edwards' views, writing,

> The consequences for Edwards' theology are far-reaching. The infinitely powerful and omnipresent God of "Atoms" is the sovereign God of Reformed theology, whose "decrees" constitute the program by which everything occurs, from creation and fall to the day of judgment. The gravity that holds the heavenly bodies in their orbits, the sinner dangling over the pit of hell, and the soul suddenly infused with saving grace are alike forms of radical dependence on the will and power of God.[36]

First, Schafer in a roundabout way gives some insight on Edwards' view of foreknowledge or, as Edwards sometimes states, "foresight."[37] As Edwards would say, the "Arminian" position looked at "foreknowledge" differently than he. The Arminian position states that God makes decisions based off the foreknown decisions of men. The argument has nuances that pertain to the actual "cause and effect" previously discussed. Edwards would not deny that God knew how men would respond; he would simply deny that the decision of man ultimately caused the final outcome. He wrote, "There are no conditional decrees in this sense, viz. that decrees should depend on things, or conditions of them, that in this decree that depends on them as conditions."[38] In simpler terms, he would say that God knew man's decision in his foreknowledge, but God's decree in eternity determined the overall effect and ultimate outcome.

> The meaning of the word "absolute," when used about the decrees, wants to be stated. "Tis commonly said, that God decrees nothing upon a foresight of anything in the creature. This, they say, argues imperfection in God; and so it does, taken in the sense that they commonly intend it. But nobody, I believe, will deny but that God

decrees many things that he would not have decreed, if he had not foreknown and foredetermined such and such other things. What we would we completely express thus, that God decrees all things harmoniously and in excellent order ... But this I say, it's improper to make one decree a condition of another, [any] more than [the] other a condition of that; but there is a harmony between both.[39]

This entire statement by Edwards reaffirms his position that God "knows and perfectly sees all things, great and small, in heaven and earth, *continually at one view; which* cannot be without infinite understanding."[40] Therefore, in his way of seeing "foreknowledge" and "foresight," in relation to personal salvation, man could not take the credit for God foreknowing his decision. On the contrary, man had to give God the credit for infinitely including him in his salvific plan that was set in stone from eternity past and into eternity future. On the topic of "irreversible decrees" he noted, "This is all that follows from an absolute, unconditional, irreversible decree, that it is impossible but that the things decreed should be. The same exactly follows from foreknowledge, that it is absolutely impossible but that the thing certainly foreknown should precisely come to pass."[41] His views on "foreknowledge" similarly reflect God's transcendent oversight of his decrees regarding election, predestination, and reprobation.

Edwards, therefore, followed his consistent Reformed line of thinking regarding justice and injustice concerning God, man, and reprobation. "It cannot be any injustice in God to determine who is certainly to sin, and so certainly to be damned."[42] This statement echoes his thoughts on reprobation without stating the word. However, Edwards specifically refers to "reprobation" in "Miscellanies" no. 704 by stating, "For there is no evil decreed for any other end but the glory of God's justice; and therefore, the decree of the permission of sin is prior to all other things in the decree of reprobation."[43] As one fast forwards from the eighteenth century into the twenty-first century, the word "reprobation" has evolved into a word that has nearly become taboo. However, for Edwards, it was simply a result and consequence of his

theological and soteriological system that rested in the Reformed Tradition of being content that all of the decrees of God were to rest with
complete trust in a sovereign God. For him, "reprobation" was not a
word that was going to be removed from his theological dictionary.

The final two words that find their way into his decrees category
are election and predestination. Edwards was quite clear and concise
in "Miscellanies" no. 62 by stating,

> The dispute, whether the decree of the means be part
> of the decree of election, [is] a very senseless one. For
> says the one, that election is absolute, that such a person
> shall have eternal life, without any consideration by what
> means. I answer, that without doubt it is so, that eternal
> life is all that is included in the decree of election; but
> effectual calling, sanctification, faith, etc., they are the
> very eternal life that they are decreed to. This and that in
> heaven be not different, but only in degree.[44]

Concerning his view on whether the decree of election was conditional or unconditional, he was again consistent with his view of
foreknowledge. He wrote, "It is very nonsense to call such a conditional election as they talk of, by the name of election."[45] Edwards
understood very well the positions of his opponents and, although
he acknowledged that it was impossible for God not to know ahead
of time who would believe, the answers in the details were different.
"Tis owned, that God did choose men to eternal life upon a foresight
of their faith. But then here is the question: whether God decreed that
faith, chose them that they should believe."[46] In a previous citation,
he had already clarified his Calvinistic position. Nevertheless, it is
interesting to question if Edwards did slip away from some of his
predecessors regarding the extent of the atonement that was later
acknowledged by Andrew Fuller. Edwards seems clear on his view of
election, but did he dabble in a sufficiency and efficiency view of the
atonement? That is, Christ's death is sufficient for all but is efficient
only for the elect. He even pondered the following as a young man:

Christ did die for all in this sense, that all by his death have an opportunity of being [saved]; and he had that design in dying, that they should have that opportunity by it. For it was certainly a thing that God designed, that all men should have such an opportunity, or else they would not have; and they have by the death of Christ.[47]

Although Edwards clarified that he believed God sees all in "one view," regarding the decrees, did he participate himself in what R.C. Sproul described as a "contradiction"[48] regarding the atonement? Was he simply, as a very young man beginning in 1722, reflecting these thoughts in his study through his "Miscellanies" and preaching particular redemption in his pulpit? In a 1728–29 sermon series from Galatians 2:20 he proclaimed, "Tis absurd to suppose that Christ died for the salvation of those that he at the same time certainly knew never would be saved."[49] Edwards preached in 1739, "But that very morn that the human nature of Christ ceased to remain under the power of death, the utmost farthing was paid of the price of the salvation of every one of the elect."[50]

The purpose of this chapter is to discuss Edwards and his approach to God's decrees. However, discovering whether Edwards vacillated in his "Miscellanies" between two opinions regarding the extent of the atonement and contradicted his overall view of God's immutable decrees is a valid question to ask as one reads the full collection of his works.

As a final thought regarding this issue, one must remember when reading Edwards' "Miscellanies" that he would at times repeat and reflect on the ideas of those with whom he disagreed. There is the possibility in the above quote[51] that Edwards was not stating apologetically his own view but perhaps reflecting on the Arminian view. The language that is found in the "Miscellanies" quote above[52] is found in similar language from the Galatians 2:20 sermon from 1728–29. However, in the Galatians 2:20 sermon he defended his position by preaching:

It matters not in this Controversy whether we suppose an absolute decree or no if we only allow that God knows all things that he knows future things before they Come to Pass as he declares he does in his word and no Christians pretend to deny But if we don't deny this it implies a plain Contradiction to suppose that Christ died for in a proper sense If it Replied that no other is Intended when they say Christ died for all then that by his death all have the offer of salvation . . . As it is evident that Christ did not die for the salvation of all.[53]

Final Triumph

The fifth and final subject to be examined is the question: Are the decrees of God sure enough to substantiate God's triumph throughout the end of history? Understanding once again Edwards' concept of God seeing "all things, great and small, in heaven and earth, *continually at one view,* assured God's final triumph in his mind. He also viewed God's decrees as the whole of God's eternal plan and God's providence as working out "the end of God's works of creation."[54] Both of these elements however, worked together like a well-oiled "machine"[55] because God is perfectly orchestrating it all from his transcendent throne.

As he contemplated God working out his decrees through providence, Edwards also began making his own calculations from historical data. He preached from creation to the completion of human history, "great events will fill up many ages, six or seven thousand years at least."[56] In his earlier "Notes on the Apocalypse," Edwards laid out a general outline of the "six or seven thousand years" that he would also later allude to in his homilies on the "History of the Work of Redemption." He referred to these key events as "remarkable periods of time: when Abraham was called, in the year of the world 2,000; Solomon's glorious kingdom settled, and temple finished in the year of the world 3,000; Christ born in the year 4,000; and the millennium to begin in the year 6,000."[57] In his "Miscellanies," he commented on the Millennium, "How happy will that state be, when neither divine nor human learning shall be confined and imprisoned within only two or three nations of Europe, but shall be diffused all over the world, and this lower world shall be all over covered with light."[58]

Hope was on the horizon as he optimistically pondered the future. There was certainly more to occur before the beginning of the millennium, but Edwards found three particular results since the time of the Reformation that were positive turns in God's decrees. First, "the Pope is much diminished in power and influence and had become less regarded by the princes of Europe than he had been before." Second, he believed that, although there was "far less persecution" on the "Protestant Church," the need for improvement still existed. Third, he was confident that a great increase of "learning" had occurred, which he also attributed to the diminishment of "popery" and the advancements in "the art of printing."[59] The last of these three not only enabled him to have access to more books from overseas, but he also was able to read the newspapers and keep up with events in the Colonies and the world abroad. As time moved forward toward the six thousandth year, he wanted every piece of information from "public news-letters ... to see if I could not find some news favorable to the interest of religion in the world."[60]

After contemplating past events and analyzing eighteenth-century contemporary world events, Edwards' thoughts went far beyond seven thousand years. After all, in actuality, God is timeless because he is eternal. People, on the other hand, live within what we call "time" but can contemplate the hope of experiencing the eternal decrees of God in eternal infinity.

When he completed his sermon series on "The History of the Work of Redemption," Edwards looked at his congregation and said,

> We have seen how it has been carrying on from the fall of man to this time. But now 'Tis complete with respect to all that belongs to it. Now the topstone of the building is

laid. In the progress of the discourse on this subject we have followed the church of God in all the great changes, all her tossings to and fro that [she] is subject to in all the storms and tempests through the many ages of the world, till at length we have seen an end to all these storms. We have seen [her] enter the harbor and landed in the highest heavens, in complete and everlasting glory, in all her members, body and soul. We have gone through time, through the several ages of it, as the providence of God and the word of God have led us, and now we have issued into eternity after time shall be no more.[61]

To the best of his ability he tried to explain in the "Miscellanies" and in his sermons that God is timeless. Man lives in small gaps in time, but only God can see the whole entire span of his decrees in light of all eternity. God always sees "all things, great and small, in heaven and earth, He is the first cause of all things" and he does "continually see all of his decrees at one view."[62] In spite of human immense limitations and refusal to often see the true splendor and sovereignty of God, he still desires to be one with his redeemed people. Edwards quoted Jesus' words, "That they all may be one, as thou Father art in me, and I in thee, that they also may be one in us; I in them and thou in me, that they may be made perfect in one" (John 17:21–23). God is moving his people in time through this world closer and closer to him. As he meditated on God's infinite nature, Edwards believed that "the nearer anything comes to infinite, the nearer it comes to an identity with God," and "He is the beginning, and the middle, and the end."[63] As a consequence, Edwards saw the singularity of God's "chief end,"[64] of what we call the end of "time," as God actually transitions us into the timeless time of his decrees. We were not with God in eternity past, but we shall give him glory in eternity future as the decrees of God perpetuate in infinity outside the bounds of what we call "time."[65]

Notes

[1] Steven J. Lawson, *The Unwavering Resolve of Jonathan Edwards* (Orlando, FL: Reformation Trust Publishing, 2008), xiii.

[2] "Miscellanies," no. 29 in *WJE*, 13:216.

[3] *WJE* 6:332, 36–37.

[4] "Miscellanies," no. 29 in *WJE*, 13:217.

[5] "The Sole Consideration, That God is God, Sufficient to Still, All Objections to His Sovereignty," in *Works of Jonathan Edwards,* memoir Sereno E. Dwight, rev. and corr. Edward Hickman (Carlisle, PA: Banner of Truth Trust, 2009), 2:107.

[6] "The Sole Consideration, That God is God, Sufficient to Still, All Objections to His Sovereignty," in *Works of Jonathan Edwards,* memoir Sereno E. Dwight, rev. and corr. Edward Hickman (Carlisle, PA: Banner of Truth Trust, 2009), 2:107.

[7] *WJE* 8:467.

[8] "Miscellanies," no. 704, in *WJE*, 18:318.

[9] "The Sole Consideration, That God is God, Sufficient to Still, All Objections to His Sovereignty," in *Works of Jonathan Edwards,* memoir Sereno E. Dwight, rev. and corr. Edward Hickman (Carlisle, PA: Banner of Truth Trust, 2009), 2:107.

[10] *WJE* 17:343–34.

[11] *WJE* 17:334.

[12] *WJE* 17:341.

[13] "Miscellanies," no. 704, in *WJE* 18:318.

[14] "Miscellanies," no. 704, in *WJE* 18:318.

[15] R.C. Sproul, *Chosen By God* (Wheaton IL, Tyndale House, 1986), 46–47.

[16] R.C. Sproul, *Chosen By God* (Wheaton IL, Tyndale House, 1986), 46–47.

[17] *WJE* 9:519.

[18] *WJE* 8:508.

[19] *WJE* 9:518.

[20] *WJE* 9:519.

[21] "Miscellanies," no. 704, in *WJE* 18:320.

[22] "Miscellanies," no. 85, in *WJE* 13:250.

[23] *WJE* 17:343.

[24] *WJE* 9:118.

[25] *WJE* 9:519.

[26] *WJE* 9:519.

[27] *WJE* 14:194.

[28] *WJE* 8:406.

[29] *WJE* 8:406.

[30] *WJE* 9:291.

[31] "Miscellanies," no. 82, in *WJE* 13:248.

[32] *WJE* 8:422.

[33] *WJE* 8:443.

[34] *WJE* 8:459.

[35] "Miscellanies," no. 87, in *WJE* 13:251–52.

[36] *WJE* 13:42.

[37] "Miscellanies," no. 29, in *WJE* 13:216.

[38] "Miscellanies," no. 704, in *WJE* 18:321.

[39] "Miscellanies," no. 29, in *WJE* 13:216–17.

[40] "The Sole Consideration, That God is God, Sufficient to Still, All Objections to His Sovereignty," in *Works of Jonathan Edwards,* memoir Sereno E. Dwight, rev. and corr. Edward Hickman (Carlisle, PA: Banner of Truth Trust, 2009), 2:107.

[41] "Miscellanies," no. 74, in *WJE* 13:243.

[42] "Miscellanies," no. 51, in *WJE* 13:228.

[43] "Miscellanies," no. 704, in *WJE* 18:321.

[44] "Miscellanies," no. 62, in *WJE* 13:233.

[45] "Miscellanies," no. 63, in *WJE* 13:234.

[46] "Miscellanies," no. 423, in *WJE* 13:478.

[47] "Miscellanies," no. 423, in *WJE* 13:478.

[48] R.C. Sproul, *Chosen By God* (Wheaton IL, Tyndale House, 1986), 46–47.

[49] *WJEO* 43.

[50] *WJE* 9:295.

[51] "Miscellanies," no. 423, in *WJE* 13:478.

[52] "Miscellanies," no. 423, in *WJE* 13:478.

[53] "Miscellanies," no. 423, in *WJE* 13:478.

[54] *WJE* 9:118.

[55] *WJE* 9:118.

[56] *WJE* 9:512.

[57] *WJE* 5:135.

[58] "Miscellanies," no. 26, in *WJE* 13:212.

[59] *WJE* 9:439–40.

[60] *WJE* 5:10.

[61] *WJE* 9:508.

[62] "The Sole Consideration, That God is God, Sufficient to Still, All Objections to His Sovereignty," in *Works of Jonathan Edwards,* memoir Sereno E. Dwight, rev. and corr. Edward Hickman (Carlisle, PA: Banner of Truth Trust, 2009), 2:107.

[63] *WJE* 8:459, 513.

[64] *WJE* 8:459.

[65] Toby K. Easley, *Jonathan Edwards: Beyond the Manuscripts* (Fort Worth, TX: Feder Ink Publishing, 2016) 90.

PROVIDENCE AND PRAYER FOR ADVANCING THE KINGDOM ON EARTH

Bonghyun Yoo

'Tis the manner of God to keep his church on earth in hope of a still more glorious state; and so their prayers are enlivened, when they pray that the interest of religion might be promoted and God's kingdom may come; and therefore that the most glorious state of the church will be in the latter age of the world.

— Jonathan Edwards, *Miscellany no. 351*

JONATHAN EDWARDS' UNDERSTANDING of reality draws from his belief in a God who is a communicative being. In "Miscellanies," No. 332, he points out, "The great and universal end of God's creating the world was to communicate himself. God is a communicative being."[1] For him, communicativeness was the most fundamental disposition or essence of God: "A disposition in God, as an original property of his nature, to an emanation of his own infinite fullness, was what excited him to create the world."[2] The divine ontological disposition, according to Edwards, sought its telos, namely, a mutual interaction between God and the world. He was convinced that his conception of God as such could answer the following question. Why would a self-sufficient and self-sustaining God create the world and conscious beings?[3] Even if God is dependent on nothing outside the inner life of the Trinity, according to Edwards, God freely chose to share his glorious and excellent reality with his created beings who are able to know and love it: "'Tis a thing infinitely good in itself that God's glory should be known by a glorious society of created beings."[4]

Moreover, Edwards' panentheistic theology of creation made an assertion that all things are in God, and God is in all.[5] In other words, God is immediately present to the world. Yet God transcends the world. Unlike pantheism, in which God is identical with the cosmos, for Edwards, God is not ontologically equal to but greater than the world. Furthermore, Edwards was a theocentric idealist in that he believed that God is the only true substance and ontologically necessary being in whom all other created beings have their existence.[6] The world is thus ideal, for it is ontologically created and sustained by divine mind.[7] Edwards' idealistic-panentheistic concept of the God-world relation established a ground for his typological imagination. He believed that "the whole universe, heaven and earth, air and seas, and the divine constitution and history of the holy Scriptures, be full of images of divine things, as full as a language is of words."[8] God can be known and seen in all the natural, historical, and scriptural types, for they are all embraced in God as the ground of all being.[9]

All types are indeed teleologically rendered as "a medium of communication by God's manner of being," which is inclined to "glorify and communicate himself" within the world.[10] For instance, Edwards held that the sun is a brighter type of the Trinity, in which God the Father is the sun itself, the Son is the brightness of the substance, and the Spirit is its diffusive heat and powerful influence upon earth.[11] For Edwards, all historical events were also typical, and he escalated them from the surfaces of history to the higher end of history in his typology. He commented that even if they might look arbitrary or meaningless at first glance, they are indeed "an orderly series of events, all wisely ordered and directed in excellent harmony and consistence, tending all to one end."[12] Last but not least, Edwards' scriptural typology was first an exegetical principle by which he could understand the unity of scripture.[13] He sought a literal and historical correspondence between persons, events, and institutions in the Old and New Testaments in terms of anticipation and fulfillment, or type and antitype.[14] This approach to scriptural typology represents the familiar path of his Reformed and Puritan predecessors, such as John Calvin (1509–1564) and Johannes Wollebius (1586–1629). Yet his scriptural typology was more dynamic than their exegeses in its nature, because Edwards did not confine it to the search for historical/horizontal correspondence or escalation within the history of the scriptures. Edwards' use of typology seemed to blur the hard line between typology (historical/horizontal) and allegory (ahistorical/vertical) in that he was most likely to insist that all types are "the inferior and shadowy parts" of spiritual meanings regarding divine wisdom and work.[15] The nature of Edwards' typology determines the scope of his typological engagement with the knowledge of God as a whole.[16]

Like general signs, types also need further validation and should be perceived and interpreted properly. For Edwards, discerning spiritual reality through types was especially important for the church because he understood some of them as prophecies pointing to the ultimate destiny of the church in the final consummation. In "Miscellanies" no. 435, for instance, Edwards described the progress and present state of history in general: "All things in heaven and earth and throughout the universe are in a state of preparation for the state of consummation; all the wheels are going, none of them stop, and all are moving in a direction to the last and most perfect state."[17] In the same entry, he then further elaborated the history of the saints in the broader context of God's providential history:

'Tis God's manner to keep things always progressive, in a preparatory state, as long as there is another change to a more perfect state yet behind. The saints in this world are progressive, and all things relating to 'em are subordinate and preparatory for the more perfect state of heaven, which is a perfect state.[18]

According to Edwards, what propels "all the wheels" of the history was indeed "a mighty wheel," an image of divine providence, "whose ring and circumference is so high."[19] History is in a constant motion from one state to another by God's immediate involvement in it. For Edwards, the historical progress toward an ultimate perfection to which the church will look forward seemed very assured, for it was God himself becoming Alpha and Omega, the beginning and the end of all things: "All the events of divine providence are like the links of a chain, the first link is from God and the last is to him."[20]

Edwards technically called the ideas with regard to God's being and providence as "first principles" in "Miscellanies" no. 350, for he regarded them as universally acknowledged in human reason, conscience, and natural laws.[21] He wrote that they are "the basis of all true philosophy, as appears more and more as philosophy improves."[22] In Edwards' intellectual context, philosophy and science indeed made considerable strides, and their new discoveries significantly affected the seventeenth and eighteenth century intellectual traditions. For instance, Isaac Newton (1643–1727), an English mathematician and physicist, led a paradigm shift from the modes of medieval thought (e.g., the Aristotelian view of nature) and laid the foundation for classical mechanics and physics. John Locke (1632–1704) was another prominent figure of modern intellectual history who made considerable contributions to the rise of epistemology and empiricism. Edwards was acutely aware of these changes and contributions to human pursuit of knowledge about natural revelation, writing that "the philosophical world makes progress in the understanding of the book of nature, and unfolding the mysteries of it" in "Miscellanies" no. 351.[23] Yet comparing to the degree of progress in the pursuit of knowledge that was achieved in philosophy and science, the church made no appreciable progress in knowledge of special revelation, according to Edwards. He commented that "the church has made no greater progress in understanding the Scripture," and he also clarified the fact by arguing that "the church is not as yet arrived to that perfection in understanding the Scriptures" in the same "Miscellanies."[24]

Why then did Edwards believe that the progress of the church's understanding of Scripture was dragging so badly? In what way did the fact that the church made little progress and even had great struggles in her pursuit of knowledge about the meaning of Scripture become a sign of the great length of time still remaining for her? The reason for such a belief was largely dependent upon his assumption that the church ought to read the Bible prophetically to grasp what lies ahead for the world.[25] For instance, he mostly understood the relationship between the Old and New Testaments in light of Messianic prophecy and fulfillment.[26] The insight of the church about the end of the age goes side by side with the gradual process of history, and the church will successively learn the future history of the world as the stages of time pass. As the church approaches closer to the "perfection in understanding the Scriptures," therefore, it could be a sign that the end is nearer.[27] Yet Edwards also warned that the church needs to pursue spiritual discernment, rather than a purely chronological quest, for the future through the Spirit's illumination in reading the biblical history.[28]

Edwards also pointed out that progressive revelation in terms of God's unfolding mystery in the future was in fact a divinely appointed wisdom for his church. He expressed the idea as follows:

> . . . how much better is it to have divine truth and light break forth in this way, than it would have been, to have had it shine at once to everyone without any labor or industry of the understanding. It would be less delightful, and less prized and valued and admired, and would have vastly less influence on men's hearts, and would be less to the glory of God.[29]

God revealed the things related to the future of the church in stages; they were not all given to her at once, for the good of the church as well as the glory of God. That is, Edwards believed that if the progressive nature of God's revelation is understood, then the church will ready herself more thoroughly before "the coming glorious times" by pondering over biblical prophecies and praying for their fulfillment more sincerely than ever (cf. 1 John 3:3).[30] It is "the manner of God to keep his church on earth in hope of a still more glorious state," as Edwards urged.[31] Moreover, if God responds to the prayers of the church and fulfills his prophecies, the glory of God will be profoundly enlarged among his people, because they would observe how God has kept his promises and thus praise him for his covenantal faithfulness that has been proven through the ages. The importance of prayer for Edwards is consistently seen in his eschatological writings. Since his early days, Edwards had started to pray for the advancement of the kingdom of God in the earthly world:

> I had great longings for the advancement of Christ's kingdom in the world. My secret prayer used to be in great part taken up in praying for it. If I heard the least hint of anything that happened in any part of the world, that appeared to me, in some respect or other, to have a favorable aspect on the interest of Christ's kingdom, my soul eagerly catched at it; and it would much animate and refresh me.[32]

It means that Edwards' personal prayer life was driven by his eschatological longing for "the advancement of Christ's kingdom in the world."[33] His prayer was also conducted while paying attention to the voices of the world in terms of the state of international affairs, particularly, news concerning the socio-political and religious progress of the Protestant church over all her enemies.[34] Edwards, a Protestant and Reformed successor, viewed the history of redemption from a militant perspective, believing that all enemies, such as Roman Catholicism, Islam ("Mahometanism"), and heathenism, will be rendered gradually powerless by the global expansion of the Christ's church, politically and spiritually.[35] In short, his prospect for the coming millennium was the final completion of the Protestant Ref-

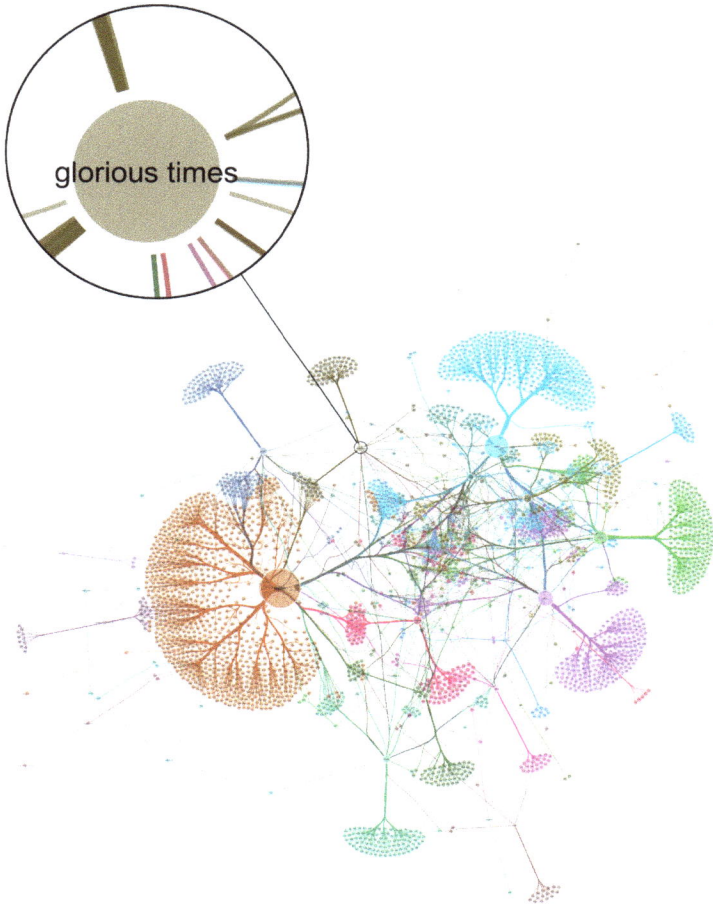

ADVANCEMENT, GLORIOUS TIMES, KINGDOM, *and* PRAYER—*a map of advance, advanced, advancement, advancements, advances, advancing, glorious times, kingdom, kingdoms, pray, prayed, prayer, prayerful, prayerfully, prayerfulness, prayerless, prayers, prayest, prayeth, praying, prays with interconnections and page locations in WJE 1–26.*

ormation on earth through "a vastly more glorious propagation of the true religion" leading up to the gradual fall of Christ's enemies simultaneously.[36] "It is a great encouragement to such endeavors, to think that such times are coming wherein Christianity shall prevail over all enemies," as he encouraged the church.[37]

He was also convinced that the "prosperity of his church" is the same as that of "his kingdom."[38] This joint end should be fulfilled with "greater earnestness and cheerfulness and faith" of God's people.[39] Hence, Edwards encouraged all the church to be united in prayer for the telos.[40] In *An Humble Attempt,* he specifically related the duty of prayer on the part of God's people to a future-oriented vision for the advancement of the church, explaining that:

> . . . it appears to me reasonable, to suppose, that something more special is intended, with regard to the duty of prayer; considering that prayer is here expressly and repeatedly mentioned; and also considering how parallel this place is with many other prophecies, that speak of an extraordinary spirit of prayer, as preceding and introducing that glorious day of revival of religion, and advancement of the church's peace and prosperity, so often foretold (which I shall have occasion to mention hereafter) and particularly the agreeableness of what is here said, with what is said afterwards by the same prophet, of the "pouring out of a spirit of grace and supplications," as that with which this great revival of religion shall begin (Zech 12:10).[41]

It was his conviction that God will be delighted with the corporate and united prayer of his people across the globe for the achievement of God's promise for the church, and the mighty works of God would be accomplished in accord with such prayer.[42] In practice, Edwards called for active involvement of the church in a global prayer network known as Concerts of Prayer. He defended it against critics who charged the practice with hypocrisy.[43] He then insisted that the church should gather together every month in visible unity and spiritual agreement to pray for that joint end, namely, the advancement of the church and thus that of God's kingdom on earth: "thy kingdom come; thy will be done in earth as it is in heaven" (Matt 6:10).

In the latter part of "Miscellanies" no. 351, however, Edwards called the church's attention to her ultimate hope in the last coming of Christ which will take the church from this earth and bring the church to the new heavens and the new earth. Before that, there would be a widespread satanic opposition against the church at the end of the millennial age. Yet the great apostasy would not last long, as Edwards believed. And soon after that, Christ will come for the decisive battle with Satan, and he will finally bring about the day of victory over rebellion and lead "his church to its highest and its everlasting glory."[44] He then concluded that that would be "the only remedy" for the church.[45] For Edwards, the ultimate hope of the body of Christ is thus not the millennium per se but the final consummation of all things in the Lord Christ.

Notes

[1] "Miscellanies," no. 332, in *WJE* 13:410.

[2] *WJE* 8:435.

[3] William M. Schweitzer, *God is a Communicative Being: Divine Communication and Harmony in the Theology of Jonathan Edwards* (New York: T&T Clark, 2012), 12–13.

[4] *WJE* 8:431–32. See "Miscellanies," no. 448, in *WJE* 13:496 and "Miscellanies," no. 204, in *WJE* 13:339.

[5] See John W. Cooper, *Panentheism The Other God of the Philosophers: From Plato to the Present* (Grand Rapids: Baker Academic, 2006), 77. See also Oliver D. Crisp, "Jonathan Edwards' Panentheism," in Don Schweitzer, ed., *Jonathan Edwards as Contemporary: Essays in Honor of Sang Hyun Lee* (New York: Peter Lang, 2010), 107–125. Crisp specifically opines that Edwards was "an idealist panentheist." Don Schweitzer also refers to Edwards' understanding of the God-world relationship as an approximately "panentheistic model." See Schweitzer, "Aspects of God's Relationship to the World in the Theologies of Jurgen Moltmann, Bonaventure and Jonathan Edwards." *Religious Studies and Theology*, Vol. 26, No.1 (2007) 20.

[6] See *WJE* 6:238.

[7] See *WJE* 9:341.

[8] *WJE* 11:152.

⁹See "Miscellanies," no. 448, in *WJE* 13:496. In "Miscellanies" No. 448, he wrote that "God's being the Alpha and Omega, the first and the last. God made all things; and the end for which all things are made, and for which they are disposed, and for which they work continually, is that God's glory may shine forth and be received."

¹⁰Janice Knight, "Typology," in Sang Hyun Lee, ed., *The Princeton Companion to Jonathan Edwards* (Princeton, NJ: Princeton University, 2005), 200.

¹¹"Miscellanies," no. 370, in *WJE* 13:441. In the same "Miscellanies" No. 370, Edwards wrote that the soul of men is another type of the Trinity. See also *WJE* 11:74. Natural types, according to Edwards, are all around us, "wherever we are, and whatever we are about, we may see divine things excellently represented and held forth."

¹²*WJE* 9:519–20. In terms of divine providence, Edwards addressed it in a similar way, writing that, "God's providence may not unfitly be compared to a large and long river, having innumerable branches beginning in different regions, and at a great distance from another, and all conspiring to one common issue. After their very diverse and contrary course which they hold for a while, yet all gathering more and more together the nearer they come to their common end, and all at length discharging themselves at one mouth into the same ocean."

¹³See Douglas A. Sweeney, *Edwards the Exegete: Biblical Interpretation and Anglo-Protestant Culture on the Edge of the Enlightenment* (New York: Oxford University, 2016), 7. Sweeney argued that the whole stage of Edwards' life was "animated by Scripture."

¹⁴See *WJE* 16:728–29.

¹⁵"Miscellanies," no. 362, in *WJE* 13:434–35. See *WJE* 11:152. See also Stephen R. C. Nichols, *Jonathan Edwards' Bible: The Relationship of the Old and New Testaments* (Eugene, OR: Pickwick, 2013), 62–69.

¹⁶See also Nichols, *Jonathan Edwards' Bible,* 62–69. He summarizes the continuity of Edwards' use of typology, arguing that "Edwards' typologizing of Scripture, history, and nature are all of one piece, explicable by reference to his philosophical commitments, in particular his idealism and his notion of being as relational and communicative within a teleology of divine self-glorification."

¹⁷"Miscellanies," no. 435, in *WJE* 13:483. See *WJE* 9:517–18.

¹⁸"Miscellanies," no. 435, in *WJE* 13:483. See "Miscellanies," no. 804, in *WJE* 18:505. In "Miscellanies" no. 804, Edwards believed in the progress of God's reign in history based upon the gospel message in which "Christ's mediatorial glory" achieved through his righteous and sacrificial works has advanced the history of redemption and bestowed upon the church "in various successive steps and degrees."

¹⁹*WJE* 9:517. See "Miscellanies," no. *ww,* in *WJE* 13:192. In "Miscellanies" *ww,* he argued that the four living creatures and the wheels full of eyes are "an emblem of divine providence" in Ezekiel's first vision (1:4–21) and the wheels of providence are "managed exactly according to these four, divine wisdom, power, goodness, and justice." According to him, each divine attribute refers to one of the four living

creatures, for instance, power for the first, goodness for the second, wisdom for the third, and justice for the last.

[20]*WJE* 9:518.

[21]"Miscellanies," no. 350, in *WJE* 13:425.

[22]"Miscellanies," no. 350, in *WJE* 13:425.

[23]"Miscellanies," no. 351, in *WJE* 13:426.

[24]"Miscellanies," no. 351, in *WJE* 13:426.

[25]See *WJE* 11:152. See also Jürgen Moltmann, *The Coming of God: Christian Eschatology,* trans. Margaret Kohl (Minneapolis, MN: Fortress, 1996), 145–46. According to him, one of the immediate criticisms concerning the prophetic interpretation of Scripture is that it takes the Bible as the book of God's providence, not that of God's promises.

[26]See *WJE* 16:728–29.

[27]*WJE* 13:426. In the note, Edwards argued that to understand Scripture fully is "the highest that God ever intended the church should come to." See also *WJE* 9:480–81, in where he claimed that the calling will be achieved in the millennial age: "There shall then be a wonderful unraveling the difficulties in the doctrines of religion, and clearing up seeming inconsistencies ... Difficulties in Scripture shall then be cleared up, and wonderful things shall be discovered in the word of God that were never discovered before."

[28]Unlike Moses Lowman (1680–1752), Edwards was relatively less concerned about chronological speculations, whereas his work A Paraphrase and Notes on the Revelation (1745) significantly influenced the formation of Edwards' exegesis on the Revelation.

[29]"Miscellanies," no. 351, in *WJE* 13:426.

[30]"Miscellanies," no. 351, in *WJE* 13:426–27.

[31]"Miscellanies," no. 351, in *WJE* 13:427.

[32]*WJE* 16:797. See "Miscellanies," no. 351, in *WJE* 13:427.

[33]*WJE* 16:797.

[34]*WJE* 5:256; "Miscellanies," no. 351, in *WJE* 13:427. See also Stephen J. Stein, "Eschatology," in Sang Hyun Lee, ed., *The Princeton Companion to Jonathan Edwards* (Princeton, NJ: Princeton University, 2005), 235.

[35]See "Miscellanies," no. hh, in *WJE* 13:186. Edwards described the Church of Rome as "the more anti-Christ, against Christ," "a viper or some loathsome, poisonous, crawling monster." See also "Miscellanies," no. 613, in *WJE* 18:146. In "Miscellanies" No. 613, Edwards wrote that the global expansion of the Christian church will "swallow up Mahometanism and root it out of the world." For more discussion on this topic, see also Gerald R. McDermott, "Islam," in Harry S. Stout, ed., *The Jonathan Edwards Encyclopedia* (Grand Rapids: Eerdmans, 2017), 338. McDermott writes that for Edwards, Roman Catholicism and Islam were "the devil's two world-historical forces stalking the earth in the latter days" against the church's latter-day glory.

³⁶"Miscellanies," no. 613, in *WJE* 18:145. See also *WJE* 5:408. In *An Humble Attempt,* Edwards wrote as follows: "As the power of Antichrist, and the corruption of the apostate church, rose not at once, but by several notable steps and degrees; so it will in the like manner fall: and that divers steps and seasons of destruction to the spiritual Babylon, and revival and advancement of the true church, are prophesied of under one."

³⁷"Miscellanies," no. 351, in *WJE* 13:427.

³⁸"Miscellanies," no. 804, in *WJE* 18:506.

³⁹"Miscellanies," no. 351, in *WJE* 13:427.

⁴⁰See *WJE* 5:314. It is written as follows: "In the text we have an account *how* this future glorious advancement of the church of God should be brought on, or introduced; viz., by great multitudes in different towns and countries taking up a *joint resolution,* and coming into an express and visible *agreement,* that they will, by united and extraordinary *prayer,* seek to God that he would come and manifest himself, and grant the tokens and fruits of his gracious presence."

⁴¹*WJE* 5:315.

⁴²See *WJE* 25:202.

⁴³Stein, "Eschatology," 234.

⁴⁴C. C. Goen, "Jonathan Edwards: A New Departure in Eschatology." *Church History,* Vol. 28, No. 1 (1959), 29. See "Miscellanies," no. 351, in *WJE* 13:427.

⁴⁵"Miscellanies," no. 351, in *WJE* 13:427. See also "Miscellanies," no. 836, in *WJE* 20:52. In "Miscellanies" No. 836, Edwards expounded a little more on the nature of the millennium as penultimate, arguing that "this is not the appointed state of her reward and happiness, and therefore won't be very long continued. The proper state of the church's rest is after the day of judgment; this that is before, is only given to the church as a foretaste, a forerunner and image of this her true rest and glory. 'Tis observable, that prelibations and images of things that are before the appointed proper season for the true thing of which they are forerunners and representations, are wont to be but short."

EDWARDS ON GOSPEL HOLINESS AS GOD'S PERFECT SALVATION

Roy Mellor

> *Holiness is a most beautiful and lovely thing. We drink in strange notions of holiness from our childhood, as if it were a melancholy, morose, sour and unpleasant thing; but there is nothing in it but what is sweet and ravishingly lovely.*
>
> — Jonathan Edwards, *Miscellany no. a*

"MISCELLANIES," NOS. *a*, 330, 341, 790, 800, 894, 1127, and 1129, ranging from early to later dates, reveal a holiness of vision, obedience and perseverance. Although Edwards remains clearly within orthodox Reformed Calvinism, there is always a hint of a tweaked approach to sanctification. In this essay I will show that Gospel holiness is vastly superior to perfection according to the capacity of our nature. The Holy Spirit is himself the communication of that Gospel sanctification which culminates in the vision of a perfect heaven celebrating a perfect God and is a powerful theme throughout all of Edwards' *Works*.

A quick glance at those *Works* of Jonathan Edwards will reveal a lack of reticence to employ the vocabulary of sanctification which is more usually associated with various "perfectionist" schools of piety. In Miscellany no. *a*, Edwards extolls the beauties of holiness: "Holiness is a most beautiful and lovely thing."[1] Then he "muses about how it is for "a sanctified soul." Here, the contrast is set up between a "sanctified soul," "the highest beauty and amiableness, vastly above all other beauties," and defilement and heathen virtues. In this very early writing from New York (1722), we have the certainty of a young "Spirit-filled" preacher glorying in the "felt-sense" of spiritual ardour. So much so that holiness is lauded as "the highest beauty;" the world around is all defilement to the soul that is sanctified. God's beauty is *almost* "too high," but not really, because the sanctified soul is "a delightful image of the blessed Jehovah."[2] The young Edwards is not uncertain as to what had happened: "I did receive the blessed Spirit as my teacher, sanctifier and only comforter; and cherish all his motions to enlighten, purify, confirm, comfort and assist me."[3]

In an early sermon (c.1723) based on Isaiah 35:8, "The Way of Holiness," which includes language reminiscent of Miscellany no. *a*, Edwards prompts the reader to consider this: "If the sinner retains his sin, and it is not washed off by the blood of Christ, and he purified and sanctified and made holy, it must be punished upon him. If he is sanctified, his sin has been already punished in the passion of Christ."[4] The Holy Spirit is immediately said to be the active agent of sanctification. Here is bold language, confident that entrance to heaven is only open to those whose sin is "washed off." The sermon then exhorts those who would enter heaven to see if their souls find pleasure and delight in the divine perfections. The "copy" should look to the "original," "the Heavenly Dove, spirit of all grace and original of all holiness" to see if the "copy" in our spirit, temper and dispositions are Christlike. You should look to Bible characters who have gone before to assess "whether you have the root of the matter in you."[5]

In Edwards' "Personal Narrative," written a decade later, the distinctive and influential character of Christian holiness is figuratively expressed:

> The soul of a true Christian, as I then wrote my meditations, appeared like such a little white flower, as we see in the spring of the year; low and humble on the ground, opening its bosom, to receive the pleasant beams of the

sun's glory; rejoicing as it were, in a calm rapture; diffusing around a sweet fragrancy; standing peacefully and lovingly, in the midst of other flowers round about; all in like manner opening their bosoms, to drink in the light of the sun.[6]

Furthermore, Edwards' cited Scriptures often cohere with those of "holiness" tendencies. In particular, we should note his interest in 1 John.[7] John Wesley frequently cited this in support of Christian perfection.[8] Edwards clearly accused John and Charles Wesley of erroneously teaching "sinless perfection," probably based on a sight of Charles Wesley's *Hymns and Sacred Poems (No 1)* and perhaps a conversation with George Whitefield,[9] so this is surprising at first. A similar shock is administered by Samuel G. Craig, editor of the 1958 edition of the Benjamin B. Warfield's *Perfectionism*. In the preface and referring to an exposition of Warfield, "Entire Sanctification," he states, "It is obvious from this exposition that Warfield was a thoroughgoing perfectionist ... he did not regard perfection as an unattainable ideal ... However, he did not believe the believer could reach this goal in this life."[10]

Was Edwards like Warfield, really a believer in Christian perfection? Contrast the truly awakened, writes Edwards, with the "high pretenders": "finding no disposition to any opinion of being now perfectly free from sin (agreeable to the notion of the Wesleys and their followers, and some other high pretenders to spirituality in these days)."[11] C. C. Goen and others have drawn attention to the difference between "sinless perfection" and "Christian perfection" in Wesley's doctrine. Geordon Hammond points to Edwards confusing "antinomian perfection" and Christian perfection.[12] What cannot be denied is that Wesley was unable to prevent a belief in the attainability of "sinless perfection" becoming a reality in many of his followers. Why was this?

Contrasting Edwards with Wesley we must always understand that sin is defined differently. One of John Wesley's most famous definitions was "sin is a voluntary transgression of a known law." He believed that "involuntary sins" were "sin, *improperly* so called."[13] It seems a million miles away from what Edwards stated sin to be: "Sin is the most cruel tyrant that ever ruled ... Sin is a woeful confusion and dreadful disorder in the soul, whereby everything is put out of place, reason trampled under foot and passion advanced in the room of it, conscience dethroned and abominable lusts reigning."[14] We know that Edwards was fully in accord with the Westminster Standards, in which "sin is any want of conformity unto, or transgression of, any law of God, given as a rule to the reasonable creature."[15] We need to remember, however, that John Taylor of Norwich (1694–1761) was a common enemy for both Edwards and Wesley. To be fair to Wesley, he never held back from asserting depravity in the human condition. But there is something in Wesley's definition of sin which skews his understanding of holiness. For Wesley, sin is (but not exclusively) about "wilfulness." For Edwards, sin always involves "lack" or "privation"—no human is *fully* as God would have us be. There was no ambivalence. In Edwards' sustained barrage of attack in one of his most difficult writings, *Original Sin,* he reveals the absolute importance he ascribed to correctly describing his subject. Edwards wanted to be sure that sin was understood as disposition as well as act. Of Adam he wrote: "His sin consisted in wickedness of heart, fully sufficient *for,* and entirely amounting *to,* all that appeared in the act he committed."[16] In these "Miscellanies," Edwards sets out how the "lack" is supplied. Put quite simply, sanctification is gifted in the Holy Spirit.

Vital to all Edwards' writing is the person and role of the Holy Spirit. It would not be exaggerating to say that on this observation hangs our comprehension of Edwards. It is not uncommon to hear of complaints that Reformed theologians downplay the Holy Spirit in their treatments of sanctification.[17] No one would ever suggest this of Edwards' holiness perspective. Pneumatology is rampant. In Miscellany no. *a*: "Oh, of what a sweet, humble nature is holiness! ... where the sun is Jesus Christ; the blessed beams and calm breeze, the Holy Spirit; the sweet and delightful flowers."[18] In Miscellany no.

330 (written in 1728) Edwards impresses on us his Spirit ontology: "It appears that the Holy Spirit is the holiness, or excellency and delight of God."[19] The Holy Spirit is this synonymy of beauty. He does not merely supply or apply holiness, excellency, delight; he is definitively this divine beauty. Although the whole created order is a communication of a beautiful God and "the Holy Spirit is the harmony and excellency and beauty of the Deity,"[20] it is in redemption that the Spirit is "the thing purchased."[21] Here is the unmistakable Edwardsean "tweak" to the doctrine of sanctification. The Holy Spirit is for Edwards the "sum of all that Christ purchased." The purchase is promised true Christian perfection:

> Christ purchased for us grace and many spiritual blessings in this world, but they are all comprised in that, in having the indwelling of the Holy Ghost. Christ purchased glory for us in another world, that we should be like God, that we should be perfect in holiness and happiness; which still is comprised in that, in having the indwelling of the Holy Ghost. (The Spirit is that river of water of life, which in heaven proceeds from the throne of God and the Lamb [Revelation 22a]). Therefore the Holy Ghost that believers have, here is said to be the earnest of the inheritance, or purchased possession [Ephesians 1:14]. The earnest is some of the same given beforehand; the purchased possession is only a fullness of that Spirit.[22]

Although there is always an "already" and a "not yet" in Edwards' preaching of holiness, the "partaking" and "communion" always begin now. These are the two key words in "Miscellanies," nos. 330 and 341. Edwards cites 1 John as evidence of our sharing in God's holiness.

Two verses which are particularly important for Edwards are: "And he that keepeth his commandments dwelleth in him, and he in him. And hereby we know that he abideth in us, by the Spirit which he hath given us" (1 John 3:24). And: " Hereby know we that we dwell in him, and he in us, because he hath given us of his Spirit"

(1 John 4:13). We are really and actually "partakers" of the divine nature and in communion with him we are made holy. In Miscellany no. 341 Edwards sees a ready explanation for fourteen omissions by the Apostle Paul: "I can think of no other good account that can be given of the apostle Paul's wishing grace and peace, or grace, mercy and peace, from God the Father and the Lord Jesus Christ in the beginnings of his epistles without ever mentioning the Holy Ghost, but that the Holy Ghost is the grace, the love and peace of God the Father and [the] Lord Jesus Christ."[23] The implicit is made explicit in 2 Corinthians 13:14 where grace and love is ours in the "communion" of the Holy Spirit who is God's communication.

It is that communication of the Spirit in the grace, love and peace of Father and Son which undergirds each of these "Miscellanies" and all of Edwards' understanding of Christian holiness/perfection. Edwards is clear: Christ's offering is the infinite price of redemption. But the "thing purchased" is the Holy Spirit. We share in "all the blessings of his purchase ... the price, and the thing bought with that price, are equal."[24]

In that "purchase" privation is reversed. The Holy Spirit dwelled within Adam and Eve producing "superior principles." But according to Edwards in *Original Sin,* "that divine inhabitant forsook the house" when they fell.[25] The loss of the Holy Spirit meant the light was switched off in the room, plunging the human race into darkness. A "fatal catastrophe" occurred which ensured the reign of "flesh" as opposed to "spirit." In the state of Adam's "probation" the Holy Spirit absolutely guaranteed perfect holiness in "the capacity of our nature."[26] Such holiness is no longer possible. "Though holiness, or the spiritual image of God, be in its principle and habit the same," the way it is gifted is different.[27] Redemption in Christ ensures that "Christian holiness/perfection" is gifted to all who are in communion with Christ: "Gospel holiness differs greatly from the holiness of man in innocency: man had the Holy Ghost then, as the Spirit of God; but now he must have it as the Spirit of the Son of God, the Spirit of a

Redeemer, a Mediator between God and us, and a spiritual husband, etc."[28]

It was absolutely necessary for Gospel holiness that the Spirit be restored and the "purchase" be made by the Redeemer, the obedient last Adam. Only Christ could render perfect obedience. The obedience God required was "universal obedience," involving the whole person without one single offence. Just one offence, even if everything else is perfect brings the whole crashing down. Why is this so? The answer is that God alone is perfect. Miscellany no. 1127 lists eleven reasons for Adam's "State of Probation," chief among which are the display of God's perfections of justice and holiness: Intelligent creatures could have had no proper idea of the greatness and beauty of God's holiness, nor of the beauty of holiness in general, for they would have had no opportunity to have compared it with its contrary, even sin or moral evil."[29] Edwards is probing the deep mysteries of God's ways, and it seems that obedience is key requirement in in both prelapsarian holiness and Gospel holiness.

In Miscellany no. 790 Edwards stresses the comprehensive nature of the obedience God requires:

> As he looks at the obedience and practice of the man, he looks at the practice of the soul chiefly, as the soul chiefly is the man and *instar totius* in God's sight: for God seeth not as man seeth, for he looketh on the heart. True godliness consists not in an heart to intend to keep God's commandments, but in an heart to do it, Deuteronomy 5:27–29. See sermon on this text."[30]

Much of this Miscellany is a meditation on John 14:15: "If ye love me, keep my commandments," and the Apostle John's own meditation in that all important Scripture 1 John. For Edwards' understanding of Christian perfection and Gospel holiness, God's love is "perfected" in this: keeping his commands from the heart. Justice is not done "by clockwork, as an act of obedience to Christ."[31] Commandments kept from the heart are "the best sign of godliness." Nor can this be played off against the "inner witness," the immediate witness of the Spirit: "Keeping Christ's commands is the highest evidence of a good estate, and yet the witness of the Spirit of adoption or love is the highest evidence: for they are both the same."[32] We know all this "by the Spirit" (1 John 3:24).

Edwards clearly wrote about "how far Exceedingly we are fallen from the state we once were in when we were in a state of sinless Perfection."[33] Such "sinless perfection" is no longer possible this side of heaven. This does not mean that the believer is mired in an anthropological pessimism of restricted grace, as is often implied by Wesleyans. On the contrary,

> 'Tis probable that some Christians have had higher exercises of love to God, than ever our first parents had, and yet were exceeding far from sinless perfection, which they had. The occasion we have to love God now is infinitely greater than that which they had. 'Tis probable that some Christians have had higher degrees of spiritual joys, than ever Adam had."[34]

As Isaac Watts said of the Redeemer: "In him the tribes of Adam boast/more blessings than their father lost."

In Miscellany no. 1129 Edwards asks why should we now be required to render obedience to God's commands when Christ has perfectly done so already. As Edwards speculates on holiness without earthly "probation," he asks why not cut straight to heaven? Being the posterity of Adam, it is essential for faith to be exercised. If the purchased paradise comes first, then faith is no longer required: "God saw fit that sanctification itself and the whole of salvation, excepting the very first act of faith, should be given as the consequence of faith, and as dependent on it as the condition of all."[35] If sanctification is first begun in heaven, then the vast array of all the facets of God's grace would not have been known. Faith would certainly not be required. Faith and God's mercies form the foundation for this beautiful display. As Edwards writes, "If holiness were first begun in heaven, there

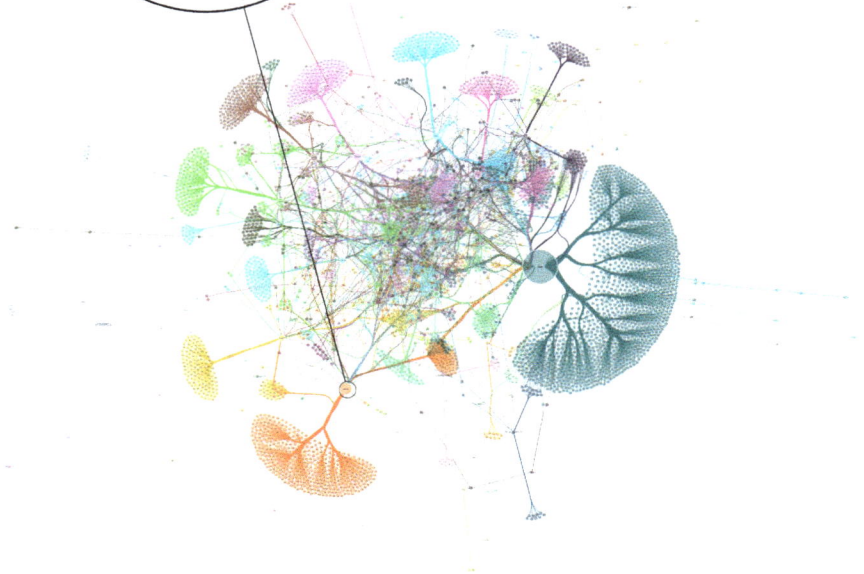

ADOPTION, COMMANDMENT, EVIDENCE, LOVE, *and* WITNESS OF THE SPIRIT— *a map of adopt, adopted, adopter, adopting, adoption, adopts, beloved, beloveds, command, commanded, commander, commanders, commandest, commandeth, commanding, commandings, commandment, commandments, commands, evidence, evidenced, evidences, evidenceth, evidencing, evidency, love, loved, lovedst, loveliness, lovely, lover, lovers, loves, lovest, loveth, loving, lovingkindness, lovingly, unloveliness, unlovely, witness of the spirit with interconnections and page locations in WJE 1–26.*

would not be that foundation laid for building it up to so great a height, nor the bringing it to so amiable a beauty in the manner of its exercise, and so no foundation for so sweet a joy."[36] Nor would it do to say that sanctification and union with Christ is post mortem. That would be to "make Christ nothing but the minister of sin and to embolden them,"[37] turning earth into hell.

Earth, however, is the territory where Christ overthrows Satan's power: "The same stage where he seemed to conquer; that he should be destroyed by the second man and head of men in the same world where he destroyed the first head of men."[38] Sin's power in all its fatal variations is defeated. The serpent's head is bruised, and Satan is dealt a finishing blow. So by virtue of the second Adam's perfect obedience, our ongoing obedience will issue one day in our perfect holiness and glorification. Our present trial or "probation" allows God to confirm all his awful majesty majesty, his hatred of sin and its dreadful power. By this, the "beauty and preciousness of holiness"[39] and its fruits are displayed in obedient and sin conquering subjects.

Far from lessening the vision of holiness and sanctification, Gospel holiness holds out for every believer a Spirit empowered life of universal obedience, fruitful in every way, by which the Spirit witnesses that we are truly children of God:

> Keeping Christ's commands is the highest evidence of a good estate, and yet the witness of the Spirit of adoption or love is the highest evidence: for they are both the same. Therefore the apostle John, where speaking of keeping Christ's commands as the great evidence of our good estate, does in the same place speak of our partaking of the Spirit of God as a spirit of love, as the great evidence of a good estate (1 John 3, at the latter end). 1 John 3:19: "And hereby we know that we are of the truth, and shall assure our hearts before him." 1 John 3:22: "And whatsoever we ask, we receive."[40]

Notes

[1]"Miscellanies," no. *a,* in *WJE* 13:163.

[2]"Miscellanies," no. *a,* in *WJE* 13:163.

[3]*WJE* 16:762.

[4]*WJE* 10:475.

[5]*WJE* 10:477–8.

[6]*WJE* 16:796.

[7]See, as an example, Edwards' use of 1 John 3.24: "Whoever keeps his command-ments abides in God, and God in him. And by this we know that he abides in us, by the Spirit whom he has given us." Especially 1 John 4.

[8]See for example: Sermon on 1 John 3.9: "The Great Privilege of those that are Born of God" in *Sermons on Several Occasions* (London: Fisher Son & Jackson, 1832) 185.

[9]See Richard B. Steele in *Gracious Affection and True Virtue According to Jonathan Edwards and John Wesley* (Metuchen, NJ: Scarecrow Press, 1994) 149.

[10]Benjamin B. Warfield, *Perfectionism* (Philadelphia: Presbyterian & Reformed Publishing Company, 1974) x.

[11]*WJE* 4:341.

[12]*WJE* 4:341. See also entry for "John Wesley" in *The Jonathan Edwards Encyclope-dia* (Grand Rapids: Eerdmans Publishing, 2017).

[13]*The Works of the Rev. John Wesley,* comp. John Emory (New York: The Methodist Concern, 1831). 1:355.

[14]"Way of Holiness," *WJE* 10:475–476.

[15]*Larger Catechism,* Q.24.

[16]*WJE* 3:390.

[17]See as examples the responses of some writers to the "Reformed Perspective" in *Five views on Sanctification* (Grand Rapids: Zondervan Publishing Company, 1987).

[18]"Miscellanies," no. a, in *WJE* 13:164.

[19]"Miscellanies," no. 330, in *WJE* 13:409.

[20]"Miscellanies," no. 293, in *WJE* 13:384.

[21]*WJE* 21:136.

[22]"Miscellanies," no. 402, in *WJE* 13:467.

[23]"Miscellanies," no. 341, in *WJE* 13:415.

[24]*WJE* 21:137.

[25]*WJE* 3:382.

[26]"Miscellanies," no. 894, in *WJE* 20:153.

[27]"Miscellanies," no. 894, in *WJE* 20:153.

[28]"Miscellanies," no. 894, in *WJE* 20:153.

[29]"Miscellanies," no. 1127, in *WJE* 20:497.

[30]"Miscellanies," no. 790, in *WJE* 18:480.

[31]"Miscellanies," no. 790, in *WJE* 18:480.

[32] "Miscellanies," no. 790, in *WJE* 18:487.
[33] Sermon Series 11, *WJEO* 48.
[34] "Miscellanies," no. 894, in *WJE* 20:154.
[35] "Miscellanies," no. 1129, in *WJE* 20:505.
[36] "Miscellanies," no. 1129, in *WJE* 20:506.
[37] "Miscellanies," no. 1129, in *WJE* 20:504.
[38] "Miscellanies," no. 1129, in *WJE* 20:504.
[39] "Miscellanies," no. 1127, in *WJE* 20:500.
[40] "Miscellanies," no. 790, in *WJE* 18:487.

EDWARDS ON THE IMPORTANCE OF THE SABBATH

David J. Arnold

> *God takes delight to honor the day and to give his blessing on this day upon that account, as princes will give gifts on their birthdays, marriage days, etc. But how much more reason has Christ to bless the day of his resurrection, and to delight to honor it, and be conferring his graces and blessed gifts on men on this day, in a joyful remembrance of his rest and refreshment from his extreme labors and sufferings on this day!*
>
> — Jonathan Edwards, *Miscellany no. 466*

JONATHAN EDWARDS' VIEW ON THE SABBATH was a dominant theme within his writings, but, unfortunately, is an overlooked one in academia. Nevertheless, the Sabbath was an important practice for Edwards, and one in which he maintained in his own life and within his ministry. As a result, the word "Sabbath," and other words related, were expounded on in his "Miscellanies."

This essay will address Edwards' understanding of the Sabbath and its importance in his "Miscellanies." A few key terms will be highlighted in order to navigate the topic. These themes are as followed: (1) Sabbath: What is Edwards understanding of the Sabbath and why should it be upheld? (2) The Christian Sabbath: How does

Edwards see the Christian Sabbath (or Lord's Day) as a vital and relevant part of the Christian faith? (3) Rest and refreshment: How does Edwards prescribe to the idea that the Sabbath is a rest and recovery day for God's people? (4) Exercise: How does Edwards see keeping the Sabbath as a spiritual exercise for further holiness and sanctification among God's people?

First, what is Edwards understanding of the Sabbath within the Old Testament framework? As an heir of Puritan stock from the early days of New England, Edwards grew up immersed in the doctrine of the Sabbath from his childhood. Furthermore, he was acquainted with Thomas Shepard's *Theses Sabbaticae,* a very influential work which helped shaped the colonies in the seventeenth century. Edwards owned a copy of Shepard's work on the Sabbath, as noted in his catalog of books.[1]

In his day, Edwards observed a growing trend moving away from a strict observance of the Sabbath, especially among young people. However, in June of 1731, after Northampton was struck with tragedy as a result of the sudden death of a young person, Edwards observes an awakening. As a result, "the youth of Northampton started meeting on Sabbath evenings for prayer."[2] This was a significant shift in the culture of Northampton, and it fueled the fire for the Great Awakening.

The question is, then, how did Edwards view the Sabbath within the corpus of his "Miscellanies"? As most scholars know, the Bible was central for Edwards and the most constant companion throughout his life. Sweeny notes that Edwards was a "Biblicist – one whose world revolved around the words of Scripture,"[3] and words such as "Sabbath," "Lord's Day," and "rest" were most certainly noted and used throughout his "Miscellanies." Moreover, within the wider context of Edwards' "Miscellanies," his view of the Sabbath was related to his view on holiness, a topic he wrote on often, because he saw it as a holy exercise for God's people.

This study seeks to show why the Sabbath was important to Edwards, what he meant by it, and how it relates to the wider context of his writings. With that said, Edwards was fascinated by how the Old Testament narratives pointed to New Testament fulfillments, including "types," and how "God designedly shadowed forth spiritual things."[4] This included the doctrine of the Sabbath. For example, Edwards states in his "Miscellanies" that the seventh day of the week was the day the children of Israel came out of Egypt. Furthermore, the seventh day and the narrative of the children of Israel leaving Egypt is a type of the redemption Christ would fulfill. Edwards writes:

> Their seventh day was the day wherein they were brought out of Egypt. Our seventh day, or first day——it's no matter by what name we call it—is the day that Christ brought us out of Egypt, out of bondage to sin and Satan; of which deliverance theirs was but a faint representation, between which and the thing represented there is as much difference as between a dim spark and the sun in the middle of the heavens, in the strength of his glory.[5]

Another example is found in Edwards' "Blank Bible," where he notes in Exodus 19:10–11 that to "be ready against the third day, for the third day the Lord will come down" (v. 11) points to the Christian Sabbath. "This 'third day' is actually the first day of the week, when God came down on Mt. Sinai."[6] Edwards understood that Old Testament narratives reveal greater truths that would be fulfilled in gospel times under Christ. "This shows, then, that God's people are to give honor to this day being the day on which Christ was to rise from the dead... The day of the Christian [sabbath] is honored above the Jewish sabbath by God's appointing the Jewish sabbath to be a day of preparation for it, as the Jewish dispensation was a preparation for the Christian."[7]

Therefore, the purpose of the Sabbath, according to Edwards, is a *memento* (a remembrance) of what God had established and what Christ has perfected in His death and resurrection. The Old Testament doctrine of the Jewish Sabbath was fulfilled in the New Testament through Christ. Edwards writes, "'Tis true the sabbath day used to be kept in remembrance of the creation of the world, but the first creation is spoiled; we have ruined it, and have reason to lament that ever we were created, except we are created again. We are truly to keep the sabbath in commemoration of the creation, but it is of the new creation."[8] Hence, Edwards observes that the Jewish Sabbath, as established in the Creation account, was a pattern of six days of work and one day of rest, which was cause to keep it. However, the work of redemption "was sufficient to supersede all the rest"[9] and should give greater cause for God's people to continue to celebrate and sanctify the Sabbath. Edwards understood that just as the Jews were commanded to keep one day as set apart to God, as a means to remember His work in creation, so the saints are to remember and call to mind the hope of the resurrection and a new heavens and earth to come (Isa. 65:17).[10]

Second, Edwards understood that the Christian Sabbath (the Lord's Day) is vital and relevant to the Christian faith. Proof of this is Edwards' sermon, "The Perpetuity and Change of the Sabbath." He says: "It is the mind and will of God, that the first day of the week should be especially set apart among Christians, for religious exercises and duties."[11] Throughout this sermon on the Christian Sabbath, Edwards reminded his congregation that "the first day of the week was preferred before any other day."[12] Therefore, Edwards exhorts, the Christian Sabbath, because it is a divine institution from the mind of God, must be distinguished within the Christian church in every culture, for all people. The reason for this is that the first day of the week is from the mind of God. It is God's institution and not man's. No one, notes Edwards, will keep the Lord's Day "conscientiously and strictly" if they do not see and observe that the first day of the week is "according to the will and command of God."[13] That is to say, if God's people don't sense the weight of the Sabbath as important to the Christian faith, it will scarcely be kept.

For Edwards, observing the Lord's Day must be a priority for God's people because the Lord has commanded it; it is His day, after all. As Shepard noted, the Sabbath is a recovery day for God's people, a day to "return, recover, and renew" their strength.[14] Edwards not only studied the doctrine of the Sabbath, jotting down its occurrences and varied themes within his "Miscellanies," but he also preached God's mind on the subject to his congregation. Edwards followed in the shoes of his Puritan predecessors, such as Thomas Shepard and Cotton Mather, who believed that if New England was to undergo a spiritual awakening, the doctrine of the Sabbath must be kept and taken seriously.[15]

Third, not only does Edwards see the necessity of God's people keeping the first day of the week as holy and for religious duties, but he also sees it as a means of rest for God's people. The Sabbath is a day for both holy rest and holy work. As already noted, Edwards was a true "Biblicist" who spent hours in his study, notebooks in reach, and quill in hand to record his thoughts on the texts which he poured over. As Edwards' early biographer Sereno E. Dwight noted, Edwards understood that if he spent the majority of his time in pastoral visitation, it would hinder his "greatest good to the souls of men," which was to spend the bulk of his time in his study.[16] Hence, Edwards saw a strong connection between worship and study.[17]

As a result, Edwards loved the ancient language of Scripture, in particular, the Hebrew language, calling it the "mother tongue of all languages."[18] In fact, in Edwards' "Blank Bible," he records approximately 150 translations of Hebrew words compared to about fifty Greek words, thus showing his preference for Hebrew.[19] And one such word is the word "Sabbatism," or "the keeping a Sabbath," which he records in his "Miscellanies" on the Lord's Day, 464.

From his study of the doctrine of the Sabbath, Edwards sees a continual thread between God's rest of creation on the seventh day (Gen. 2:3) and Christ's rest from His work of redemption at the resurrection. "They are spoken of as parallel," writes Edwards, "particularly with respect to the relation that they bear to the keeping a sabbath amongst God's people, or with respect to the influence these two rests have as to sabbatizing in the church of God."[20]

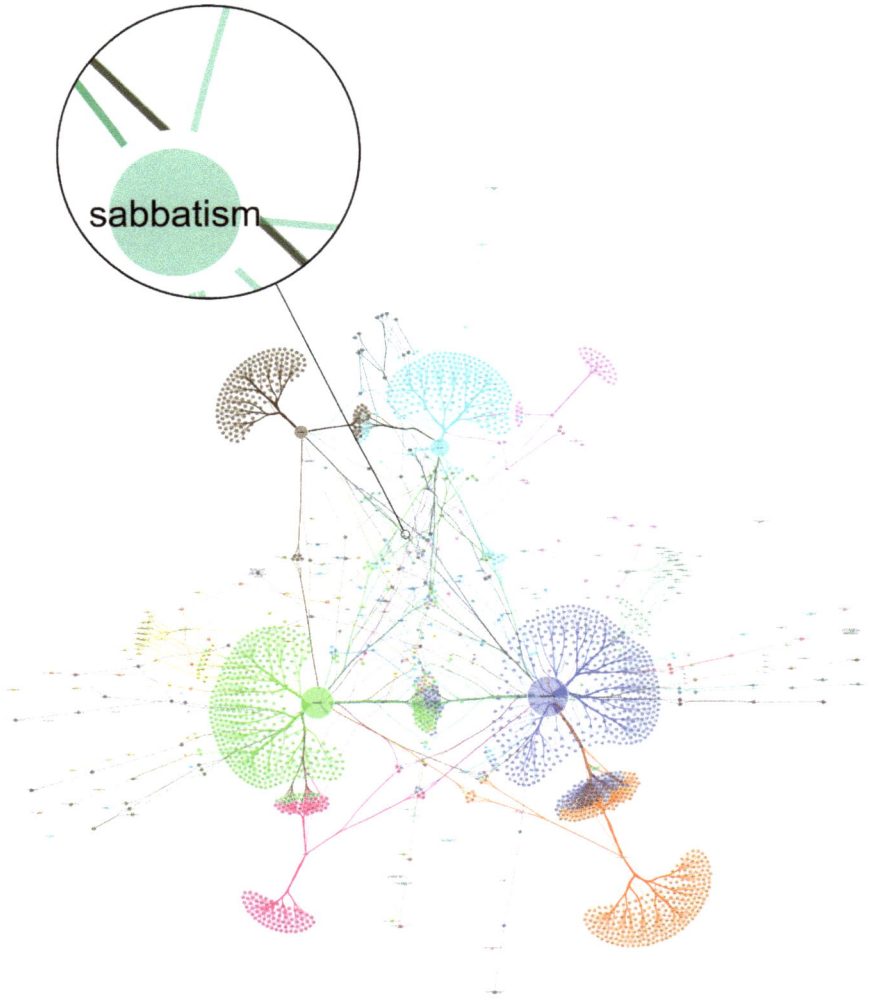

CREATION, LORD'S DAY, REDEMPTION, and SABBATH—*a map of creation, creations, lords day, redemption, redemptions, sabbatarians, sabbath, sabbaths, sabbatical, sabbatism, sabbatizing with interconnections and page locations in WJE 1–26.*

Because Edwards owned *The Practical Works of Richard Baxter,* he most likely read Baxter's classic bestseller, *The Saints' Everlasting Rest,* which expounds on Hebrews 4:9.[21] Like Baxter, Edwards understood that Hebrews 4:9 points to an enjoyment and rest beyond what the Israelites experienced in the wilderness. "The word in the original," writes Edwards, "here in the Hebrews 4:9 translated 'rest,' is *sabbatismós;* the word translated 'rest' in the Hebrews 4:10 and Hebrews 4:11 verses and other places of the context, is not the same, but is *katápausis.* So that here is an evident reference to God's blessing and hallowing the day of his rest from the creation [to] be a sabbath."[22]

The Sabbath day, Edwards notes, is not only a day of rest but a day of refreshment, when God's people should "delight to honor the day and to give his blessing on this day upon that account, as princes will give gifts on their birthdays, marriage days, etc."[23] And the reason God's people should do this is because of the resurrection of Christ, a day of utmost celebration, honor, and a "day of great joy."[24] Not only was Sunday the day of our Lord's resurrection, but it was also the day of His refreshment, where He finished His work. How much more should it be for God's people? Is it not, as the Puritans called it, the market day of the soul? For Edwards it certainly was a celebratory day, and most likely, his favorite day of the week, a day in which he prepared for all the week. Thus, Edwards writes, "Be partaker with him in the rest he rested."[25]

Finally, Edwards sees Sabbath-keeping as a vital exercise for God's people for further holiness and sanctification. First of all, Edwards understood that man can serve God better at certain, specific times, which he calls *cæteris paribus.*[26] *Cæteris paribus* is Latin for "all else being equal," or perhaps a better definition is "holding all things constant." Logically, Edwards understood that when God's people hold constant attention on religious duties and meditation upon the Lord at a particular time and prepare themselves beforehand for this particular time, they are all the better when that time comes. In other words, "if a man long beforehand devotes such a day for a particular study, he can devote himself to that study much the better for it when the time comes."[27] Therefore, Sabbath preparation is an important exercise if we are rightly to keep the Sabbath as holy.

"The Israelites in all their solemn feasts were to remember and praise God for their redemption out of Egypt, as seems by Psalms 81:1–7. How much more should Christians commemorate that infinitely greater redemption of Jesus Christ, of which the other was but a shadow, by keeping a holy day," writes Edwards.[28] Edwards would have agreed with the advice George Swinnock gave for preparing for the Lord's Day when he wrote, "If thou wouldst thus leave thy heart with God on the Saturday night, thou shouldst find it with him the Lord's Day morning."[29]

Edwards understood that when one is devoted to the Lord and religious duties at a specific time, *cæteris paribus,* it enhances the experience and helps in its enjoyment. The Sabbath is meant to be enjoyed, and to be enjoyed as God intends. To do so requires both seriousness and intentionality. Edwards states the following in his "Miscellanies": "I need nothing to convince me that 'tis evident to the light of reason, that there ought to be a time set apart to be spent wholly in the service and worship of God and the more immediate duties of religion amongst all nations, yea, in gospel times."[30] And then in his sermon on the Sabbath, Edwards says almost the same thing, which shows continuity in his thinking about the Sabbath as a day set apart for growth in holiness and religious duties. "It is sufficiently clear, that it is the mind of God, that one day of the week should be devoted to rest, and to religious exercises, throughout all ages and nations."[31]

In conclusion, Edwards kept the doctrine of the Sabbath with utmost care and therefore devoted time to write about its importance and practice throughout his "Miscellanies." The aim of this study was to show Edwards' view of the Sabbath within the context of his "Miscellanies," and then attempt to connect that to his other writings. For Edwards, the glory and enjoyment of God is supreme. As such, Edwards wrote substantially on the Sabbath throughout his life because he understood its importance in regards to God's glory.

"The key to understanding Jonathan Edwards," wrote Iain Murray "is that he was a man who put faithfulness to the Word of God before every other consideration."[32] Edwards was not detoured from his understanding of what God's word says about the Sabbath, in spite of the Enlightenment age in which he lived. Unfortunately in many Christian churches today, the Sabbath has become almost obsolete, considered an archaic practice. The truth is, the church can learn from Edwards on the importance of the Sabbath and what God's word has to say about it. After all, says Edwards, the Sabbath is from the "mind and the will of God;" and if it's from His mind, the church must conform accordingly.[33] Edwards reminds the church that first and foremost, the Sabbath should be kept and upheld. Second, the Christian Sabbath, the Lord's Day, is the true Sabbath for God's people and is therefore is vital and relevant to the Christian faith. Third, Edwards sees the Sabbath as a day of rest and refreshment for God's people and should be honored by all Christians in every nation. Fourth and finally, Edwards sees the Sabbath as a spiritual exercise for further holiness and sanctification for God's people. These themes within Edwards' "Miscellanies" are a much-needed reminder of why Christians should take the Sabbath seriously in the twenty-first century. Edwards is, in this author's opinion, a fresh voice to a topic that desperately needs reviving.

Notes

[1] See "Catalogues of Books," in *WJE* 26:101.

[2] George Marsden, *Jonathan Edwards: A Life* (New Haven: Yale University Press, 2003), 155–56.

[3] Douglas A. Sweeney, "Longing for More and More of it? The Strange Career of Jonathan Edwards' Exegetical Exertions," in *Jonathan Edwards at 300: Essays on the Tercentenary of His Birth,* ed. Harry S. Stout, Kenneth P. Minkema, and Caleb J.D. Maskell (Lanham, MD: University Press of America, 2005), 25.

[4] "Miscellanies," no. 119, in *WJE* 13:284.

[5] "Miscellanies," no. 28, in *WJE* 13: 215.

[6] "Blank Bible," in WJE 24:233.

[7] "Blank Bible," in WJE 24:233.

[8] "Miscellanies," no. 28, in *WJE* 13: 215.

[9]"Miscellanies," no. 495, in *WJE* 13: 538.

[10]"Miscellanies," no. 28, in *WJE* 13: 215.

[11]Jonathan Edwards, "The Perpetuity and Change of the Sabbath," in *The Complete Works of Jonathan Edwards,* Vol. 2 (Peabody, MA: Hendrickson Publishing, 2011), 93.

[12]Edwards, "The Perpetuity and Change of the Sabbath," 93.

[13]"The Perpetuity and Change of the Sabbath," 94. Note: throughout Edwards' sermon on the Sabbath, he consistently repeats the phrase "the mind and will of God," as to drive home the point to his congregation the seriousness of Sunday.

[14]Thomas Shepard, *Theses Sabbaticae or the Doctrine of the Sabbath* (London: Forgotten Books, 2015), 261.

[15]Cotton Mather recorded in his Diary, "Tis true concering both Persons and Peoples, That if Religion desireably flourish, Sabbaths will bee duely kept. But Religion will decay and wither, if Strictness about the Sabbaths do go." *Diary of Cotton Mather* (London: Forgotten Books, 2015), 29–30.

[16]Sereno E. Dwight, "Memoirs of Jonathan Edwards" in *The Works of Jonathan Edwards,* Vol. 1 (Peabody, MA: Hendrickson Publishing, 2011), lxxx.

[17]"As Edwards saw it," writes Marsden, "the discipline of work was part of his worship to God, an offering of his time to God." *Jonathan Edwards: A Life* (New Haven: Yale University Press, 2003), 133.

[18]Robert E. Brown, "Biblical Languages (Hebrew and Greek)" in *The Jonathan Edwards Encyclopedia,* Ed. Harry S. Stout (Grand Rapids: Eerdmans, 2017), 70.

[19]Brown, "Biblical Languages (Hebrew and Greek)" in *The Jonathan Edwards Encyclopedia,* 71.

[20]"Miscellanies," no. 464, in *WJE* 13:507.

[21]"Catalogues of Books," in *WJE* 26:5, 385.

[22]"Miscellanies," no. 464, in *WJE* 13:506.

[23]"Miscellanies," no. 466, in *WJE* 13:507.

[24]"Miscellanies," no. 466, in *WJE* 13:507.

[25]"Blank Bible," in *WJE* 24:1143, note on Heb. 4:11.

[26]"Miscellanies," no. 43, in *WJE* 13:224.

[27]"Miscellanies," no. 43, in *WJE* 13:224.

[28]"Miscellanies," no. 1207, in *WJE* 23:131.

[29]As quoted from J.I. Packer's *A Quest for Godliness: The Puritan Vision of the Christian Life* (Wheaton: Crossway, 1990), 257.

[30]"Miscellanies," no. 160, in *WJE* 13:310.

[31]Edwards, "The Perpetuity and Change of the Sabbath," 94.

[32]Iain Murray, *Jonathan Edwards: A New Biography* (Edinburgh: Banner of Truth Trust, 1987), 471.

[33]Edwards, "The Perpetuity and Change of the Sabbath," 94.

Edwards on Glory as the End of Creation

Brandon James Crawford

> *For the sum total of the glory that God is to receive is infinite;*
> *for he will be glorified to all eternity, and those that shall*
> *render him his tribute of glory will, to eternity, be increasing*
> *in their knowledge of his glory, and so in the degree of their*
> *love and praise to eternity.*
>
> — Jonathan Edwards, *Miscellany no. 1099*

Introduction

WHAT WAS GOD'S CHIEF PURPOSE in creating the world? What was his purpose in populating the world with intelligent creatures (i.e., human beings)? What goal is he pursuing as he governs the world and regulates the lives of its creatures? From the other side, what should human beings have as their highest end? What thoughts should dominate their minds? What should reign in their hearts and have the chief rule in their behavior?[1]

These are the kinds of questions that occupy thoughtful minds. For Edwards, these questions were all-consuming. Over the years, he devoted reams of paper to his answers. In his "Miscellanies" alone, he approached the question of God's end in creation about three dozen times, his entries stretching across the timeline of his adult ministry.[2]

Though the entries differ in length and emphasis, Edwards' answer to the basic question was consistent: God made the world for his glory. What follows is a brief summary of this concept as developed in Edwards' "Miscellanies" entries, with some additional consideration given to the practical implications of Edwards' ideas for the Christian life.

God is Infinitely Glorious in Himself

Before discussing God's end in creation, it is important to understand something of Edwards' conception of the nature of God himself. For Edwards, as for all orthodox theologians, God is *glorious*. To speak of the glory of God is to speak of "all that is great and good in the Deity, including the excellent sweetness and blessedness that is in God, and the infinite fountain of happiness that the Deity is possessed of."[3]

This last statement is emphasized particularly well in the "Miscellanies." Edwards routinely explains that one aspect of God's glory is his utter and complete happiness in himself, needing no one and no thing outside of himself to bring him joy. His happiness in himself comes about in these two ways: "(1) by appearing or being manifested to himself... in his Son, who is the brightness of his glory; (2) by enjoying and delighting in himself ... in his Holy Spirit."[4] In other words, God's infinite happiness in himself is owing to the fact that he exists in Trinity—Father, Son, and Holy Spirit—and within this divine community, there is perfect companionship and delight. The Father sees his perfections manifested in the person of his Son, and rejoices in that display through the Holy Spirit. This is God's glory *ad intra;* also called his "peculiar glory" by Edwards.[5]

Because God is completely glorious and happy in himself, he is a radically self-sufficient being. In fact, the above is basically how Edwards would articulate the doctrine of divine aseity, and it puts into context Edwards' understanding of God's relationship to the world. In short, Edwards was adamant that God does not need the world, or affirmation from the intelligent creatures of the world, in order to be fulfilled. He does not need the world for *anything*. The world, in fact, is completely dependent on *him*—*so* dependent that the world would not even exist were it not in a state of "continuous creation" by God.

Edwards expresses his belief in the continuous creation of the world in Miscellany no. 346, where he states that "It [is] most agreeable to the Scripture, to suppose creation to be performed new every moment. The Scripture speaks of it not only as past but as a present, remaining, continual act. Job 9:9; Psalms 65:6, Psalms 104:4; Isaiah 40:22, Isaiah 44:24; Amos 5:8; and very commonly in the Scripture."[6] This is admittedly a rare doctrine among Reformed theologians, but for Edwards it was a necessary correlate to the doctrine of divine aseity. Since God is the only self-sufficient being, all else must be directly dependent on him for continued existence. Direct dependence on God for continued existence means that the world must be maintained by the ongoing operation of God's power, with the world continually existing as an "immediate production out of nothing, at each moment."[7]

God Created the World *Because* of His Glory

God is infinitely glorious and happy in himself, needing nothing at all from the world. In fact, it is the world that needs him! So why did God create the world? And why does he renew it every moment through this act of continual creation? For Edwards, the beginning of the answer lies in the fact that God is *good*—which is a facet of his glory.

God's goodness is his desire to share his happiness with others. As Edwards explains, "To be perfectly good is to incline to and delight in making another happy in the same proportion as it is happy itself, that is, to delight as much in communicating happiness to another as in enjoying of it himself, and an inclination to communicate all his happiness."[8]

God did not create the world in order to make himself happy, then, but to make others happy.[9] That is to say, God created the world because one aspect of his glory is his desire to spread his joy. This is a concept worthy of reflection. In Edwards' worldview, creation is the product of the overflow of God's happiness. If this is true, it means that the physical universe is inherently *good*. Its existence is a consequence, not of blind impersonal forces, nor of a war between gods, but of an eruption of Trinitarian love. This places love at the very heart of created reality. Additionally, it means that whatever ugliness we may find in the present world cannot be original to creation, but alien to it. This, of course, is the very point Edwards makes in works like *Original Sin*.

God Created the World *for* His Glory

Before making intelligent creatures, God fashioned an inanimate universe. Through this act, God published his glory. Or, stated another way, through this initial act of creation the divine glory eternally enjoyed within the Trinity was now, for the first time, being manifested outside of the Trinity. And this was good. Indeed, "the display of the divine glory is . . . most excellent. 'Tis good that glory should be displayed . . . 'Tis an excellent thing that that which is excellent should be expressed."[10] Because God delights in the perfections he sees within himself, he also delights in his perfections displayed outside of himself. His glory *ad extra* is a happiness in himself, as he sees himself reflected in the things he has made. Thus, through the act of creation, even before intelligent beings were introduced, God was bringing glory to himself.

But God's plan for the world also included the creation of intelligent beings, for his desire was to *share* his happiness in himself with others. This required creatures capable of perceiving and enjoying the manifestation of his perfections as he himself does. As Edwards explains, "The great and universal end of God's creating the world was to communicate himself. God is a communicative being. This communication is really only to intelligent beings: the communication of himself to their understandings is his glory, and the communication of himself with respect to their wills, the enjoying faculty, is their happiness."[11]

So, just as God is glorified in himself in two ways; namely, through his knowledge of himself in the Son and his delight in himself through the Holy Spirit, so God intended to glorify himself through human beings in two ways: "(1) by appearing to them, being manifested to their understandings; (2) in communicating himself to their hearts, and in their rejoicing and delighting in, and enjoying the manifestations which he makes of himself." Both of these may be called his glory "in the more extensive sense of the word, viz. his shining forth, or the going forth of his excellency, beauty, and essential glory *ad extra.* By one way it goes forth towards their understandings; by the other it goes forth towards their wills or hearts. God is glorified not only by his glory's being seen, but by its being rejoiced in, when those that see it delight in it."[12] Indeed, "by the glory of God seems to be meant the flowing out of his goodness, or the communication of his fullness of happiness … The glory of God implies … manifestation and communication, the latter called grace, the former, truth."[13]

Once again, this should not be construed to mean that God needed to create in order to bring himself either glory or happiness. We have already established that God has been infinitely glorious and happy in himself from all eternity. "The creature's happiness does not add anything to God's happiness, any more than God's being glorified in the view of the creature and by the creature adds something to God's happiness." The relationship between God's happiness in himself and the creature's happiness in him should instead be understood this way: When God shares his happiness with others, and they are made happy by that gracious communication, God is doing something that is inherently good. And God enjoys the good that he sees in himself in the sharing of his happiness with others. So God is not being made happy by his creatures, but is entirely happy *in himself* as he sees his own glory reflected in the happiness of his creatures.[14] And it is his happiness in himself, as he sees his glory reflected in creation, that explains why he made the world.

In another of his "Miscellanies" entries, Edwards states it like this:

> It is said that God hath made all things for himself [Proverbs 16:4], and in the Revelation [Revelation 4:11] it is said, they are created for God's pleasure; that is, they are made that God may in them have occasion to fulfill his good pleasure, in manifesting and communicating himself. In this God takes delight, and for the sake of this delight God creates the world. But this delight is not properly from the creature's communication to God, but in his to the creature; it is a delight in his own act. Let us explain the matter how we will, there is no way that the world can be "for" God more than [this]; for it can't be so for him, as that he can receive anything from the creature.[15]

To further emphasize the point, Edwards is saying that God's pleasure in the creature's enjoyment of him does not mean that God needs them in order to be happy, or even that his happiness can be increased by them. Infinite happiness by definition cannot be increased. Instead, God derives pleasure from his creation because of what he sees of himself in the creation. He takes pleasure in his own goodness as it is manifested in his dealings with the world. "He takes pleasure in his glories being manifested and respected because this is a thing fit and amiable in itself, that his glory should be manifested and respected."[16]

These facts should come as welcome news to humanity. In the Edwardsean worldview, God has made the enjoyment of himself, the *glorification* of himself, the chief end of creation; and yet, he is doing so by means of the communication of good to human beings. He finds happiness in himself through the happiness of his creatures. The inescapable conclusion is that God's mission to glorify himself and the creature's desire for happiness are not at odds with each other. Indeed, humanity was created to *be happy,* according to Edwards, but to be happy in the enjoyment of the One who made them.

This thought, if it took hold, would have the potential to significantly alter the way many people perceive God. Far from working to cultivate their terror, the God of Edwards works to carry human beings to the heights of joy. He does not seek his glory at their expense, but through their happiness in him. Such a view also has the potential to improve one's sense of worth. True, God does not *need* human beings, but they are wanted by God, which is why they exist. Human beings are also uniquely precious among the creatures of God in that they are the only creatures capable of self-consciously bringing him glory through their perception of his perfections and their rejoicing in all that he is. The Edwardsian worldview has the further benefit of giving to human beings a lofty purpose. They were created for the glory of God—to see the grace and truth of God in the universe and to rejoice in all that he is for them.

But what about that portion of the human family which does not, and will not, delight in that Triune glory? What about that portion which is "dead in trespasses and sins," hostile to the God of glory? According to Edwards, even that part of the human family contributes God's plan to glorify himself. This is because God's plan for the world was to use it to manifest the *full range* of his glory: not just his mercy and grace through his work on behalf of the saints, but also his holiness and justice through his dealings with unrepentant sinners.

This is not to imply that God is the author of sin, but it does affirm that sin was factored in to God's good plan for the world. As Edwards writes in "Miscellanies," no. 553, "Even sin and wickedness itself comes to pass because God has a use for it, a design and purpose to accomplish by it. Things don't happen merely to fulfill the desires or designs of some other being, some adversary of God. But all that is or comes to pass, 'tis of God's will and for his pleasure that it happens, for his ends."[17]

But of course, God is chiefly glorified when human beings are made happy in him, "rejoicing in the manifested glory of God," "admiring it," "loving God for it," and capable of "expressing those affections and dispositions wherein consists their praising and glorifying

God."[18] Because no human being today is naturally inclined toward this, being under the dominion of sin, God's ultimate purpose for creation also included the plan of redemption through his Son.

God Created the World to Magnify His Glory *in Christ*

Creating the world was a Trinitarian work. At the same time, according to Edwards, the world was a *gift* from the Father to the Son as his reward for redeeming sinners—for making sinners happy in him.[19] Here the doctrines of creation and redemption meet. In Edwards' understanding, God's dealings with all things external to himself are subordinate to the plan of redemption, which is the chief means by which God is fulling his end of glorifying himself in the world.

Stated another way, God created the world, and governs it as he does, for the purpose of preparing a bride for Christ—a huge company of humanity redeemed and loved by Christ, and who would love him in return. Through this bride, God will successfully communicate the *fullness* of his happiness to human beings, and they will, in turn, achieve the highest levels of happiness in him, bringing him glory. God's plan to prepare a bride for Christ is thus the means by which God intends to glorify himself in the world. And this, too, is good: "It is a thing in itself infinitely valuable and worthy of regard that God's glory should be known by elect creatures to all eternity. The increasing knowledge of God in all elect creatures to all eternity is an existence, a reality infinitely worthy to be, in itself worthy to be regarded by him to whom it belongs . . . "[20]

In summary, through the inanimate universe, God manifests the glory of his wisdom and power, which brings him delight. Through his dealings with unrepentant sinners, he manifests the glory of his holiness and justice, which brings him delight. Through the plan of redemption, he displays the riches of his grace and mercy in Christ to the Church, which brings both him and them great delight. Through the display of each aspect of his glory, God is glorified. He rejoices in

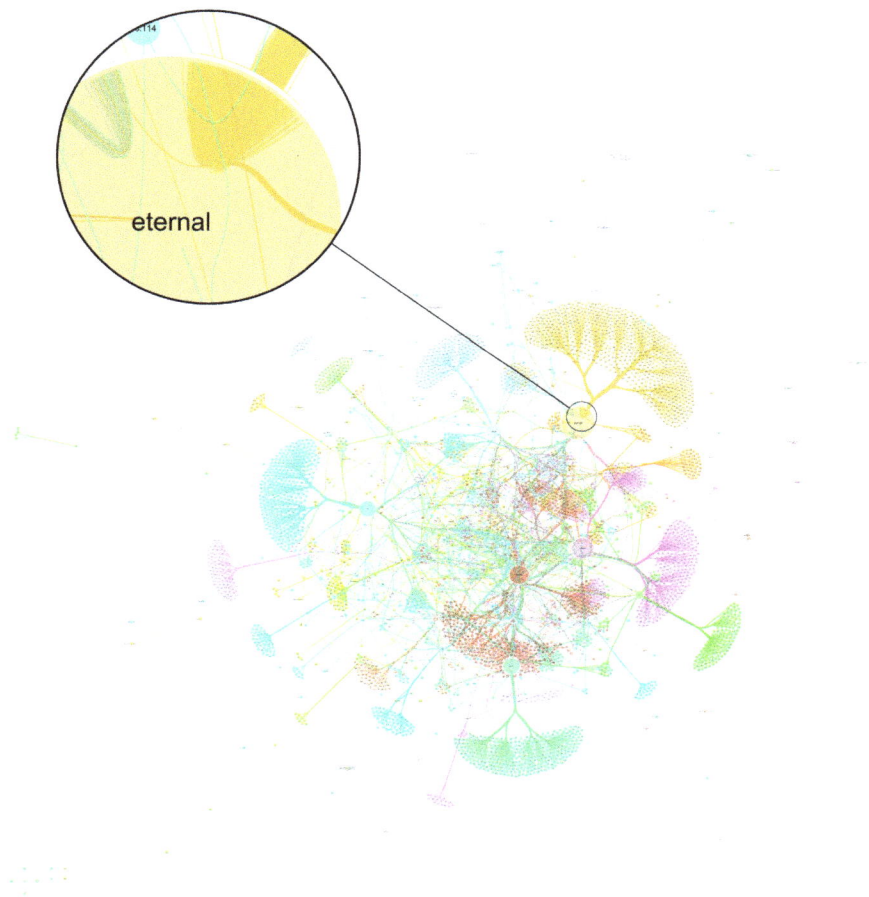

DECLARATIVE GLORY, ETERNITY, FITNESS, INFINITE, and WORTH—*a map of coeternal, coeternity, declarative glory, eternal, eternally, eternals, eternity, fit, fitly, fitness, fits, fitted, fitter, fittest, fitting, infinitates, infinite, infinitely, infiniteness, infinites, infinity, praiseworthiness, praiseworthy, thankworthy, unfit, unfitly, unfitness, unfitnesses, unfits, unfitting, unworthily, unworthiness, unworthy, worth, worthies, worthiest, worthily, worthiness, worthless, worthlessness, worthwhile, worthy with interconnections and page locations in WJE 1–26.*

the manifestation of the splendor of his own perfections. He rejoices in it all, and Christ's bride receives good through it all. "He will be glorified to all eternity, and those that shall render him his tribute of glory will, to eternity, be increasing in their knowledge of his glory, and so in the degree of their love and praise to eternity. So that God's declarative glory, as it is in God's view, is truly an infinitely great thing."[21] In the Edwardsean worldview, here is the inducement to turn from sin and become part of the pure bride of Christ: the Church is the home of those who have been made happy in God through their response to the atoning work of Christ. Here alone may a person find his true purpose, and find that happiness he was created to experience.

Connections with Other Works in the Edwards Corpus

The themes discussed in this chapter are prominent in Edwards' "Miscellanies," but are certainly not exclusive to them. Readers interested in exploring these themes in the rest of the Edwards corpus would do well to begin with the following documents.

Edwards' most extended discussion on the aseity of God is found in his *Discourse on the Trinity*, the entirety of which is based on the thesis that "God is infinitely happy in the enjoyment of himself, in perfectly beholding, and infinitely loving, and rejoicing in, his own existence and perfections."[22] For more on Edwards' doctrine of continual creation, which for Edwards is logically correlate to the aseity of God, the reader should consult the appropriate section in his work entitled *Original Sin*, which provides an extended philosophical defense of the doctrine.[23]

On the question of why the infinitely happy God would determine to create, what his chief end was in creation and where mankind's chief purpose lies, the reader should consult his *Dissertation Concerning the End for Which God Created the World*. In this great masterwork, written toward the end of his life, Edwards argues that both reason and revelation prove that the universe exists to promote the glory of God and to advance the happiness of human beings; and that these aims are not two, but one. As he says near the end of that work, "In the creature's knowing, esteeming, loving, rejoicing in, and praising God, the glory of God is both exhibited and acknowledged; his fullness is received and returned. Here is both *emanation* and *remanation* . . . the beams of glory come from God, and are something of God, and are refunded back again to their original."[24] For more on the happiness of God and his creatures in the "Miscellanies," the reader should consult the many "Miscellanies" entirely devoted to "happiness."[25]

For a further discussion of God's plans to glorify himself in the world through the work of redemption by Christ, the reader should consult Miscellany no. 327(a), which states, in part, "the infinite love which there is from everlasting between the Father and the Son is the highest excellency and peculiar glory of the Deity. God saw it therefore meet that there should be some bright and glorious manifestation made of [it] to the creatures, which is done in the incarnation and death of the Son of God . . . "[26] And, for an explanation of how all of human history has been made subservient to God's plan to glorify himself through the redemption of Christ, the reader should consult Edwards' unfinished work, *History of the Work of Redemption,* which takes the reader through every dispensation of human history, showing how each relates to Christ.

Conclusion

Edwards approached the question of God's end in creating the world throughout his "Miscellanies." Though the entries differ in length and emphasis, his answer to the question remained the same. He answered that God did not create the world in order to make himself happy, for he is infinitely happy in himself, and has been from all eternity. Rather, God created the world because of his glorious goodness, which desires to share his happiness in himself with others. And God created the world *for* his glory. Specifically, he created the world in order to glorify himself by displaying the full richness of his attributes to intelligent creatures, making those creatures happy in him, in the Church, through Christ.

Notes

[1] Compare to the introductory comments of Edwards in "Miscellanies," no. 1266(a), *WJE* 23: 213.

[2] The first entry to directly address this issue, "Miscellanies" no. 104, was written in the early 1720s. The last entry, "Miscellanies" no. 1266(a), was written in the early 1740s. For dating of Edwards' "Miscellanies" entries, see "The Dating of Edwards' Early Manuscripts" in *WJE* 13:59–90.

[3] "Miscellanies," no. 1082, in *WJE* 20:465–66.

[4] "Miscellanies" no. 448, in *WJE* 13:495–96.

[5] "Miscellanies," no. 327(a), in *WJE* 13:406.

[6] "Miscellanies," no. 346, in *WJE* 13:418.

[7] *WJE* 3:400–01.

[8] "Miscellanies," no. 96, in *WJE* 13:263–64.

[9] "Miscellanies," no. 332, in *WJE* 13:410.

[10] "Miscellanies," no. 699, in *WJE* 18:282.

[11] "Miscellanies," no. 332, in *WJE* 13:410.

[12] "Miscellanies," no. 448, in *WJE* 13:495–96.

[13] "Miscellanies," no. 1094, in *WJE* 20:482–83.

[14] "Miscellanies," no. 1151, in *WJE* 20:525.

[15] "Miscellanies," no. 448, in *WJE* 13:496.

[16] "Miscellanies," no. 1140, in *WJE* 20:517.

[17] "Miscellanies," no. 553, in *WJE* 18:97.

[18] "Miscellanies," no. 1266(a), in *WJE* 23:213.

[19] "Miscellanies," no. 148, in *WJE* 13:301.

[20] "Miscellanies," no. 1225, in *WJE* 23:157.

[21] "Miscellanies," no. 1099, in *WJE* 20:485.

[22] *Discourse on the Trinity,* in *WJE* 21:113.

[23] *WJE* 3:400–401.

[24] *WJE* 8:531

[25] Including "Miscellanies," nos. 87, 97, 106, 198, 233, 272, 477, 721, 741, 934, and 1059.

[26] "Miscellanies," no. 327(a), in *WJE* 13:406.

INDEX

Below is a brief index of persons, doctrines, and topics.

Adoption, 296
Allegory, 279
Already, not yet, 293
American Revolution, 213
Ames, William, 129
Analogy, 112
Ancient Chinese
    and the patriarchs, 179
    notion of Christian doctrines,
        172
    on repentance and restoration,
        176
    philosophical classics, 177
    sages, 181
    social ethics and morality, 171
Antichrist, 201
Antinomianism, 190
Antinomy, 263
Arminianism, 165, 188, 190, 228
Ashcraft, Michael, 213
Astrology, 90
Astronomy, 90
Augustine, 205

Bale, John, 205
Barbee, David, 158

Barrow, Isaac, 9
Baxter, Richard, 188
    The Saints' Everlasting Rest, 307
Beatific Vision, 234, 241
Beauty, 109
Bezzant, Rhys, 159
Book of Nature, 105
Boston, Thomas, 189
Bourn, Samuel, 10
Brainerd, David, 150
Breck, Robert, 3
Brightman, Thomas, 205
Bushnell, Horace, 19

Caldwell, Robert, 36, 54, 55
Calvin, John, 181, 233
Calvinism, 235
Chauncy, Charles, 42
China
    Edwards' favorable view, 170
Chinese philosophical classics
    Edwards' enthusiasm, 181
Christian perfection, 291, 293
Christology, 222, 239
Clarke, Samuel, 10

A Demonstration of the Being and Attributes of God, 70
The Scripture-Doctrine of the Trinity, 3
Clockwork vision, 106, 108
Cocceius, Johannes, 185
Coleman, Benjamin, 202
Comets, 89–100
    apocalyptic symbols, 90
    common providences, 94
    final judgment, 93
    misery of damned, 92
    Newton's Comet, 99
    presages, 94
    prove world will end, 98
    the cycle of life, 97
Communication, 110, 289, 293, 294, 313, 318
    fundamental disposition of God, 277
Confucianism, 170
    Edwards' idealization, 182
Confucius, 171, 175, 176, 179
Constantine, 205
Continuous creation, 131, 132, 313
    direct and indirect acts, 138
Contradictions, 263
Conversion, 157
Correspondences, 110
Cotton, John, 202, 203, 227
Covenant of grace, 187–189, 191
    faith as condition of salvation, 194
    marriage, 193
Covenant of redemption, 187, 191, 194
    conditional language, 190
Covenant of works, 186, 188, 189, 193, 194
Covenent theology
    soteriology, 186
Craig, Samuel G., 291

Created minds, 134–138
Creation, 201, 246, 278
    because of God's glory, 313–314
    consciousness, 251
    for God's glory, 314–318
    God's glory, 249, 314
    goodness as motive, 251, 267
    highest end happiness, 252, 322
    intelligent beings, 248, 249, 314, 322
    to magnify God's glory in Christ, 318–320
Crisp, Oliver, 20, 119, 123, 128–132, 141

Davenport, John, 202
Davis, John, 224
Decrees, 257
    antecedent and consequent actions, 261
    cause and effect, 260–265
    final triumph, 272–274
    individual salvation, 267–272
    knowledge, 259–260
    no contradiction, 264
    optimism or pessimism, 265–267
    subordinate and ultimate ends, and chief end, 266
    theological framework, 259
Deism, 162, 163, 178, 212
DeJong, Peter, 186
Descartes, Rene, 100–101
Devotional world view, 106
Dickson, David, 185
Divine action, 119
    exceptional operations, 127
    immediate and mediate, 122, 123
    methodological operations, 127–128
    mixed operations, 126–127
Divine aseity, 312, 320

Divine covenants, 185, 186, 195
Divine grace, 194
Divine inspiration
　　heathen and pagan
　　　　philosophers, 163–164
Dwight, Sereno E., 305

Eliot, John, 202
Emblematic world view, 108
Emlyn, Thomas, 42
Ends
　　ultimate and subordinate, 253
Enlightenment Rationalists, 22
Erskine, John, 41
Evangelical feminism, 59
Evangelism
　　cross-cultural, 150
　　methodology, 165
　　preparatory element, 151
　　theology, 150
Excellency, 27, 109, 252, 267, 293
　　beauty, 27
　　decrees, 257
　　love, 29
　　origin in aesthetics, 27

Faith, 193, 296
Fall, the, 164, 176, 177, 180, 259,
　　265
　　man's understanding broken,
　　　　260
Federal theology, 187
Fifth Monarchy, 228
Fixed laws, 123
Fu Xi, 179

Gale, Theophilus
　　The Court of the Gentiles, 90
Garden of Eden, 259
Gentry, Kenneth, 222
　　Three Views on the Millennium
　　　　and Beyond, 223
Goen, C. C., 210, 291

Goodwin, Thomas, 228
Great Awakening, 211, 302
Great Chain of Being, 113
Grotius, Hugo, 228
Grudem, Wayne, 59

Hammond, Henry, 228
Happiness, 233, 246, 250, 267, 314
　　business of true religion, 248
　　definition, 235
　　God's complacence, 252
　　perception of God's excellency,
　　　　252
　　progressive in Heaven, 240
　　rejoicing in God, 254, 317
Harmony, 108, 110
Hastings, Ross, 44
Heathenism, 282
　　virtues, 290
Heaven, 248
Hell
　　criticisms, 9
　　four theses, 9–12
History of redemption
　　three ages, 212
Hobbes, Thomas, 10
Holiness, 157, 190, 289, 291, 296,
　　298
　　highest beauty, 290
　　spiritual image of God, 294
Hollis, Isaac, 120
Holmes, Oliver Wendell, 41

Imagination, 115, 239
Inner witness, 296
Islam, 282
Israelites, 179

Jackson, John, 176, 177
　　Chronological Antiquities, 175
Jang, Kyung-Chul, 214
Justification by faith, 186, 189, 195

Kepler, Johannes, 94

Kimnach, Wilson H.
    "doctrinal precision", 115
Knijff, Cornelius van der, 190
Knowledge of God, 241
Knox, John, 181

Laozi, 174, 175, 179
Laws of nature, 120
Lee, Sang Hyun, 43, 129
Leibniz, Gottfried Wilhelm, 170, 177
Locke, John, 2, 280
    The Reasonableness of
        Christianity, 80
Lord's Day, 305, 308
Lord's Supper, 161
    converting ordinance, 159, 167
Luther, Martin, 181

Mather, Cotton, 202, 203, 211, 305
    Threefold Paradise, 205
Mather, Increase, 160, 202
    Kometographia, 94
Mayhew, Jonathan, 3, 42
McClymond, Michael, 215
McDermott, Gerald, 151, 162, 163,
    165, 215
Means of grace, 167
Mechanical philosophy, 101, 106, 212
Mede, Joseph, 203, 228
Mencius, 175
Messiah, 180
    person and work, 177
Microcosm and macrocosm, 106
Millennium, 242, 282
    Christ's spiritual reign, 202–203
    civil millenialism, 213
    conversionist millennium, 212
    earthly and future, 199
    Edwards' calculations, 202, 205
    Final Judgment, 205
    four assertions, 200–201
    four comings of Christ, 206
    futurist, 205

    golden age, 205, 223
    inchoate, imperfect, 203
    Jews, 228
    literal thousand years, 200, 201,
        210, 221, 224
    millennial society, 215
    post-millennialism, 206, 209,
        210, 213, 222, 228
    preterist, 205
    progressive millennialism, 213
    prophetical day, 225
    restoration of Israel, 206–207
    Sabbatism, 210
    social reform, 205
    technological advances, 215
Miller, Perry, 186
    on covenant theology, 185
Milton, John, 2
Missional nation, 211
Mixed mode causation, 132–141
Modern missions, 150
    Edwards' impact, 150
More, Henry, 9
Murray, Iain, 309
Music, 109
Mystery, 67, 263, 295
    natural senses, 69
    progressive revelation, 281
    Trinity, 70
Mythologies, 180

Natural religion, 170
Natural theology, 178
Natural typology, 112
Neonomianism, 188, 190
New England theology, 186
Newton, Isaac, 2, 94, 228, 280
Noah, 179

Occasional meditation, 108, 115
Occasionalism, 123, 132, 144

Packer, J. I., 263

Panentheism, 278
Paradox, 263
Parker, Thomas, 205
Parousia, 227
Patterns, 109
Pauw, Amy Plantinga, 34
Perfection, 289
Petto, Samuel, 189
Pierpont, Sarah, 233
Poetic spirituality, 113, 114
Prayer, 282
    global network, 284
Predestination, 158
Preparationism
    Creator's preparation, 161–166
    creature's preparation, 153–161
    definition, 152
    outside Christendom, 165
Prisca theologia, 162, 163, 165
Probation, 298
    Adam's, 295
Progressive revelation
    Chinese classics, 179, 181
Providence, 110, 211, 223, 224, 236,
    263, 264, 272, 279, 280
    Bible as book of God's, 287

Rahner's Rule, 44
Ramsay, Chevalier, 3, 172, 174–177,
    180
    "Discourse upon the Theology
      and Mythology of the
      Pagans", 180
Reason, 66, 320
Redemption, 201, 294, 318, 321
Reformation, 284
Reformed *ordo salutis*, 156
Regeneration, 177
Reinscripturation, 115
Revealed theology, 170
Revelation, 66, 321
    agreeableness, 81–83
    natural and divine, 163

necessity, 83–87
Revivals, 211, 224, 235
Ridgley, Thomas
    Body of Divinity, 238
Roman Catholicism, 282

Sabbath, 301, 302
    a remembrance, 303
    Lord's Day, 304
    rest and recovery, 305
    spiritual exercise, 307
Salvation
    election, 270
    foreknowledge, 268
    predestination, 270
    reprobation, 269
Sanctification, 157, 289, 293, 296,
    298
Schweitzer, Don, 213
Scripture, 109, 111, 266, 280
    attributes, 80
    church's understanding, 281
    meditation, 115
Secondary causes, 139
Semi-Pelagianism, 165
Shepard, Thomas, 202, 203, 305
    Theses Sabbaticae, 302
Shuckford, Samuel, 170
    *Sacred and Prophane History of
      the World Connected*, 179
Sin
    human accountability, 264
    permitted by God, 264
Sinless Perfection, 291
Skelton, Philip
    Deism Revealed, 70, 170, 175,
      177, 179
Soteriology, 223, 267
Soul, 250
Spiritual awakenings, 224
Spiritual Brethren, 251
Spiritual knowledge, 113
Sproul, R. C., 261, 263

Starke, John, 60
Stein, Stephen, 221, 227
Stoddard, Solomon, 157, 159
    "harvests", 159
    The Safety of Appearing at the
        Day of Judgment, The
        Efficacy of the Fear of Hell,
        and A Treatise Concerning
        Conversion, 160
    Stoddardeanism, 160
Strobel, Kyle, 20
Strong, A. H., 189
Studebaker, Steven, 36, 211
Swinnock, George, 308

Taylor, Edward, 160
Taylor, John, 292
Theological anthropology, 161
Tillotson, John, 80
Tindal, Matthew, 10
    Christianity as Old as the
        Creation, 71
Total depravity, 157, 165
Trinitarian apologetics, 42
Trinity, 113, 174, 180, 214, 234, 278,
        318, 320
    analogical language, 37
    Augustinian model, 31–34
    claims outside Christianity, 3
    criticisms, 2, 22, 41
    Edwards' four orders, 44–53
    elliptical, 56–58
    Eternal Functional
        Subordination, 59–60

ethics, 23–24
love, 314
mystery, 263
natural religion, 30
paradox, 263
perichoresis, 56
rational arguments, 4–7
self-communication, 13
Social model, 34–36
transcendence, 25–26
types in creation, 4
work of redemption, 43
Twisse, William, 228
Typology, 211, 278
    exegetical principle, 279

Ware, Bruce, 59, 60
Warfield, Benjamin B., 291
Watts, Isaac, 296
Wesley, Charles, 291
Wesley, John, 291, 292
Westminster Confession of Faith, 187,
    194
Westminster Standards, 292
Whitby, Daniel, 202, 228
Whitefield, George, 291
Wigglesworth, Edwards, 42
Willard, Samuel, 202
Wilson, John, 228
Wilson,John, 210
Winthrop, John, 211
Witsius, Hermann, 185
Wolff, Christian, 170, 171, 177
Wycliffe, John, 205